Anthology

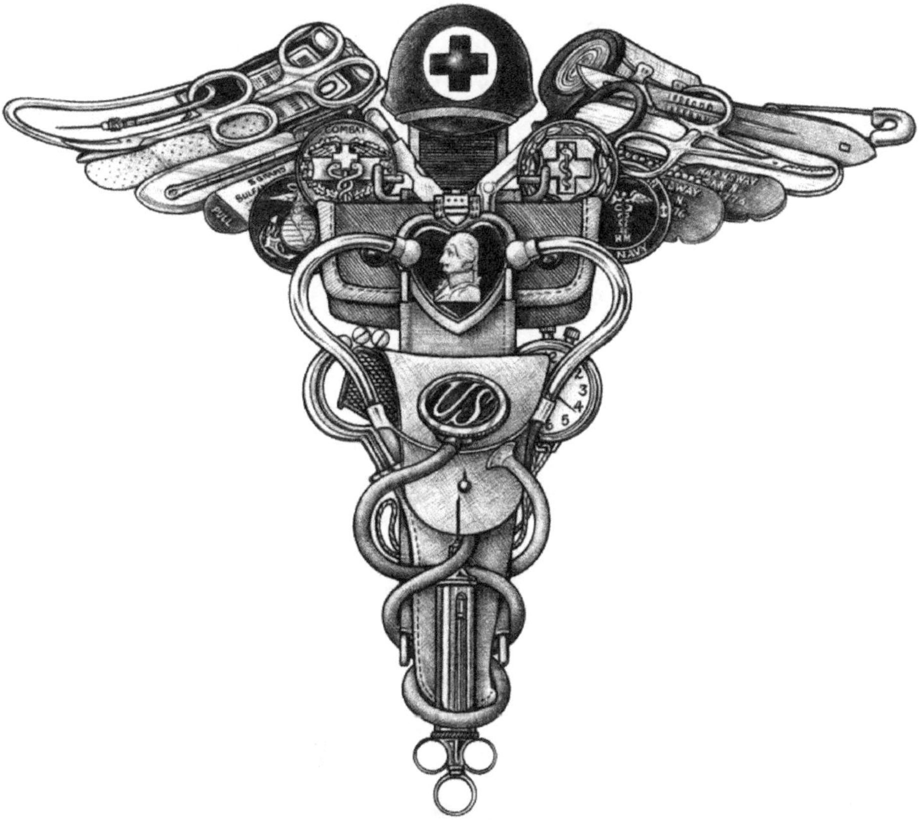

Tales of the 85th Evacuation Hospital Phu Bai, Vietnam

Anthology

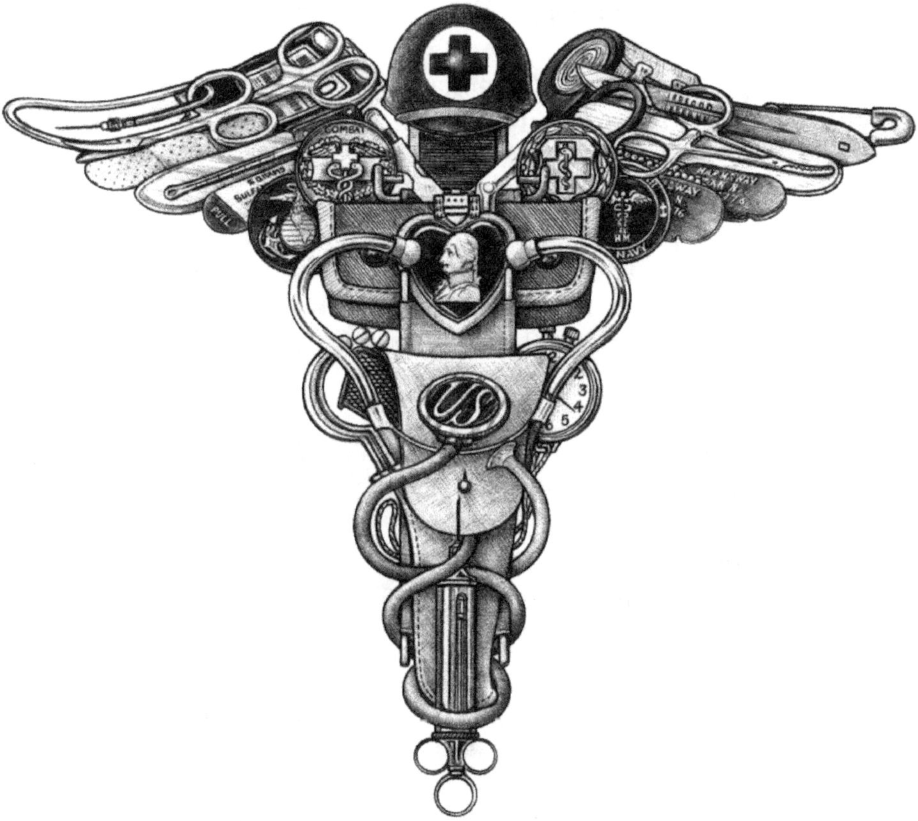

Tales of the 85th Evacuation Hospital Phu Bai, Vietnam

Copyright ©

First publication in 2024 by 1st Battalion Publishing
1stbattalionpublishing@gmail.com

ISBN 979-8-9874744-3-3

This book is a compilation of stories and events that occurred during the Vietnam War to those who served at the 85th Evacuation Hospital. All photographs and quotes within this publication were provided by the author(s) and reprinted with their permission or permission received to reprint. All authors have retained their individual rights to their works in perpetuity.

Title page artwork (Caduceus) used with permission of Don Stewart
www. dsart.com

Editor: Angel Giacomo

Cover Art designed by Angel Giacomo

Library of Congress Control Number: 2024904948

Printed in the United States of America

First Edition: 2024

Table of Contents

Contributing Authors of the 85th Evacuation Hospital (Phu Bai, Vietnam) Reunion Group

Lisa Abend

Jay Barrett

Beverly Brockschmidt

Michael Clark

Liz Conyers

Margret Furey

Gary Gingell

Kathy Gunson

Patti Hendrix

Margi Jackson

Robert Jackson, MD

Gus Kappler, MD

Vaughn Owens

Rose Marie Patin

Arthur L. Phillips

Kathryn Riley

John Martin Streeby

Michael Tucker

Duane Wall

Photographic Contributors of the 85th Evacuation Hospital (Phu Bai, Vietnam) Reunion Group

Michael Clark

Kathy Gunson

Robert Jackson, MD

Gus Kappler, MD

Rose Marie Patin

Arthur L. Phillips

John Martin Streeby

Michael Tucker

Dedication

In honor of the military of the United States of America and all those who have served her in times of war and peace and whose memory we continue to honor.

"Youth is not entirely a time of life; it is a state of mind. Nobody grows old by merely living a number of years. People grow old by deserting their ideals. You are as young as your faith, as old as your doubts, as young as your self-confidence, as old as your fear, as young as your hope, as old as your despair." – General Douglas MacArthur

Foreword

It was my extreme honor to assemble this collection of stories from the 85th Evacuation Hospital in Phu Bai, Vietnam. Within these pages, you'll find out how much duty in the Vietnam War affected the men and women who answered the call to serve before, during, and after the war.

Each story is a mosaic piece, contributing to a larger external image of sacrifice, camaraderie, brotherhood, and the unshakeable bond of the human spirit. From the medics to the nurses to the surgeons navigating the chaos of the operating room and the support staff, each one ensured the hospital's seamless operation—a vital thread in the intricate tapestry of wartime healthcare.

We pay tribute to the unsung heroes who, amidst the flying bullets and boom of artillery fire, held hands with the wounded and offered solace to the living and the dead.

These are living testimonies of the sleepless nights and ceaseless adrenaline—narratives of anguish, hope, and triumph over the cruelty of war and the injuries it inflicts on the human body and soul.

Welcome Home!

Angel Giacomo

Brief History of the 85th Evacuation Hospital

The 85th Evacuation Hospital has a long and proud history of service. It was formed on 29 December 1928 as part of the Ninth Corps in the Regular Army and activated on 20 March 1944 at Camp Maxey, Texas.

The hospital was moved to Camp Swift, Texas, in November 1944 and later transferred to Camp Kilmer, New Jersey, staging for overseas deployment through the New York Port of Embarkation.

The 85th Evacuation Hospital arrived in France on 22 January 1944, was assigned to the Fifteenth Army, and supported Allied forces in France. The unit entered Germany on 3 April 1945, operating for the duration of the war. It was deactivated on 4 February 1946 at Ellwangen, Germany.

The 85th Evacuation Hospital was reactivated on 17 December 1954 at Fort George G. Meade, Maryland, where it trained and participated in several large-scale exercises. In February 1957, the hospital was moved to Fort Polk, Louisiana. The 85th Evacuation Hospital was transferred to Fort Hood, Texas, on 4 May 1959 and assigned to STRAC on 1 July 1960. (STRAC - The Strategic Army Corps - A command of the United States Army with a mission of high readiness. Motto: Skilled, Tough. Ready Around the Clock.)

The 85th Evacuation Hospital (SMBL) arrived in Vietnam on 31 August 1965. On 1 September, the hospital was established approximately seven miles west of Qui Nhon and began receiving patients on 5 September 1965, officially opening on 10 September 1965.

On 10 October 1965, the 85th moved into Qui Nhon. The 528th Medical Laboratory, the 48th Medical Detachment, and the 463rd Medical Detachment supported it.

In 1969, the 85th Evacuation Hospital moved from Qui Nhon to Phu Bai on the northwest end of the airfield, adjacent to Highway 1, 12 km southeast of Huế. The unit was supported by the 616th K A surgical team attached to the 48th Medical Detachment and the 326th Medical Unit. The hospital remained in Phu Bai until its closure in January 1972 by the Commanding Officer, Major Robert F. Jackson, MD.

The patch of the 85th Evacuation Hospital displays the words "Miracularum Laborantes," which, translated from Latin, means "Miracle Workers." And Miracle Workers they were with a 95% survival rate.

My Story

By

Arthur L. Phillips

I, Arthur L. Phillips, arrived at the 85th Evac Hospital in April of '70 as a SFC 91C. Arriving from Fitzsimmons Medical Center, Denver, CO, I was assigned to the ER department. Captain Roger Hopkins was the OIC (Officer in Charge), and MSG Israel was the NCOIC (Non-Commissioned Officer in Charge).

I was later reassigned to SICU/Recovery as the Wardmaster, replacing SFC Rosevelt Walker's DEROS. CPT Joann Cashman was the HN. After 5-6 months, I was reassigned back to the ER until my DEROS (Date Estimated Return From Overseas) in April '71.

Staff members that I recall assigned to the 85th during my tour are Colonel Sukioma, Hospital CO, Major Cho, Hospital XO, 1SG Bradley, SFC Billy Mitchell, SFC Joe McClain, SFC Moses Harris, SP6 Jeff Brailey, 2nd LT Vicky Gilman, 1st LT Johnson, Captain Brown, MD, Major Coan, surgeon, LT. Colonel Quinn Becker, surgeon, who later became the Surgeon General of the Army, Major Abend, surgeon, PFC Leroy Pugh, SP5 Railey X-ray tech. SP4 Woolf, 2nd LT Patricia Walsh.

Events that I recall during my tour were from May to June '70 during the Cambodian invasion. Numerous casualties (WIA/KIAs). Bob Hope's visit during the Christmas "Stand Down" and casualties from friendly fire on Christmas Eve '70.

One casualty, I recall, had unintentionally walked into a helicopter tail rotor and survived. After leaving Vietnam, I was reassigned to Brooke Army Medical Center in San Antonio, TX, as assistant Chief Wardmaster and then a 91C instructor. Several years later, I met the tail rotor casualty, and after numerous cosmetic surgeries, he had recovered. I also recall caring for a teenage POW while assigned to SICU. He was transferred to Huế Provincial Hospital, and we learned later the young casualty was shot and killed by a South Vietnamese soldier upon his arrival at Huế.

Never understood why we never received enemy fire, though we were just over the wire from the Phu Bai/Huế Airport runway. During the night shift downtime, we would climb to the top of the water tower located outside the ER and observe firefights in the distance at the base of the mountains to our west.

The South Vietnamese training center was located approximately 1/2 mile north of the 85th at the end of the runway. Transporting casualties to the Naval hospital…the USS *Sanctuary* docked in the South China Sea, the 95th Evacuation located in Da Nang, and others to the 3rd Field hospital in Saigon. We received numerous casualties from the 18th Surgical Hospital located in Quan Tri.

I recall the 44th Artillery and the HQ company, 3rd Brigade, 101st Airborne, was on the west side of Hwy 1 and received "incomings" often.

Attached is a photo of me taken near my hooch in the lower EM living area. It was standard protocol. All newly arriving Senior NCOs were required to be housed in the lower EM hooch area to deter drugs and local females from entering the compound at night. The senior NCOs were permitted to relocate up the hill as new Senior NCOs arrived to replace those who had arrived earlier. I moved into the "Seven Heaven" hooch.

During my tour, I worked during my off time as the 85th Evac Hospital NCO Club Manager.

I retired after 26 1/2 years as a CSM on 1 December '87 after serving as the 1SG of the 601st medical company, Republic of Panama, CSM of the 56th Medical Battalion, Fort Ord, CA, and CSM of 3rd Army, Fort McPherson in Atlanta, GA.

Arthur Phillips

85th Evac Hospital Vietnam

The Brockschmidt Family

Orders for Vietnam - June 1970
El Paso, Texas, William Beaumont General Hospital

The news came as we thought it would. Fred had orders for Vietnam, so it began "Training for the Military Wife." We developed a list of things I, as a military wife and mother of two small children (two-year-old and six-month-old girls), would need to know and do. The military did not allow spouses to live on post when the husbands were sent to Vietnam, so we had to find a house and set up the move. We found a house to rent in a civilian neighborhood. The landlord moved into a new house and wanted to rent his property for the first time. We signed a contract with an estimated time of ending. Now that we had a home with a yard, I needed to learn how to mow with a hand-push lawnmower, trim rose bushes, and keep the flowerbeds alive. Fred always paid the bills; however, I was always aware of our finances. I just needed to take over the checking account duties, automobile car tags, insurance, car maintenance, etc., etc., and then some.

A neighbor on one side was very friendly and made me feel at home in the neighborhood. The neighbor on the other side was a very nice older woman, but I never saw her much. Other neighbors didn't appear to be the friendly type. I visited friends and attended church on post for company. After Fred left for Vietnam, I joined the Geographical Wives Club, which allowed me to get together with other spouses in the same situation. The club was a blessing as I needed adult conversation, and it gave me a break from the children one evening a month. I remember a presenter from the Sheriff's Department who explained how to stay safe, and if we felt threatened or endangered by someone trying to enter our home, it was "OK to shoot them, but just make sure that a part of their body was over the threshold of your door." He was actually quite serious. I would practice getting my rifle out and what I would do if anyone tried to enter. Note: the bullets were in a separate place, and I never actually loaded the gun. However, the Mother Bear in me would have evolved if I was truly threatened.

Letters were written every day, and I looked for mail in return. It took a while to receive the letters from Vietnam. They were so welcomed when they arrived that I read them repeatedly. It was difficult raising the children by myself. I remember our two-year-old had night terrors. She was extremely close to her daddy and missed him very much. There was nothing I could do but pray for his safe return.

I was a nurse and worked part-time on the evening shift at Southwest General Hospital. I was fortunate to have the lady at church who took care of the nursery as my babysitter for a few nights a week. One evening, while working on the medical-surgical unit, I was standing and turning my head to look at someone when things went black. It was only a split second, but it caught my attention. This had occurred a couple of times that week, so I asked a colleague of mine to take my blood pressure. It was 70/50. I decided to see a doctor as this was not normal. While explaining my symptoms to the doctor, he took my blood pressure sitting, lying, and standing. He asked me if my husband was in Vietnam, and I replied, "Yes, he is." He told me he would order some tranquilizers for me since my husband was in Vietnam, and I might need to take them. My standing blood pressure was 160/80!

I Was Livid! How dare he try to push pills on me! I said, "No, I Do Not Need Them!" I later wondered if he always wrote prescriptions for tranquilizers for women whose husbands were in Vietnam. Since it was time for my annual GYN checkup, I made an appointment with a friend of ours, a GYN physician. I shared my experience with the previous doctor. My doctor told me there was nothing wrong with me. I was physically good and needed to eat more protein, cheese, meat, etc. He also noticed I had lost a few pounds. Protein was the answer, and I never had any more blackout spells.

R & R

Fred and I decided to wait until nine months to go on R&R, so we would only have three months until he would come home. I was very excited and made reservations at the Royal Hawaiian Hotel on Waikiki Beach, which I thought would be very romantic. When the military bus drove up and our husbands came out, we all cheered and ran to our husbands. Many happy tears were shed that day. Greeting and holding my husband tight in my arms was wonderful.

On the way to the romantic hotel, Fred told me about the incident on the bus on the way to meet me. A car had apparently backfired, and all the soldiers on the bus hit the floor! This was a natural reaction because they felt like they were back in Vietnam. We arrived at the hotel and had a nice room; however, it only had a tub and not a shower. We were able to keep the lovely shutters open to enjoy the breeze and hear the surf. Oh, such romance. BIG MISTAKE! Every time Fred heard a noise, the waves, or someone on the beach, he would look to see what was happening. He also wished he had a shower in the room. It was a pretty sleepless night. In the morning, I could tell he was uncomfortable with my romantic setting, so I said, “We are moving!” I called the Ilikai hotel and got us a room on the 23rd floor with a shower and no noise. This was the “Romantic Room we needed.” He enjoyed his shower every single day!

That night, we dined at the Ilikai, and the rest of the week was undeniably lovely and romantic! I realized, then, how difficult it was to live in a war zone, never knowing what would happen next or who to trust. This began my understanding of men and women after being in a war zone.

ORDERS

They never came! Fred kept waiting. However, the orders were not received, and the landlord was pushing to get a date to advertise his house to rent again. I remember Fred saying he finally asked the chaplain for assistance since he was getting nowhere with the office for orders. Meanwhile, the landlord brought various people to see the house. One woman was interested. So much so that she wanted to move in with me with her son. She noticed I had a third bedroom and assumed it would happen. The bedroom was full of boxes we had stored until our next duty station. Of course, I declined that idea, so the landlord returned to advertising.

There was a great deal of pressure on us to get orders and to get away for a few days; I took a trip to Roswell, New Mexico, to visit my sister-in-law, whose husband was also on an overseas tour of duty. My sister-in-law lived on Post in Roswell. We had a nice visit, and then it was time for the children and me to return to El Paso. When I drove up, several neighbors came to my car and asked if I was OK. They said the Red Cross had been trying to reach me! I almost lost my composure. Suddenly, the neighbors were talking to me and were concerned. The Red Cross was looking for me? What did this mean? Was Fred OK? I contacted the Red Cross immediately. The message was, “Orders will arrive soon.” Apparently, the neighbors were always watching the kids and me.

However, they never made an effort to connect until now. They were very friendly, and in retrospect, I am glad they were there. For the next two weeks, I had amicable neighbors.

END of Duty in Vietnam June 1971

Finally, orders came, and we were transferred to Madigan General Hospital in Tacoma, Washington. The year without Fred was quite difficult. Daily prayers to keep him safe and other men and women serving. We both had faith and believed in prayer. I know that is what got us both through this journey. I felt I had passed the test; I was now a real military wife! I learned to handle all situations that occurred. Thinking back, it made me stronger, wiser, a multitasker, and really appreciate military life. We were and still are all family. With all the knowledge and chores I learned, Fred said it was OK for me to continue paying the bills, mowing the lawn, etc. LOL. Ironically, I agreed with him as I enjoyed the exercise and was thankful to continue.

We were very blessed the year he was gone as we both made it through, and our love continued to grow.

With the Lord's help, we made it through a tough year with the blessings of being safely reunited.

The 85th Evac Hospital in Vietnam was a blessing in disguise, for we have an extended family that we love dearly and treasure their friendship. We lost Fred to cancer on August 10, 2021.

By Beverly Brockschmidt
10/27/2023

My Dad

By
Margret Furey

I was born in 1972, so I never knew a life when my dad was in Vietnam. I did, however, know a life with my dad after Vietnam. Growing up in a military family, we were fortunate enough to be able to travel to different places and experience other cultures.

One thing that continued through our travels was that my father always knew his surroundings and ensured his family was safe. When we would go to a hotel, we never stayed on the first floor as it was too easy for "someone" to access the room. When we went to a restaurant, my dad would sit with his back to the wall so nobody could sneak up on him, and he could see who was approaching his family. I always felt protected and safe. In hindsight, I think a lot of my dad's protectiveness came from being in Vietnam. Don't get me wrong, I believe had my father not been in Vietnam, he still would've been very protective, but I think this was on a different level.

I probably only asked my dad a few questions about Vietnam as I grew up because I knew he did not like to talk about it. (I knew this because I had older sisters who had asked questions or heard my dad telling them he didn't want to talk about it.) When I was in high school, I asked my dad a couple of questions about war, and he told me he never wanted me to experience it.

I am fifty-one years old now, and have heard stories, read books, and watched documentaries about soldiers in Vietnam and their return. I hope they all know their sacrifice was not in vain, that they were, and are still, appreciated. A line on my father's headstone says, "We all love and respect you." I think this not only goes for my favorite Vietnam veteran, my father, Colonel Fredric Rollen Brockschmidt, U.S. Army retired, but it goes for all veterans who have served our country.

Margret Furey
10/21/2023

The Longest Year

By Rose Marie Patin and Kathryn Riley

"Oh, my dear, I see your husband is back from Vietnam. It certainly doesn't seem as if he's been gone a year." My neighbor was being friendly, and her smile was warm, but it was all I could do to remember that I was a lady and not let her have that well-deserved rap in the mouth.

Believe me, what she said was about the worst thing you could say to a woman who has just survived that year. I know. I've been over the route.

Maybe it doesn't seem like a year to you, lady, but it's been a year and then some. To be exact, it's been three hundred and sixty-five twenty-four hour days—give or take a week or two in either direction. Honey, it's been an eternity.

It has been knocked out and fallen out teeth, well-known and obscure rashes, dozens of stomach aches, flu, tonsillitis, and wall-to-wall chicken pox. It's children who miss their daddy terribly. It's fixing an especially nice dinner to cheer the whole family up on a rainy Sunday and having your oldest say, "Remember how much daddy likes roast beef...I wish he were here."

It's thunder, lightning, and wind storms at 2 A.M., tornado alerts in the basement with candles, and crabgrass in the lawn.

It's mountains of bills and payments and paperwork—insurance premiums, tax forms, registration blanks, and license plates, all of which were written by the men who invented double-talk and double-think—in collaboration, of course.

It's a leaking roof and appliances that all give out in the same week. It's repairmen who can't possibly come for at least two weeks. "Two weeks—I'll be up to my hips in dirty diapers in two weeks." "What do you mean you don't stock parts for that model anymore?"

It's the nights. Those long and often sleepless nights when you dare not take anything to sleep—who would hear the baby, and what if there was a phone call or a prowler?

It's at night when you wonder and worry the most about him. Where is he? Is he safe? What is he doing? Is he using his mosquito net and taking all his pills? Your imagination gets wilder as the hour grows later, but it won't let you speculate on anything worse than dysentery or malaria—as if that isn't enough to give you nightmares.

And then there are the ever-present news reports. Some days, you feel like canceling all the newspapers and boycotting the radio and TV. It makes you hate "you are there" news coverage.

It's the desolate feeling you get when you watch a tender love scene in the late movie you are watching because you can't sleep because you drank too much coffee and haven't had a letter for a week.

It's the overwhelming sense of absolute total responsibility for the children's safety, health, training, discipline, education, and general welfare. Should I let him build that tree house? What if he falls out and breaks something? If I get her a bicycle, can I depend on her to always think of the rules and not get hurt—or worse?

It's been your year to tell etiquette writers how to write letters—hundreds of them. Cheerful, newsy, documentary, silly, sexy, sad, irate, and lonesome letters. Letters to write when you couldn't think of anything new or unsaid. Urgent letters—"Did you or did you not pay that bill before you left? Must know soonest."

It's being a non-person in a neighborhood of families and seeing your children get that "look" when they see a friend's daddy drive off with the family on a Sunday afternoon to real or imagined delights. It's having your eight-month-old mimic say *daddy* like a parrot but not knowing what it means.

It's crank telephone calls or unlisted telephone numbers, pickets, and people who tell you that "We don't have any business over there anyhow," and people who don't even know or care that we're "over there." It's people who say, "My dear, you are so brave! I just don't know how you manage," which for some reason annoys you beyond belief.

It's the joy of finding another one—a wife who waits. One with children and a dog, one whose congenial company brightens your Monday morning and with whom you can safely gripe and worry. One who knows all the terminology. Not only does she know all the MOSs, but she also knows Nha Trang from Hai Phong and all other points in between.

The only thing that keeps you going is pride in him, faith in God, and a short-timer's chart. So please, lady, don't say, "It doesn't seem like it's been a year." It's been the longest year in recorded history.

Memories From A Vietnam Soldier's Wife

Major Joseph Patrick Patin

Trauma Surgeon

85th Evacuation Hospital, Phu Bai, Vietnam

By Rose Marie Patin

INTRODUCTION

- He joined the Berry Program, enabling him to complete a surgical internship and residency.
- Received orders in July 1969, reported to Fort Sam Houston (to learn to be a soldier).
- First duty assignment was Ft. Huachuca, Arizona
- Received orders to RVN July 1970
- Assigned to 85th Evac Hospital, Phu Bai, as Chief of Surgery

PHU BAI MEMORIES SHARED

- "The soldiers received the best and most up-to-date care. The surgeons were well trained and brought the best care to the soldiers."
- Sometimes operating nearly 24 hours a day.
- Lost 50 pounds, stating, "Those damn malaria pills gave me the runs."
- Using his skills as an apprentice bricklayer (he worked with his contractor father on job sites during the summer college semesters to earn money to pay his tuition), he organized the "building of an outdoor brick fireplace for barbeques."
- Out of boredom, he began running the perimeter of the hospital grounds. Long-distance running became a passion during his tenure in Phu Bai, and he challenged himself over the years to run many marathons in Boston, New York, Houston, Atlanta, St. Louis, Orlando, Baton Rouge, and New Orleans.
- Accompanied Bob Hope and the USO crew on rounds in the hospital.
- Heat, mosquitos, and more heat!
- Listening to 8 track recordings of one- and two-year-old son and daughter!
- Planning R&R visit to Hawaii
- Being scared!

MEMORIES OF WIFE

- Joining Red Cross Waiting Wives Club. At twenty-six years old, I was "in charge" because I was an officer's wife and expected to comfort and support enlisted men's wives. We bonded instantly.
- Having complete control over finances and decisions with household, car, and children!
- Writing letters daily and then waiting for the mailman to bring a letter from Vietnam.
- R & R Reunion!!!!
- Keeping busy! Loneliness! Praying!
- The joy of his return!!!

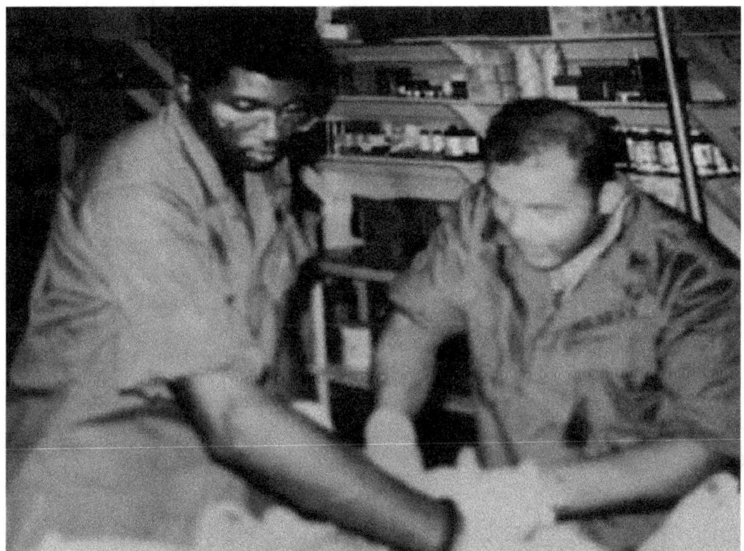

Dr. Joseph Patin with SP4 Alphonso Guy in the trauma room.

Remembrances of Phu Bai from the perspective of a Wife

By Liz Conyers
(wife of Captain Cary Conyers, M.D.)

Cary and I were not married when the Army came calling: either three years of service in the U.S. at a medical clinic or one year in Vietnam as a partially trained General Surgeon, and one year at a U.S. Army hospital.

So, what to do?

We decided (or I should say - Cary decided) to choose the Vietnam option.

Marriage was postponed until his return. He did not want to "make me a widow" (his words, not mine).

The war was winding down in '71 when Cary left for Phu Bai.

He remembers arriving at the 85th Evac Hospital in a helicopter and someone aboard asking, "Do you know what Phu Bai means?"

All was quiet; then the reply: "Valley of Death!"

After Cary got settled, I began sending him regular care packages full of goodies from local vendors: cheeses, meats, sweets - which he shared, I am told, with hooch mates.

Often, the owners of the local markets where I purchased the food would donate free items after I told them where I was sending the food. They were very generous.

I tried to do this at least every two weeks since Cary was not fond of the mess hall!

In addition, I tried to write letters almost every day ... just news about my day-to-day life while missing him.

I knew he was busy with his medical duties at the 85th, but I must say... I did expect more than FIVE letters from him over the course of the year!

The five I received, however, did not disappoint—each was a dissertation on one particular topic.

For example:

"Walking to the Latrine (or Shitter, as he called it) during the Monsoon Season"

or

"Visiting a Local Orphanage" (which he did often with others from the 85th) to help treat the children.

He asked in that letter if we could adopt ten babies or toddlers from the orphanage. I took that as a proposal of marriage!

I said, "YES!"

Of course, he also wrote about all his co-workers in detail, showing how much he admired them.

I felt as though I knew many of them before actually meeting them at the Las Vegas reunion.

All very special!!

When I greeted Cary at the Philadelphia airport in August 1972, one year later, I didn't know what to expect.

We kissed and held each other for a long time. I drove us home to my apartment, where he stayed for three weeks, during which time he saw no one, including his mother and brother.

He slept, read, went for walks…and we united!

It took a while, but he eventually re-entered the "normal" world—little by little.

Vietnam changed Cary—he fully admits—but in a good way.

True, he became more serious about life in general, but also more passionate—about his surgeries, his patients, and especially about us!

We are still together, have two wonderful children, and better for it—fifty-two years later!

Alone The Entire Way

By
Jay Barrett

Every time I travel, I remember the lonely trip to the 85th Evac Hospital. It gives me a sense that everything will work out. It also helps me to understand what I see as a critical factor in the mental illnesses exhibited in my Vietnam veteran patients at the Veterans Administration Hospital where I worked for nine years.

Every person who went to Vietnam went alone. There were no comrades, no one to share the trip into the unknown. No one to help process the experience. My parents both served in World War II. My mom was a nurse who trained and traveled with her unit to the Philippines. My dad was a B25 pilot who traveled to Okinawa with his flight crew. For most other wars, soldiers traveled with a unit with people they knew and could share. Not this war. We went alone, and each had our own 365 days to survive.

I went to nursing school at Duke University without knowing anyone. I traveled from basic training to Kansas by myself, again not knowing anyone there, so I felt that being alone on this trip would be difficult. I was smart and courageous enough to figure it out as I went. But I really was unprepared for the experience.

My mom drove me to Logan Airport in Boston and stayed until I boarded my flight to San Fransisco. My sister told me Mom broke down and cried on the way home. She had some idea of what I would be facing. She had been so supportive and proud of me that I thought that I would be okay, and I didn't appreciate her anxiety.

I remember that it was uncomfortable to wear a uniform when traveling in 1971. At school, we hid the fact we were in the military because of the anti-war movement throughout the country. Because there were fare breaks for soldiers in uniform, I had traveled this way before and heard comments from people disparaging our soldiers. With the draft in effect, I wanted to scream out that most did not have a choice and the war was not their fault.

I had been stationed at Ft. Riley in Kansas and had gone home for three weeks before heading west. I did not receive much in the way of directions for where to go for my transport overseas. Someone had told me to look for a kiosk that arranged transport to Travis Air Force Base. My flight arrived late, and few people were around to ask for help. One worker directed me to a back corner where there was an empty stall with a sign for troops needing a bus ride. I stood there, unsure what to do next, with my suitcases, in my summer uniform, twenty-three years old and alone. I think I said a prayer, and behind me came a young man with his gear.

"Are you heading to Travis?" he asked.

He was a lieutenant like me.

I must have looked lost.

"Me, too," the other man continued. "I think this is where we get the bus, outside. There is a phone over there to call and alert them that we are here."

I know I could have figured it out, but, boy, was I happy to have someone to help make the trip easier.

The bus finally came, and the driver asked whether we wanted to go to the Officers' Quarters to try to sleep or to the terminal area. It was past midnight, and my companion said that since most flights take off in the middle of the night, we should go to the terminal. Good, because I wouldn't know that.

We got to the "terminal," and I use the word loosely. My companion found some other helicopter pilots sitting around a small table. We joined them and found a place to "sign in." I remember playing spades with these guys and getting more and more tired. We all felt that would help us sleep on what would be a long trip.

The boarding announcement happened in the middle of the night, and we headed out. We must have been given tickets because my new "friends" were scattered throughout the plane.

I sat in my assigned seat and realized I was the only female soldier on this flight. That was a bit unnerving as I listened to the eighteen and nineteen-year-old young men around me talking about their last night at home with their buddies. They made some very macabre jokes about heading into death.

We arrived in Anchorage, Alaska, and deplaned to await the next leg of our journey. My new pilot friends and I found a bar. Even though it was early morning, we had a Bloody Mary to toast our trip. Amazing that they had opened the bar for us at such an early time. Someone was aware of our journey.

When we boarded our next plane, I was again anxious about being the only female. I knew this would be the status for the whole year. We flew to Japan and changed planes again for the last leg of the trip. With 250 soldiers, I couldn't find the pilots who obviously found other fellowship. We were all a bit quiet on the last flight. It could have been due to tiredness since it meant many hours since we had last slept well. Or it could have been the realization that our next stop was Vietnam.

It was raining when we arrived in Saigon. During the walk from the plane to the terminal with our armed escort there was a loud explosion. Most of us hit the tarmac. Upon looking up, the guard was laughing.

"Just thunder, newbies!" he admonished.

It wasn't that funny to us. Then the smell hit me. I don't know what it was, just that it was horrible. I wondered if I would ever get used to it and asked the guard about what it could be.

"Vietnam, ma'am," was all he said.

I found my pilot "friends," and we located transport to the in-processing site. I signed in and was given a room to catch up on my sleep. In-processing began the next day with my in-country assignment.

I schlepped my bags to a tiny and smelly room. Rough as it looked, I couldn't wait to lie down. Without even disrobing, I dropped onto the lumpy mattress, and it did not take long before I realized that the sheets must never have been washed after many sleepers. It was nauseating. I had no choice but to cover my nose and drop off to sleep. The next night, I made a pillow of my jacket that smelt musty but not of human smells.

The following morning, I found the "mess" and had some coffee. I discovered there wasn't anywhere to wash the sheets. But by then, my nose was blocked up so the smell wasn't so bad. Not!

I reported to the area to get my assignment and begin in-processing. I said I would go anywhere but Phu Bai because I had a friend there whom I did not want to see. We had become very close at basic training. He flew a "Dust-off" for the 101st. After he had written about his helicopter going down and having to evade the enemy for three days, my self-defense kicked in and changed my feelings for him. My father died when I was fifteen. I could not face that kind of loss again.

They listened and assigned me to Cam Ranh Bay. Most of the cases there dealt with drug addiction, which was not quite what I wanted to have for my experience. With the military, you go where they send you. I would make the best of it.

I fully in-processed with finance and personnel and went back to await my transport. That night, I awoke to shouts and lots of rifle fire. I wasn't sure what to do. My thoughts were that we were being overrun. I remember being very afraid until someone shouted, "Happy July 4th!"

I took a short breath (it still stunk) and went back to sleep, thinking about how hot and scary this place was.

The next day I was called in and told that my orders had changed. I was being sent to the 85th Evac at Phu Bai. So much for asking me about my choices. Because I was in a different area, I had to out-process before heading north. I don't remember eating much or sleeping very well. The atmosphere was less than fun. There were no other females there the entire time I sat there doing a lot of waiting.

Finally, at two o'clock in the morning, I was awoken by the words, "Get a move on. There is a plane going to Da Nang."

A jeep took me to the Air Force Base. Again, as the lone female, I joined a group going to Da Nang on a C-130. We were packed into the cargo area and sat on the canvas-covered benches on both sides of the big plane. No actual seats and cargo in the middle.

When the pilots found out I was in the back, they invited me to sit in the cockpit. The one advantage of being a young woman where there were few American women. The flight did not go well as we ran into a typhoon and had to land in Chu Lai until the storm passed. Luckily, a major from the First Cav approached me when we disembarked. He invited me to accompany a group to the Officer's Club to wait for the next plane. Next Plane? Oh, yes. The plane we came in on had to return to Saigon. The pallets with our belongings were dropped onto the runway.

I had my first Rusty Nail, recommended by my host. We played Spades for hours while awaiting clearance to journey on. Finally, we were called. But it meant we wouldn't arrive in Da Nang until after midnight. Great! With the ever-present curfews, I had no idea what I would do when I got there.

I had been told that in the terminals, men would be walking around with towels on their shoulders. The right shoulder meant they were selling drugs. One on the left meant they were buying drugs. Of course, all the men had towels wrapped around both shoulders!

I collected my two suitcases and the duffel bag issued in Saigon that contained my helmet, flak jacket, and jungle boots. My major friend took pity on me as I looked lost. He invited me to ride with him to the Red Cross location. From there, as directed, I could contact the 95th Evac Hospital in the morning. As we rode in a jeep through the streets, the driver and the major carried M16s. We found a room for me. I thanked the major. He wished me well and said I wouldn't see him in the morning as he was leaving early. After another twenty-three hours of traveling, I fell asleep—on clean sheets!

The next morning, I found a Red Cross worker who showed me a phone I could use to call the 95th. The hospital sent a jeep to take me to in-process and then back to the Red Cross to await a ride to Phu Bai. All I knew about Phu Bai was that it was way to the north in the country, and the base was where the 101st was stationed. I still didn't know what I would find, but since people had helped me so far, I was hopeful I would make it to the 85th. I soon discovered why everyone gave me pitiful looks when I told them where I was headed, even as they said, "Phu Bai is alright!"

After another night in Da Nang, a worker told me I had a ride to Phu Bai. I had no time to worry about it because a jeep was waiting to take me to the hospital where a helicopter was waiting. I was greeted by a young Warrant Officer who ran me out to the chopper and helped carry my bags. The pilots had great fun, talking about their nightly jaunts and passing around a pair of red panties. My luggage was sitting in the middle of the chopper, unsecured. As they did dips and turns, I worried it would fly out. We finally landed at the 85th. My journey was over. It was July. The temperature was somewhere around 100 degrees. The dust rose when we landed. I looked at plywood buildings with metal rooves and a *Welcome to Phu Bai* sign.

I climbed out and saw two men coming out—to welcome me.

Lieutenant Colonel Garlic held out a hand and immediately began apologizing. "We thought you were a male, so we have you set up in the male officers' area. We'll have to see what is available."

Great – another hurdle.

I soon found myself walking on the corrugated metal walkway (held up by empty ammo boxes to avoid the monsoon rain flooding) to a "hooch" that would be my home. It was made of plywood, with a metal roof, and stood on stilts – again for the flooding. (During monsoon season, I watched a gray rat swim underneath!) I also found out that I had one-fourth of the small building.

"Sorry, we didn't have it all set for you. Let us know what color you want, and we'll leave paint on the front step for you. Maybe you can find someone going home who can sell you an air conditioner. Come on over to the mess hall at lunch, and we'll introduce you to everyone." Lieutenant Colonel Garlic gave me directions, and I saluted as I was alone again.

There was a boarded-up window that someone had used for A/C. There was a single metal bed and a small closet. The bare essentials. It was right across from the latrine and showers, which was nice. I took my stuff in, made the bed with the bright-colored sheets I brought, and decided I wanted green walls. Sure enough, a can of paint and brush were left on my step the next day. After days of travel, I was "home."

I believed that since I had made it this far, with all the bumps in the road, I would be okay. That was until the second night there when an incoming round landed close enough to spray dirt on my metal roof…

My Military Career

By

Margi Jackson

My military "career" began on June 30, 1971. Army orders arrived in a big envelope containing many pages. This big envelope was totally unexpected. At the time, we lived in Dayton, Ohio, as my husband completed a four-year surgery residency that day. Many retired military families lived in our neighborhood, which was near Wright- Patterson AFB. I excitedly ran next door to show my neighbor Ann. She grinned and told me we weren't moving to San Francisco. In a few short weeks, we were on our way to Fort Sam Houston. We had three children, ages eleven, six, and seven months. The weeks there flew by, and soon, the three kids and I were on a plane headed back to Ohio so the boys could start school. In a couple of weeks, my husband came home for a few days before leaving for Vietnam. So, our lives changed forever on a beautiful Sunday afternoon in September.

I was accustomed to being alone with the children as residency takes many nights of "call." I had just about decided I'd had enough of this "aloneness" and contemplated ending the marriage someday. But instantly, this was different for both of us. We missed each other desperately, and he "courted" me all over again. I faced each day with renewed vigor.

My days were busy, jam-packed. We had a son in junior high who played soccer and basketball. We had a second-grade son who was also busy. And then, there was Susie, the baby. My husband's father had passed away two years prior, and I also had my mother-in-law to care for as well.

Meanwhile, the love letters kept coming and kept me going. Soon, the Christmas presents for the children from "Dad" arrived, and we made it through Christmas without him. In those days, the only means of communication were mail and an occasional short-wave radio call. There was no internet, Skype, Facetime, etc. But those love letters kept going and coming.

Soon, we were planning a trip to Hawaii for rest and relaxation. I sold his car to afford the trip, farmed out the children, and traveled with another friend whose husband was also in Vietnam. We go back to Hawaii fairly often and always go to Fort DeRussy. It's changed a lot, but those wonderful memories don't.

Time can pass quickly, even when sometimes it doesn't feel that way. In April, he could take a leave for ten days, and Susie didn't remember him. He quickly won her little heart again. A patient who was critically wounded was med-evaced home, which allowed him a few more days of leave. A few weeks after another return to Vietnam, this time the fourth, I got a phone call from an acquaintance telling me she was so sorry to hear my husband's helicopter went down. I calmly thanked her and called a colonel I knew at Wright Patterson AFB who, within minutes, assured me it wasn't true.

On his seventh birthday in June, I found Tom asleep on the floor, burning up with a fever. I did my best to lower the fever for the next few hours and throughout the night. The next morning, I learned he had meningitis and was hospitalized for several days. Our older son, Bob, was twelve years old and took over the total care of his baby sister, who was eighteen months old. I don't know what I'd have done without him! Tom recovered, life went on, and finally, the Vietnam tour ended, and we moved to Fort Knox, Kentucky. I loved Army life there. However, I was accustomed to making all the decisions. Now Bob went to work at nine and home at two, only on call every 9th night. But the adjustment went smoothly. I would have been thrilled had he chosen to stay in the Army. However, our Vietnam experience had only begun. While there, my husband met a wonderful Vietnamese family. When Vietnam fell, they were trapped there. In 1977, this family miraculously escaped to Thailand and eventually made it to Indiana, where we still have the original ten children calling us Mom and Dad and now grandchildren and great-grandchildren.

This story of escape took many months, miracles, and hard work for everyone involved, but they, to this day, are a true joy in our lives. These days, we enjoy our other children, grandchildren, and one great-grandchild. But most of all, we enjoy each other. GOD HAS BLESSED US RICHLY!

Margi Jackson
Vietnam veteran spouse

Vietnam, Here I Come

By
Kathy Gunson

I was scheduled to leave Eugene for Travis Air Force Base in Northern California on 4 January 1971 at 0730 hours. My stepfather, Lloyd, had breakfast and coffee waiting for me when I crawled out of bed, more likely fell out of bed. A restless night left me blurry-eyed and staggering. Excitement? Fear? Both? Neither? I tried to appear calm and collected, but my heart was attempting to execute its escape from my chest. That would have been a foul sight, my heart falling onto the table, leaving bloody prints as it bounced with each beat. My stomach, not to be left out of this unraveling emotional state, felt as though I had swallowed an enormous ball of ice. Yes, I was scared.

As I walked into the kitchen, I saw Mom standing over the breakfast nook heat vent, her nightgown billowing and undulating with the rise and fall of the warm air, a comfort for cold feet on a chilly morning. Coffee cup cradled between her hands, looking about as bright-eyed as I was, I knew she had not slept either, for her daughter was going off to war. In 1941, Mom had sent a husband off to war. He did return home, injured but intact for that. Looking back over these past 47 years, I cannot even begin to imagine the sick dread and anguish she must have felt with my decision to volunteer for Nam. Oh, Mom, if only I could apologize now even though you no longer can hear it. I earnestly apologize and am so sorry for having put you thoughtlessly on that merry–go–round again.

When goodbyes have been said and pulling away from family and daily routine has begun, the conversation becomes difficult and stilted. I would not be wrapped up in their daily lives for a while, nor would they be in mine, so what exactly do you chat about? Certainly not plans for tomorrow. I distinctly remember we three made a stab at a conversation about the weather. However, how much can one talk about fog?

Murmuring to her eggs, Mom asked, "Do you have everything packed? Not forgotten anything, have you, sis?" She didn't want to look at me, casting a glance, only to look away more quickly. She was terrified for me, an easy read on her face. I definitely had misgivings about my decisions, but I hoped my face was not an open book, with trepidation and heartbreak printed across my forehead.

My pride would not let me show or voice my fears or the despair slowly curling its sinister arms around me. I wanted to leave my parents feeling that I was more than willing to face this challenge head-on, confidently journeying into the unknown. But what if Mom or Dad or my brothers or others died while I was gone? Would I forever rue my decision to bow out of their lives as I selfishly sought adventure and excitement? My family was my rock and my world, and I knew I was just as important to them. Yet, with a carefree flick of my hand and a toss of my hair, I decided I'd like to go to war. And if the same scenario were to be repeated, I would make the same decisions, but perhaps with a little more finesse and awareness of the impact it would have on others.

However, in 1971, I needed to fluff my feathers, spread my wings, twitch my tail, and leap off the home branch to fly with unfettered freedom.

Thick fog masked the surroundings of our neighborhood as we drove away, heading for the airport. The comfort of being able to see the middle line and shoulder of the road did nothing to ease concerns about our inability to see beyond ten feet in front of the car. Did planes take off in this weather? Good question. I was not a good flyer, having been on a plane maybe four times before this trip, so the fog was adding to an already heaped pile of anxiety. Man alive, why does this need to be happening?

Accompanying me to the boarding line, my stepfather lugged my humongous duffle bag. We once again hugged, kissed, hugged again, and said goodbye. However, all this hugging and kissing was interrupted when the terminal PA system squealed loudly, followed by the announcement, "All aircraft have been grounded temporarily due to weather conditions and poor visibility. The National Weather Service is unable to give us information as to when the inversion might lift. Please check back during the day to find out your departure time."

Now what? The three of us headed back home, spending the next thirteen hours playing cards and dominos and secretly wondering when this delay would end, leaving us to get on with life. We were in a holding pattern, and the stirring of emotions was wearing. I was fearful of being considered AWOL, absent without leave, punishable with time in the brig, reduction in rank, forfeiture of pay for a prescribed period, or giving up my firstborn to the government should I fail to report at my appointed departure time to Vietnam. I had absolutely no idea who to get hold of for further instructions if that happened. We didn't cover these kinds of unforeseen events in basic training.

There was great irony in my decision to join the Army, let alone volunteer for a tour in Vietnam. All through my childhood, I suffered such homesickness that even an attempt to spend a night with neighborhood kids in our card table tents would quickly end with me, heart in my throat, running for home. Notification of Girl Scout summer camp registration rendered me a puddle of tears. "Mom, I'm afraid to go. Please don't make me."

Of course, she never did. My mother was ever so loving and understanding. However, upon entering my sophomore year at the University of Oregon, Mom insisted I live on campus for at least one term in preparation for transition to Portland and the University of Oregon School of Nursing the following year. I had survived the trials of separation from my mother's bosom, and now, 4 months as a newly graduated nurse, I was heading 12,594 miles west into a war. I was scared witless but also leaning forward like a masthead on the front of a ship, eager to grab an adventure with both hands.

Atmospheric inversions had to let go of their hold on the universe at some point, and ours did around 8 o'clock that evening. Back to the airport, the ticket counter, the boarding line, and the final hugs and kisses, I found my seat and sighed as the plane left Mahlon-Sweet Airport behind. My mom's parting words were, "Phone me as soon as you get to Vietnam." I didn't give that request a second thought. Of course, silly Mom, I would find a pay phone when I arrived in Vietnam and fill you in on the trip.

Upon arriving in San Francisco an hour later, I soon discovered that Travis Air Base was not a cab drive away but a one-and-a-half-hour drive north. I didn't feel I even began to have enough money for cab fare and remembered I needed to report at a designated time. Panic was starting to set in.

The following is my first letter home, written on 5 January 1971 at 6:30 pm. We boarded an aircraft chartered by the government to transport troops and equipment to Vietnam. More particulars will be coming forth about Flying Tigers Airlines and their attempt to fly us to Vietnam in a timely manner. A good heads-up for you is the statement, "Oh shit!"

This disclaimer is bold, so you will remember this caution and put it to good use, forestalling all gnashing of teeth or unparliamentary language, i.e., evil speaking as you read or choose not to read my letters home. I was 23/24 years old and hell-bent on fibbery (oh, I love this word, fibbery, meaning to deceive), protecting Mom from my reality of life at the 85th Evacuation Hospital. I was blatantly truth-guarding. Furthermore, my spelling, grammar, and hyphenation skills were not of journalistic quality at that age. However, friends have insisted I enclose the letters, so try to grin and bear it. You will find peats and repeats in this narrative, but come to the end, I think you will understand why. Thank you.

5 January Tuesday

Dear Mom, Dad, and Kirk, plus everyone else.

Well, we're up, up and away. I'll give you in detail the accounts of my waiting. Arrived in San Francisco in one piece. Finally managed to find a Porter to carry my bags to the bus (transport to Travis), which I was told was only a block away, and was actually 5 blocks away. Bought my ticket and stood outside in the elements freezing my bippy off for 30 minutes. Then I was forced to lug my baggage to the bus, but some kind soul with a chip on his shoulder put it in the baggage compartment since I would have been forced to lift that duffle bag over my head and heave.

The trip to Travis was about an hour and a half. We drove through part of downtown San Francisco, got to see a tattoo parlor. Arrived at Travis and lugged the bags around again for a half hour. Finally went to change into my fatigues. When I walked out of the bathroom, I must have turned every head in the place. I wanted to run and hide, not because I'm beautiful but because the Army pant suit is so ugly.

The plane was to leave at 1:00 am. At 12:30 am we lined up for 30 minutes only to stand. At 2:15 am they said our flight would be delayed. At 4:15 am they began to load us. I waited in the loading line for an hour, had just sat down in my seat when an announcement came to exit the plane. At 6:00 am we were still sitting in the terminal. They finally loaded us on buses. First, we were driven to the Brigadoon only to find they had no vacancy. Finally ended up at the Voyager in Davis, California. They sent us to the bar, only to send us back out and in line again. I finally got a room, ate breakfast, and went back to the room and cried for an hour.

I turned off the light in the room. Saw what I thought was the bed, made a leap, and landed on the floor. Nearly broke my knee and two fingers.

Ate lunch and spent 2 hours in the bar playing bridge. They loaded us again at 4: 00 pm. The bus driver gave us a guided tour of the sites along the road, and then we sat for another hour in the buses at the terminal before we loaded the plane.

I did phone Mom from Davis, California.

"Are you in Vietnam already?

"No, I'm in Davis, California, wherever that is."

"What are you doing there?"

"Oh, just hanging out. I'll write it all in a letter. I love you, Mom. Say hi to Dad for me. Bye. Wait I do have a funny for you. I turned the light out in my room and made a flying leap for the bed but had misjudged its location and distance, so landed on the floor with a resounding thud, spraining my fingers and some toes and scraping my knees, but I'm ok. I wonder what the people in the room next door thought about the noises coming from my side of the wall. Ok, I love you, bye."

(Note to reader. When telling Mom about this "funny," I did not divulge my feelings of despair, the fall proving to be the proverbial straw that broke the camel's back. I felt I had no other recourse but to dissolve into a weeping heap of loneliness and misery. Woe is me; woe is me. I was tired, hungry, and hurt, all cope having flown out the window.)

This zany excursion to Vietnam did not stop with our departure from Travis Air Base. Boarding a DC-8 passenger airliner, part of the fleet of Seaboard World Airlines, 269 exhausted, grumpy soldiers crowded into tiny seats, chins resting on knees. On the other hand, feeling quite smug, I quietly applauded my short stature, finding it mighty handy, and demonstrated an extraordinary ability of employing and evolving a soft, un-segmented body like a snail, curling in my seat for warmth and comfort.

Sitting eight across with a narrow aisle passing down the center, we were packed like sardines. The fuselage was originally designed with 3 seats on each side of the aisle. If the need for a toilet happened, the afflicted would have to turn sideways, sidling up the aisle like a crab. We had two bathrooms for 269 GIs and the flight crew. The desperate could not scuttle or skitter, the aisle being the only place for standing and stretching. Definitely packed like sardines, that's what we were, and by the end of the third day, Odeur de Parfum of sardine was the scented trail left by each of us. Because Seaboard Airlines was a government contract flight service, the amenities on board were sparse, as indicated by the lack of seating comfort. We did have 4 flight attendants and meal service, but that was all she wrote. Complimentary drinks and packs of peanuts were sorely lacking. The flight time was estimated at fifteen hours, plus refueling in Anchorage and the Yokota Air Base in Japan.

Departing California at 6:30 pm (1830 military time) in the evening, we landed in the pitch dark at the Anchorage airport, January in Alaska, hosting six hours of daylight between 10 am and 4 pm, so we did not have an opportunity to view the surroundings. Two hours sitting on the runway gave thought to "something must be wrong."

Back at Travis, our flight had been delayed seventeen hours; a bad radio was the culprit. Now, I didn't think fueling an aircraft would take two or more hours, but then again, I did not have a lot of airplane operational savvy. As my seatmates and I discussed this conundrum, a squeal on the PA was followed by an explanation. "We are currently experiencing aircraft malfunction. You will disembark, load onto the yellow school buses, and be taken to billets for rest and to await further orders."

Phone call home sometime in the late evening on January 5th from Anchorage.

"Hi, Mom."

"Hi, Sis. Are you in Vietnam?"

"No, I am in a very nice suite at the Anchorage Hilton. We do not know how long we will be here. There are problems with our plane. I'm going to get some sleep, then head to the bar for breakfast and a card game. We do not have access to our personal items, so I'm feeling pretty gritty, and my teeth have fuzz, but I have a lovely bathroom, so am going to soak in the tub before I hop into bed."

"You nut head. Would you please get into bed before you turn your light off and not just leap towards it in the dark? You are going to hurt yourself, and then you will be sorry."

"OK, Mom. I love you, and we'll talk later."

"Yes, phone me from Vietnam."

Breakfast at the hotel came and went, and as dinner time approached, we received orders to board the bus. Heading back to the plane for the continuation of our disrupted flight, the return route skirted a horrifying sight: a crumpled, blackened, burned aircraft that had crashed two months prior. This bit of scenery proved to be quite unsettling, considering the problems we were having with our transportation. In addition, I am certain those from the crash who were not injured were then sent to Vietnam on the next flight out.

The military's unofficial motto is like that of the Postal Service, "Neither snow nor rain nor heat nor gloom of night stays these couriers from the swift completion of their appointed rounds." Add plane crashes and other disasters into that slogan. At the time, we were not given much information about this crash. Subsequently, I am enclosing information I gleaned from newspaper reports.

> "The DC-8, ferrying 229 military personnel to Vietnam, crashed on takeoff. The pilot appeared to be trying to abort the takeoff when the nose of the plane suddenly dropped down on the end of the runway. Numerous explosions and a fireball followed the impact. Forty-six GIs lost their lives, with multiple burn causalities flooding the hospital."

Once again, on our way to the Orient, we were to fly to Japan, but after 6 hours, we landed in Honolulu and were asked to deplane and twiddle our thumbs. The terminal bar was very, very appealing. I put down quite a few whiskey sours in a short amount of time. My utility pants pockets also proved quite roomy, and two glasses of these sours fit snuggling in one pocket. A few beers tucked here and there, and I was ready to roll. We were ordered to line up, sit down, line up, sit down, so we played musical chairs for another three hours. Finally, the bird was ready, and we flew toward the land of the Rising Sun, more than a little drunk and becoming travel-weary.

Entertainment on the plane was nonexistent unless you happened to have a deck of cards. Two cards were laid face up on the table. The gamble is that the rank of the third card from the deck will fall between the two already played, the suit being of no importance, but rather the rank of the third card determining win or loss. If the third card does not match the rank of either card on the table, you win the pot, but if the third card matches either, you pay double.

The moment for my time in the spotlight arrived. I drew a deuce, and since the gambler in me felt lucky, I bid $100 because I had a ten-point spread between an ace and a deuce. I mean, what were the chances I would lose? Yep, you can see the writing on the wall. I lost and had to pay $200. I guess I had money on me because this little incident was burned firmly in my memory.

7 January 1971 Thursday, 9:35 pm. Japanese time (2135 military time)

Well, I've now seen Alaska and smelled the air of Japan. By now, you've probably received the postcard from Alaska. Nothing much more to say on that.

Ah yes. Are you ready for an attitude check concerning Seaboard World Airlines?

1. *Attitude check: This airline sucks.*
2. *Positive attitude check: This airline positively sucks.*
3. *Negative attitude check: No airline sucks like this airline.*
4. *Religious attitude check: This goddamn airline sucks.*

We landed in Yokota, Japan, at 7 pm and sat around in the plane for 2 hours, which was to be only an hour's stopover. It's a 5-hour flight to Vietnam—yippy skippy.

One thing nice about the trip over, I've met some mighty fine people, people that I would have never meant otherwise. We're having some turbulence so that's why the crooked writing.

I hate this crummy plane. So far we've only had to have the radio and an engine replaced. I can't say I'm not scared because I am.

I've had diarrhea the entire trip—not because of Nam but because of this plane. Oh well, I know I'm in the hands of God.

I have to now fill out a Declaration Certificate. I declared $3.75—rich, huh. Well, can't write any more till I find some paper.

As of now I've had---

1. *3 offers for the bedroom. That's not bad; there will probably be more before I land.*
2. *5 offers to be someone's girl*
3. *2 offers for marriage*
4. *24 hours of sitting*
5. *3 hours of sleep*
6. *10 cups of coffee, 1 hot chocolate, 2 cokes, 1 candy bar, breakfast, lunch, and constipation*

At the moment the plane is dancing, I'm bored, and the dumpy stewardesses are trying to get dinner ready.

All in all it hasn't been unbearable. Everyone is in the same boat so spirits are pretty good. I've got my shoes off and my feet up.

We slept a lot and visited a bit but most everyone was quiet, lost in thought about home and a hopeful return to that home at the end of the tour. The thought of death or injury would wander in and out of my awareness, eliciting a gulp and a grimace. While en route, I learned to play a card game called Acey-Deucey.

There are only 5 female military and 8 stewardesses. And as for looks, even in our ODs we've got the stewardesses beat 10 to 1.

Will write later and tell you about Alaska.

(Note to reader. Please excuse this smug little shit behavior. I was a 23-year-old who felt she had the world by its short hairs. Those poor stewardesses were on our flight from Travis to Vietnam, on their feet, working non-stop, held prisoner to our needs, wants, and complaints while we lollygagged in our cramped seats. It wouldn't be beyond reason to think they all resigned from their jobs after this gawd awful trip. I take my hat off to you ladies and thank you for your service to us.)

My Alaskan journey never got written. On 8 January 1971, in the wee, dark hours of the morning, we landed in-country at Bien Hoa Airbase (pronounced Ben Wah), where my energy became focused on what would come next. Having never been on assignment in the military, let alone a war zone, I felt scared and fraught with great angst.

I was in unfamiliar territory, feeling quite vulnerable, and on a journey without a map.

Leaving the plane via a seemingly very long and very exposed staircase, we were quickly ushered into a corrugated metal building. The graveled floor lent the hastily constructed edifice a sense of fleeting permanence. Dangling from the overhead beams, two bare bulbs struggled to spill rheumy light into the room. A door, opposite the one through which we had entered, displayed an exit sign, suggesting someone exercising his or her twisted sense of humor.

We were instructed to proceed toward the "exit" and into the waiting bus. The bus doors were kissing the building's doorjamb, said proximity immediately discouraging any thought of executing a hasty left or right face and a bid for freedom. The bus, a machine gun mount on top, chicken wire stretched across the windows, and machine gun mounted jeeps in front of and behind the bus, escorted us down a dark and eerily quiet road to heaven knew where.

The chicken wire was to deflect grenades and other explosives lobbed through the windows, but it wouldn't stop bullets. I felt my only defense against a bullet through the forehead was to wear my steel pot. With my duffle in my lap for additional protection, I hunkered down into the seat as far as I could. I wanted to curl up on the floor, but no one else around me seemed bothered by the prospects of an attack, so I tried to suck it up and be brave, or somewhat brave, brave enough for me.

A relatively short ride ended at the 90th Replacement Battalion on the road to Saigon between the village of Bien Hoa and the huge base at Long Binh. There, we would be given our unit assignment, heralding the opening of a new chapter in our lives.

The processing building at the 90th, a step up from the reception "center" at Bien Hoa, would be my first introduction to the incredible fundamental ingenuity of design employed by the military. These buildings were meant to be temporary and utilitarian, so they were rife with inherent design problems in that they were energy inefficient, had a low fire rating, and were susceptible to pests, lots of pests.

The 90th processing building had wooden walls composed of slats, each one at an angle so the wind could blow through and ventilate. Wire screen was stretched across the inside of the walls, the tin roof and concrete floor complimenting the austere structure. This was an excellent idea for the heat of the season, but Vietnam could also become quite cold and damp.

Filling out form upon form—My Will (Egads!), identifying marks should I bite the dust, direction for sending my pay home except for a small allowance to be dispensed to me by the paymaster, and any other directives deemed necessary by the Army, my pencil was quickly ground to a nub. I was tired and hungry, a member of a horde of grumbling, pissed-off soldiers. We would not be given billets or a meal until we "processed in." I wanted to lay my head on a pillow and would be willing to sleep on concrete if necessary.

Understand, other than medical personnel, the rest of our flight buddies were being assigned to units, issued weapons, and proceeding on their journeys into the bush, their mission to search and destroy the enemy. I'm wondering if they were hoping this "processing" would go on endlessly.

The compound at the 90th Replacement Battalion sorely lacked hospitable charm. Located on flat ground in a rural area, not a blade of grass was in sight, just dirt and lots of it. If at one time there had been flowery beds of color in this dull landscape, they had disintegrated, every surface being distressed, pounded into oblivion, courtesy of thousands of boots. A few trees here and there dotted the landscape, and you were welcome to share them with the ants, so the buildings and bunkers provided the greatest amount of shade.

At every opportunity, dirt seemed to creep into all parts of the uniform that were not stitched closed. Sifting down through the grommets on my boots, it found purchase between my toes, dusting my feet a lovely brown, grinding into the crevasses of my skin, and filling the gaps under my nails. Gritty, moist creases rested behind my knees, and a path of grime snaked down my neck. We got dirty just being, not kicking up dirt, just being.

Dawn came thick with heat, weighing down as though it had substance. Breakfast eaten, I went off to find some entertainment because the suffocating heat and humidity made sleep an impossible pastime. I joined a GI sit-in, each of us leaning against sandbags, passing a bottle of Wild Turkey whiskey up and down the line, when I heard a thud near my right shoulder. A small trickle of sand was making its way out of a tear in the bag, a tear put there by a sniper's bullet.

Terrified, with my innards now roiling with spastic convulsion while "OH SHIT, OH SHIT!" was trying to crawl out of my mouth, I sheepishly asked the guys if we could move elsewhere.

But they laughingly said, "Nah, don't worry about Charlie. If he shoots one of us, then we shoot him, so as long as he sends a bullet our direction once in a while, he is doing his job."

With my anxious pleading, we finally moved to an area between buildings because I just knew that when the sniper pulled that trigger the next time, he would hiccup and accidentally shoot me. I told Mom before I left that nurses were not killed in Vietnam. I didn't want to lie to my mom.

The nursing billet at the 90th was situated near the base's northern perimeter. A lovely ripcord razor wire enclosed the backyard and a two-hole outhouse shared space within these confines. I never did like outhouses. The distaste continues to this day. I'm not just bothered by the dark hole from which the fumes of hell regurgitate but have an unfounded fear of serpents falling into this pit of excrement, coiled, waiting to exact revenge on the unwitting who is sitting.

My snake phobia has plagued me all my life. As a child, I knew beyond a shadow of a doubt that a python lay in wait under my bed and another in my clothes closet. Mustering all the courage I could pluck, I would drop to the floor, whipping the bed skirt up, looking for the scaly demon.

Well, it might not be under the bed, so in all probability, it slithered into the closet. Pulling the closet door open did not allay my fears. With great trepidation, I would rummage through the debris on the closet floor, testing my irrational resolve that snakes regularly visited me. And finally, with exhaustion settling in, I would brush my hand across the top of the bedspread in a final search for a reptilian body. I do not know how long I carried on with these bedtime activities, but I am pleased to say I no longer look for snakes in my bed unless I am camping in snake country.

8 January 1971 5:45 a.m.

*Well, I'm here! Arrived without a welcome from Charlie. Traveled 7 miles to the Detachment area with a guarded convoy. Received our funny money and a few other things. Was escorted to nurses BOQ (*Bachelor Officers Quarters*). Went out to take a shower in ice-cold water, thus woke up.*

The weather is quite nice. In fact I'm sitting here shivering a little bit. We're all sitting here saying what's that noise, who's outside. All in all it's quite quiet—knock on wood. I've lost 5 lbs since I left home—

not to my dismay. Haven't had anything to eat or drink for a while. We are actually having fun.

My room is plyboard walls and floor, hard cot, and a bright light. There are no doors and only a screen door on front. In a sense it's almost cruder than camping, the building seems to move when someone walks—I think it's me.

Will write again. 10 to 1 this afternoon, but for now would like to get this off. I'm just fine-in body, soul, and spirit. I found when our lip starts to quiver, the morale of the guys goes down so, I shall keep it stiff. Hopefully by Monday I'll get a chance to have 8 hrs of sleep.

The Good, the Bad, and the Ugly

By
Michael Tucker

My story: it was the best of times, and it was the worst of times. The best were the movie nights, compound barbecues, and flying to Da Nang on a Huey for a refrigerator. As crazy as it seems, I did do that. Refrigerators were a must. Taking the Chinook to the beach for some R & R on the weekends.

At the 85th, we were one big family as far as I was concerned. Everyone was equal in my eyes—enlisted and officers alike. Except for our racist CO, how I hated him, but I kept my mouth shut and accepted things as they were.

I had a shaving profile because if I shaved, I would break out with shaving bumps (ingrown hairs on my neck). Dr Patin gave me a script for a profile. A profile is a military exemption from shaving. One morning during a monsoon, Colonel Sukiyama was touring the enlisted men's area and saw me. That afternoon, I was called to his office.

I immediately knew why, so I shaved. He asked me about the profile, and I explained why to him. His reply was, and I quote, "Black men have tough skin and don't need a shaving profile." I was not allowed to be exempt from shaving.

The worst of times was when we had incoming casualties then all hell broke out. I will never forget those days, long hours in the OR and limb-burning duty.

The smell of burning limbs is still with me to this day, along with the terrible images of wartime injuries. I went to Vietnam Nam as a kid and returned as a man; I was grateful for that.

If I had to do it all over again, I would do so with no changes. I will never forget Vietnam, no matter how hard I may have tried in the past. Today, I embrace the fact that I served over there and will always cherish "the Good, the Bad, and the Ugly" of my experience.

I thank God for all the wonderful people I met during my tour at the 85th Evac. Forever in my heart and soul.

Michael Tucker, RN
Formally Spec 5 OR Tech

Vietnam Experience with a little pre and post-history

By

Vaughn Owens

I was drafted in July of 1969. I never thought I would be taken because of being deaf in my left ear. They were turning guys away for high blood pressure, flat feet, and other maladies, but not me.

I was sent to Ft. Leonard Wood for basic training. After basic training, out of one hundred GIs, I and one other guy were sent to Ft. Sam Houston for medic training. I thought because of my hearing, I would not be sent to Vietnam but would stay stateside or maybe be sent to Europe. Fooled again and received orders for Vietnam.

Arrived in Vietnam on 6 Jan 1970. What in the hell have I gotten into? I got off the plane onto a bus with barred windows and an escort with an M-16. Hot.

Housed in barracks with hundreds of other GIs waiting for orders. My first orders were to Quang Tri 18th Surgical Hospital. I had no idea where that was, so an E-6 pointed it out on a map. “OH MY.” I hopped on a plane and flew to Danang, where my orders were changed to the 85th.

85th Thoughts and recollections: In no particular order.

I was assigned a hooch (wonderful accommodations) with Johnny Cates and a couple of other short-timers, names I don’t remember. Johnny was the mail Clerk, and I was assigned to him as his replacement.

For most of my tour, my hooch mates were Marty Jacquot, Joe Manikowski (sp), and Ron Ziglar (sp).

Colonel Sugiyama, Captain Nelson, First Sergeant. A big man, I forgot his name.

Concertina wire surrounded the compound.

There was an airport next to the hospital, planes coming and going, and Sky Crane helicopters moving cargo.

Pulling perimeter duty at night around the compound and outer perimeter.

Helicopters brought wounded at all hours.

My mail headquarters where mail was delivered twice a day.

Getting a driver's license to drive a deuce and a half for picking up and delivering mail and an M-16 to protect the mail.

Getting blamed for delivering a Dear John letter.

Our little chapel, which I'm sorry to say, I didn't use much.

Monsoon rains always had a damp bed.

Mama San always tried to get us to eat some of her awful food.

MPC (Military pay currency) Play money. I still have some.

Outhouse for toilets (smiley the shit burner who took care of them) and hope the wind was blowing away the stench.

Flush toilets and real showers.

Water fights with the fire extinguishers.

Sports: Basketball in the motor pool, softball, and football with a trip down to the 95th for a game (I don't remember who won).

Lots of Pabst blue ribbon and Schiltz beer with the old pull tabs, and somewhere, you still used a church key.

Shows with Oriental bands singing our favorite songs (not the greatest, but with enough beer, they sounded great).

Taking patients to see the Bob Hope Show at the 101st Airborne and his troop coming to the 85th. I still have signed pictures of Bob Hope, Gold Diggers, Lola Falana, and Johnny Bench.

Care packages from home with goodies and tapes let me know what was happening back home. I still have some of the letters my mother saved.

Stereo equipment, reel-to-reel, and cassette tapes were sent from Japan. I still have some of the equipment and recordings.

Stress between African Americans and whites at times.

Ladies of the night smuggled on the compound.

Tended bar at the Officers Club for a period of time.

Being promoted to SP4 & SP5 during my tour didn't mean much except more money because I wasn't staying in the Army.

Rides in a Chinook to swim in the South China Sea.

Having a buddy from home giving me a chopper ride and letting me fly it for a brief moment.

Lots of pot and some heroin. I often wondered after I left what happened to some of those guys who used the heroin.

The letter I sent home spoke about how my tour might make me rough around the edges or crude in my actions.

Agent Orange (didn't know what it was at the time, but sure do now, suffered prostate cancer).

That last plane ride out of Vietnam. What a war hoop when it left the ground.

I probably have forgotten more than I have remembered. We tend to do that. Time heals. I'm not as bitter as I once was as a 22-year-old kid. I did a lot of growing up in a year.

I have a wonderful wife, two great-grandchildren, and two wonderful grandchildren. Life has been good.

Vaughn Owens

Patti Hendrix: My Sister/Hero/Adventurer

By

Gary Gingell

I was blessed with wonderful parents and three great sisters. A solid family full of warmth and love. My three older sisters had a positive effect on me. I dearly love Bonnie, Patti, and Sally (deceased).

Patti had a special influence. In the midst of growing up, I spent a summer with her in Hawaii as mentioned below.

I remember when she was going to college and then St. Luke pursuing her nursing career. She joined the army to help pay for her education. (Patti never shied away from adventure.) Even though there was a war going on, I did not think too much about it as they don't send women into battle...

She had a really sweet Cougar XR7. She always had cool cars: an MG, Datsun Z, etc., which obviously meant if she drove cool cars, she was a cool sister.

When she left for her army assignment in Hawaii, she kept in touch by writing letters to her little brother. As time passed, she invited me to visit her if I got good grades. As luck would have it, I made the grades and went to see her in June of 1970 at Tripler Army Hospital base. I had never been out of Ohio or flown, so traveling was a unique experience. Especially when I got bumped off the plane in L.A.!

WOW, what a fun place Hawaii was as a thirteen-year-old kid. It was such a wonderful experience. We got to roll around in her Austin Healy Sprite! Another cool car.

She taught me how to body surf, snorkel, and basically grow up. While she worked, I hung out at the Olympic-sized pool on the base. We toured a Nuke Sub at Pearl with one of her boyfriends. I dove off a large rock in Waimea Bay, and the Waimea Water Falls rocks. Saw my first ever concerts there—Neil Diamond and the Four Tops.

Being there with Patti, I really grew up. We hung out with the other doctors and nurses, which meant going to the Officers' Club where everyone except Patti was drinking. We went to the beach with a cooler filled with Olympia beer courtesy of the docs. Of course, the docs showed me how to drink beer on the beach and wine coolers at the Officers' Club.

In short, it was the experience of a lifetime for me. To share it with my sister Patti was extremely special.

I saw the war on the news but did not comprehend what it was all about or how it had or would impact many of the people we were with in Hawaii—including MY SISTER.

They all acted so normal!!

In early August, Patti told me I would have to cut my trip short because she was shipping out to the Vietnam War! I was more than a little pissed. I whined to her, "Couldn't you go in September so I would not be so inconvenienced???" She said that was not an option. I still did not grasp the gravity of where she was going and what she would be doing.

I was extremely grateful for my time with Patti and all the doctors and nurses I met in Hawaii. They were all awesome!

I got home and watched the war on TV but now had a different outlook. MY SISTER was there! She wrote often and never mentioned any danger. I figured they would not send her into battle and the hospitals must be in "safe" areas.

Later in life, I learned there was really no "safe" place in Vietnam and that Patti was very far north toward the DMZ. Not safe by any means. I guess they call it a "Forward Evac Hospital" because it is "Forward." As in near the battle areas.

Patti and John married in Vietnam and came home for a celebration. America might not have treated Vietnam vets with the honor they were/are due, but our neighborhood sure did! Everyone in the area showed up for the celebration at our house. Some were WWII vets and could definitely relate to the Vietnam Vets—Patti and John. War is War.

It was the first time I met Lt. John Hendrix. When they arrived and took their luggage into the house, he called me into the bedroom and showed me his .357 Magnum that he carried on the plane home! He said he never left home without it. It's a different world now. Their short stay ended, Patti and John returned to the war, and I went back to school. What a contrast in environments!

As life progressed, I learned a little about some of the dangers she faced on the base, her "walks" to the local orphanage, and even flying with John. These are not things that were forthcoming. They had to be pried from her. I believe God kept her safe on those walks and visits to the orphanage as she cared for his children. I'm sure many were orphaned by the war.

I am certainly not surprised she "sort of" disobeyed orders and left the base to help the kids. That is what defines Patti as the loving, caring person she is.

My lifelong friend Dan Welcome's brother, Jim, lost a leg to a mine in Vietnam. I did not immediately connect this to what Patti was doing there.

Eventually I realized that Patti had a front-row seat to all the horrors that war can bestow upon young men in battle. Patti was part of an exceptional team of people trying to put the young soldiers' broken bodies back together while facing the dangers of being IN A WAR ZONE. She worked on the Jim Welcomes and others who had worse outcomes. Many would go on to have PTSD that negatively affected their lives.

As life progressed, Patti dealt with John's PTSD issues, and tragically, she endured the greatest fear any mom or dad faces: the loss of a loving child. She has an inner strength that is all too rare. I am proud of her beyond words. The word *Hero* comes to mind, but it is too brief a description to fit Patti. That word often describes one incident or act whereas Patti lived a life full of such acts. She is much more than simply a *hero* to me and has inspired me throughout the decades.

I had the privilege of joining her at a couple of her Vietnam reunions and was awed by the doctors and nurses I met whom she served with. They all served through the horrors of war with Patti. WHAT A SPECIAL GROUP OF PEOPLE!!!

I salute you all!

My sister Patti: The adventure continues...

(As a side note: In 2021, I retired from Cleveland P.D. as commander of Special Services that included the narcotics, gang, and SWAT units. I responded with SWAT to all barricade and hostage situations and ran the Op. Occasionally, we would encounter someone suffering PTSD from various recent wars, including Vietnam. The negotiating group was also part of my team. They had all received intensive training, part of which dealt with PTSD. We were also very fortunate to have access to the V.A. and other groups that could assist us when dealing with PTSD-affected people. I believe this helped us mitigate situations that might have turned out differently in the 70s and 80s.)

Gary Gingell
March 2024

The Boot in the Burner

By
John Martin Streeby

They moved the man from the operating table to the gurney. All instruments and needles had been accounted for. There was blood, and there were scrub sponges and paper wrappings on the floor and blue-green sheets held together with towel clips.

When the patient was gone, the floor was washed, and the debris pushed to the drain in the center. The walls and table were washed with alcohol, and the big overhead light was wiped off and swung up out of the way. When they were finished, a man took away the plastic sack that had been by the operating room door.

He carried it across the helipad to the incinerator. He could feel splinters tearing the plastic, and when he pushed the sack into the small door of the incinerator, a bone splinter scraped his knuckle, and he closed his eyes and pushed the bag in the rest of the way with his foot, and closed the door. The incinerator was hot, and he could smell the plastic sack burning and then the boot inside.

To Preserve the Fighting Strength

By
John Martin Streeby

the light was bad
hey said
he was carried away
he died
they beat his chest
but he died
Ray gave one last hard smack on the chest with his fist
but he was dead
the doctors laughed at Ray
he was so short and the table was high for the doctors
Ray said it was a shame that such a young boy should be dead
dead weight
he had foamed at the mouth
a reaction to an overdose of morphine
he was a Viet Cong
the Viet Cong were very sensitive to morphine
taking him from the operating table
and putting him on the gurney
we were very clumsy
that was a shame too
we rolled the gurney out through the emergency room
and everyone looked
he was covered with one of the blue-green sheets
that Ray had taken from the warmer
we took him to the dead shed
we were in a hurry
there was no blood
I don't know what happened to the body
after we left it at the dead shed by the helipad

To My Wife

By
Michael D. Clark

Here's to my wife, I love her so,
although I left her long ago
she still remains deep in my heart.
And now that we're a world apart
I know what it is to be alone,
and we together must be strong
to make it through this hardest year,
separated in two worlds of fear.
But I know our love will carry us through,
for in our hearts we are not two
but one individual for all our lives.
And here is to my wonderful wife,
whom I pray will be all right
'til I come home from a drawn-out fight
with which I don't at all agree.
Why can't people just let us be
together to live our lives in peace
as civilized members of the human race?

Michael D. Clark, October 1970
(Written shortly after arriving in Vietnam.)

Searching for Dad

By
Lisa Abend, daughter of Dr. Mel Abend

Originally printed in AFAR Magazine (October 25, 2013)
Reprinted with permission of the author, Lisa Abend.

It was the three drunk men who pointed the way. Or, to be more precise, it was the boy who pulled up on his motorbike while I was talking to the three drunk men (all of whom, in truth, were far too inebriated—at the cocktailish hour of 10 a.m.—to do anything more than slurp at the cubes of coagulated pig's blood that floated in their bowls of soup).

Leering, they passed the photograph of the beautiful woman, its once sharp lines now faded, to the boy on the bike. She had worked at the military hospital where my father was stationed in 1970, and although she was not the person I most wanted to find, I had brought her picture from home because I thought she might lead me to the person who was. Looking at the image, the boy on the motorbike remembered a woman one village over who had worked at the hospital during the war and married an American doctor.

My translator, Phuoc, and I set off down the dirt road that the boy indicated, across the highway and past the rice paddies. The heat was dense and fierce, and I soon gave up trying to wipe away the sweat that dripped steadily down my neck. We came upon a man walking home from the fields, and Phuoc asked him for directions. The man pointed his machete at a two-story house farther down the road. Like many of the homes in Thuy Phu, a commune just outside Phu Bai, its living room was open to the street, so we stood politely on the steps, shooing chickens away from our feet while Phuoc inquired of the four women inside, "Is there someone here who married an American during the war? A doctor?" The oldest one nodded. She introduced herself as Van Thi Cúc and invited us inside.

I could hardly believe my luck. I was in Vietnam without a single contact, and yet on my first excursion, I had found one of the two people I was seeking. Taking off my shoes and stepping inside, I allowed myself to hope that this first, near-miraculous discovery would lead to a second.

"Here she is," Cúc said with a smile. I looked around the room expectantly, but none of the other women came forward. Then I noticed that Cúc's gaze was fixed on a photograph on the wall. It showed a middle-aged Vietnamese woman, her dark hair curled into neat waves, leaning into a man with a marked resemblance to the actor Elliott Gould. She was clearly not the one in my photo. "But he's not a doctor," Cúc said with a cluck any Jewish mother would recognize. "He's a dentist."

***

What was I doing in a stranger's living room in a tiny village in central Vietnam, parsing professions and looking at family photographs? In a sense, I was searching for my father.

He had died the year before. His last few days were spent at home, propped up in a bed that had been positioned in his study so he could look out through the windows at the Georgia pines. Sitting with him as he slept, I was struck by the obvious, but no less profound, realization that my father existed outside of me. It was a thought that probably comes to all of us, eventually: that our parents have lives that have nothing to do with us, their children. In those last few hours, I wished I had known him better, the Mel Abend who was not my father.

As my family and I prepared for the funeral, we went through old photo albums, including the one my dad had brought back from his year as a surgeon in an evacuation hospital during the Vietnam War. He went to Vietnam when I was about six, and growing up, the album had simultaneously attracted and terrified me, for it was filled with gory photos of mangled bodies on operating tables. But what I noticed now, as an adult, were the images of a young Vietnamese boy, no more than six years old himself, sitting up in bed with a beatific smile on his face. I recalled my father telling me that the boy had been near an explosion and was brought to the hospital still impaled on the post that had cut through his torso. My dad had operated on him, and now, in these photos, the boy was sitting up, smiling. Here was someone whose life my father had dramatically affected, and who had known my dad at a time and in a way that I never could. He would be in his 40s now. I wondered if I could find him.

My quest started, logically enough, in a hospitality suite on the outskirts of Las Vegas. In 1970, my dad was stationed at the 85th Evacuation Hospital in Phu Bai. Forty-two years later, the staff held a reunion. Now in their 60s and 70s, the doctors, nurses, and medics gathered in Las Vegas with what felt—even to this outsider—like relief. Decades later, most of them still didn't talk about the war with family or friends. My dad, who could otherwise chat about anything, had never done so either. "No one who wasn't there could understand what it was like," Gus Kappler, a thoracic surgeon who had helped organize the event, told me.

The high point of the weekend was a slide show that, with its images of helicopters and guys in fatigues flashing peace signs, seemed familiar, almost iconic. But for Gus and the other vets, the images on the screen weren't icons but memories: the mud, the lack of hot water, the drain in the operating room floor where the blood from surgery was washed down, the football games, the boredom, the Bob Hope show, the "designated driver" they would appoint to stay sober in case any casualties arrived.

I learned some things about my dad. The man whom I had seen smoke exactly once in my life was photographed doing surgery with a cigarette dangling from his mouth in front of a sign that read OXYGEN. NO SMOKING. The concert-level pianist who gave up the instrument permanently when I was in fourth grade played so well in the officers' club that the others dubbed him "Magic Mel." When a newly arrived nurse finished her first, brutal night in the OR, my dad told her to go outside and hit something, just to get the rage and fear out of her system. And when one of the medics asked him what to list as "cause of death" for a particularly tragic delivery of body bags, my dad had insisted, "Murder."

None of the veterans remembered the boy. But looking through a stack of black-and-white photos that I had brought, Kathy Gunson—the same nurse whom my dad had told to go hit something—recognized a Vietnamese woman. "She was the bartender at the officers' club," Kathy said. "She might have known that boy."

***

Five weeks later, I flew to Ho Chi Minh City. An expat friend based in Asia told me that everyone still calls the city Saigon, but it was hard to reconcile the images that name conjures with the bustling, prosperous metropolis dotted with Louis Vuitton outlets and cupcake shops that I encountered. Working up the courage to traverse the busy, crosswalkless streets, I managed to make my way to the War Remnants Museum. I had read that the museum's contents—fetuses deformed by Agent Orange floating in formaldehyde, grisly photographs of napalm victims—presented a rather one-sided version of the war. But the exhibitions were so heavy-handed, and the decades-old Communist slogans so far removed from the bustling commerce going on outside the door, that they seemed almost ironic.

I left the next morning for Huế, the large city nearest to Phu Bai. Home to Vietnam's last emperors, it stretches languidly along the Perfume River. I knew that Huế had been the site of some of the fiercest fighting during the war; it was the scene of a bloody battle and horrific massacre during the 1968 Tet Offensive launched by North Vietnam against the U.S.-supported South. But 45 years had done a lot to erase any trace of that past. Driving into the city, all I saw were tire shops and fancy homes under construction. I checked into a hotel in the backpackers' district, where the welcoming staff had an adorable penchant for leaving animal-shaped towel sculptures on the bed.

I met Phuoc the next day. He was friendly but no-nonsense, with a cool efficiency to him that I found reassuring. I handed him the photograph of the boy and explained the nature of my quest. Phuoc didn't seem to find any of what I said very remarkable. He did not remind me of how many people had been killed in the war or point out how many had emigrated after it. He did not, in other words, tell me I was crazy. He simply asked to borrow the receptionist's helmet, strapped it to my head, and ushered me toward his motorbike. "OK," he said. "Let's go look."

As we careened through the streets of Huế, the tourist bars advertising air-conditioning and cheap beer gradually gave way to furniture shops and street markets overflowing with flowers and fruit. Phuoc told me he had worked with U.S. veterans groups, leading them on tours and translating at encounters with former Vietnamese soldiers. "Sometimes they even meet North Vietnamese," he shouted above the motorbike's din. "It's always very meaningful for them to realize they don't have to feel that hostility anymore." I wanted to ask more, but I was too busy concentrating on maintaining my death grip on his bike. We narrowly missed colliding with a teenage girl who had balanced her phone precariously between her handlebars. She was texting as she drove.

We retraced the path I had taken in from the airport. Phuoc pointed to the mountains where Camp Eagle, the base for the 101st Airborne, had been located. We passed a rusted gate blocking a dirt road that seemed to lead nowhere. "That was the hospital," Phuoc said. We circled back. Behind the gate there was only jungle.

We pulled in to the village of Phu Bai and chose a street to follow at random. It was hard to get a sense of the place: Expensive-looking two-story houses with balconies stood next to cement-floor shacks, and streets ended abruptly in rice paddies. With no name or address to go on, our only strategy was to approach anyone who looked old enough to have been alive during the war.

At our first stop, a man in his 60s invited us to pull up a chair around the outdoor stove where his daughters and granddaughters were cooking. Phuoc explained our mission. The man looked at the photo a long time, then looked carefully at me. He said something long and complicated, and I turned with anticipation to Phuoc. "He said 'no,'" Phouc said.

I was incredulous. "All that talking and he just said 'no'?"

"Well," Phouc expanded. "'No, I have never seen him.'"

I handed over a second photo, this one of the woman that Kathy, back in Vegas, had told me tended bar in the officer's club. This time the answer came faster. It was no again.

As Phuoc and I stood to leave, the man mentioned a house a few doors down; the owner had been friends with some American GIs. We stopped by. No one there recognized the boy or the woman either, but again, everyone seemed to want to send us off with some kind of lead—a man who had worked at the base, say, or a woman who had been injured and sent to the American hospital. With each meeting, I would run through the same cycle of emotions: nervousness at approaching a stranger, hope as they contemplated the past, disappointment when it became clear they didn't recognize anyone, and then, unexpectedly, a light balm of gratitude at their willingness to take my search seriously and send me off with another suggestion. In this way, one person led to another until, finally, Phuoc and I found ourselves in Van Thi Cúc's living room, the one with the chickens outside and the photograph on the wall.

Cúc told me that the woman in the photo was Thuat, her sister-in-law, and that she had moved to the United States in 1972. Before that, Thuat had worked at the hospital, doing laundry and other jobs. She might know the woman or the boy I was looking for. I asked Cúc if she had contact information and she sent one of her granddaughters searching through a stack of papers in a credenza otherwise stuffed with Barbie dolls. The girl came up empty-handed. "But you could talk to her nephew," Cúc said. "He should know how to find her."

We met the nephew, a sullen man in his 20s named Can, in the café he owned near the main highway. Phuoc asked him about his aunt, and Can abruptly stood up and disappeared into the back to fetch some photos. I used the interval to gaze at the mural that covered one of the café's walls: a nude woman floating inside an egg that, in turn, hovered near a waterfall while white chickens observed the scene. I was trying to figure out the message—had the chickens laid the egg the woman was floating in?—when Can returned with a phone in his hand.

"Here," Phouc translated. "You can talk to his aunt."

I did a quick calculation in my head: It was 1 a.m. in Boston, where she lived.

"I'm so sorry to disturb you at this hour," I stammered into the phone.

"It's okay, I couldn't sleep anyway," came the voice on the other end. "I'm in the hospital."

"You're in the hospital?" I was feeling more sheepish by the moment.

"Yes, I'm having a tumor removed tomorrow." Thuat paused. "It's benign, though."

I was in a roadside café in a village in Vietnam, talking to a distant insomniac about the growth she was about to have removed. And no, she didn't remember a woman who had tended bar in the officer's club.

In the following few days, I adopted a routine. In the morning, Phuoc and I would go to Phu Bai and follow a daisy chain of connections that inevitably led nowhere. In the afternoon, I would take in Huế's sights in an attempt to put myself in my dad's place, to see what he had seen. I hiked out to the Thien Mu pagoda, where the lovely gardens were thick with butterflies. I ate dumplings that put the glue in glutinous rice and watched schoolkids practice tae kwon do with militaristic precision. I rode a dragon boat down the river and was predictably ripped off after I refused to buy a handpainted bookmark from the captain.

One night, while eating dinner at a vegetarian restaurant on the grounds of a pagoda, I was hit on by a monk, despite the fact that he was about 20 years younger than I and, well, a monk. His name was Hanh, he was waiting for friends, and he wanted to know what I was doing later that night. I looked up from my hot pot to notice that all the Westerners had by this time cleared out of the restaurant; except for the waitresses, Hanh and I were alone. Just as the situation was about to get really awkward, a bus pulled up in front and began disgorging dozens of passengers clad in identical brown robes. The place filled with monks, who bowed to each other jovially as they took their seats. "My friends," Hanh said. I was off the hook.

And the war? The past I was searching for revealed itself only in bits and pieces. Walking along the river one day, I found a vendor selling dog tags, the names—Brian Carson, Michael Danzinger—still legible. I had a beer one night at a bar that seemed to owe its tremendous popularity among Australians solely to its name: The DMZ. One afternoon, I visited the Forbidden City, former home to the emperors and today a compound of graceful, crumbling pavilions surrounded by a carpet of weeds and wildflowers. I eavesdropped shamelessly on a tour group and heard their guide say, pointing out one ruin, "American shells did that."

Wandering through Huế, where the hot bustle of shops and traffic would unexpectedly cede to tree-lined streets almost poetic in their stillness, I thought often of my father. Curiosity was one of his most pronounced personality traits, and I know he would have wondered, as I did, who thought to adorn the fat, brightly painted statues at the Thien Mu pagoda with real facial hair. He was a great eater and, like me, would have loved strolling through the market, peering at open vats of strange, fermenting things. And, as someone who delighted in family celebrations, he would have been just as charmed as I was by the high-cheeked couple posing in the street like fashion models for their wedding pictures as their parents looked on, beaming. But in many ways he became more mysterious to me in Huế. By the time I was old enough for such things to matter, my father was an experienced traveler, however when he'd arrived in Vietnam, he had never been much of anywhere. I had trouble imagining what a young man from an insular neighborhood in Boston would have made of the cone-hatted vendors balancing baskets of limes across their shoulders like human scales, or the monks with their massive, flapping fans. It was impossible, as well, to imagine this lovely, prosperous country torn apart by war. Whenever I asked about it, people always answered vaguely: Yes, it was terrible, a tragedy for all involved, but things are better now. It was as if everything from that time—the violence, the fear, the physical artifacts themselves and my father's experience of them—lay out of reach.

Toward the end of my 10 days in Vietnam, I went to Da Nang, a coastal city about 60 miles south of Huế, to see a nun. I had become convinced, based on no evidence other than my own desperation, that the boy I was seeking had been an orphan. Sister Xavier had run the Kim Long orphanage in Huế during the war, and now lived in a home for retired nuns. Well into her 90s, she was hard of hearing and frail enough to require a wheelchair. But she glowed with a kind of contentment I've not often come across. She took the photo, looked at the boy, and said he was very beautiful. "Did you know him?" I asked. "Oh, yes," she replied confidently. At that moment, a novice interrupted us, bearing glasses of weak tea. When I tried to turn the conversation back to the boy, Sister Xavier couldn't remember what we had been talking about.

Why had I wanted to find the boy in the first place? My father had saved his life, but I didn't need him to tell me my dad was a hero; I already knew that. I had told myself I was looking for the perspective of an outsider—someone who would have known my father intimately but in a different way than I had. I thought that by shifting the frame, by adopting someone else's viewpoint, maybe I would come to see my dad more clearly. But if I'm being honest, it wasn't just my dad I was hoping to see. I also wanted to see myself through my father's eyes, to know, with just a little more certainty, who I had been to him. In his letters home during the war, he barely mentioned me or my siblings. But the boy he operated on would have been more or less the same age as I was, the daughter he had left safely behind.

***

Why had I wanted to find the boy in the first place? My father had saved his life, but I didn't need him to tell me my dad was a hero; I already knew that. I had told myself I was looking for the perspective of an outsider—someone who would have known my father intimately but in a different way than I had. I thought that by shifting the frame, by adopting someone else's viewpoint, maybe I would come to see my dad more clearly. But if I'm being honest, it wasn't just my dad I was hoping to see. I also wanted to see myself through my father's eyes, to know, with just a little more certainty, who I had been to him. In his letters home during the war, he barely mentioned me or my siblings. But the boy he operated on would have been more or less the same age as I was, the daughter he had left safely behind.

I wondered if all those photos of the boy smiling from his hospital bed were a substitute for the ones of birthday parties and Halloween costumes he couldn't take that year. Or if he had thought of me while he tended to the boy, if he had been especially careful with him because he recognized that, in a different world, it could have been me on the operating table.

In any case, I didn't find much of the war, and nothing at all of the boy or the woman I had gone looking for. But I found something else. A group of haunted men and women in a Las Vegas hotel had led me to the boy on the bike with a good memory, and he had led me to the older woman who was willing to pick up her phone in a far-off hospital room. It went on and on, and it made me think: What was that series of random, interlaced, seemingly endless encounters if not a metaphor for life itself? Maybe I didn't find another Mel Abend, the one who existed outside my memory of him. But I did find a chain of people willing to help me, a stranger on a quixotic quest. I found connections, maybe not to my father, but from one person to another, and from them to me. And isn't connection, after all, a buffer against the things that haunt us—a year at war, the past that disappears, the death of someone we love?

Maybe there was no Mel Abend who existed apart from the father I knew. Maybe the only way I could know him—maybe the only way any of us can ever know anyone—was as the sum of these branching connections.

On the last day, Phuoc and I went back to Phu Bai. We spent that morning as we had the ones before, following the bread crumbs that elderly strangers cast before us. At one house, a couple invited us to sit at their dining table. It abutted a household shrine containing a photo of their son in uniform. He had been killed during the war.

As we were leaving, the woman suggested another house, a few doors down. A local physician lived there; maybe he knew the American doctors. We walked over. A handsome man in his 70s named Vo Kim Mai and his equally handsome wife welcomed us in. They were both dressed in pajamas: his of striped cotton, hers of purple silk. A puppy gnawed at my feet as we sat to talk. By now, I had given up on finding the boy, and I adopted a different conversational tack. I didn't explain about my father or show the photos. I simply asked the doctor if he had known any American soldiers during the war. He told a long story about a GI who was always trying to get others to drink with him. Mai outfoxed him by pouring his drink into a napkin.

I tried again. Had he known any of the surgeons at the military hospital? "Oh, yes," said Mai. Malaria was very bad back then, and once he had flown in a U.S. helicopter with an American doctor to bring medicine to a village. Did he remember the doctor's name? No, he did not. I pulled my iPhone out of my pocket. On it, I had copied a photo that one of the 85th Evac vets had given me back in Las Vegas. It depicted six of the surgeons, dressed identically in fatigues and standing in a row. I showed it to Mai and asked if, by chance, any of these men were the one with whom he had flown in the helicopter. He didn't hesitate. "That one," he said. And he pointed to my father.

The Criminality Of Agent Orange

By

Gus Kappler, MD

It is mid-March 2024.

At least seventeen of the 85th Evacuation Hospital '70-'71 personnel suffered from Agent Orange-related diseases. As a result, seven have died.

I boast of being afflicted by colon cancer, sixty-four Basal Cell skin cancers, Melanoma of the right cheek, Chronic Lymphocytic Leukemia, and most recently, Atrial Fibrillation with right-sided heart failure.

For a year, I operated on the devastatingly wounded 101st Airborne grunts.

Why am I being punished for saving lives and serving honorably?

Our military sprayed fifty-four thousand gallons of Agent Orange herbicides over the Phu Bai area before my arrival. This amount does not include spraying from helicopters, trucks, and by hand.

The term Agent Orange represents a "Rainbow" of herbicides. Their fifty-five-gallon drums advertised broad stripes of Orange, Blue, Green, Pink, Purple and White.

Agent Blue contained Arsenic.

Agent White contained Picloram.

Agents Orange, Green, Pink, and Purple contained a form of Dioxin.

Indeed, all the Agents cause cancer. Dioxin is extraordinarily carcinogenic and avidly mutates genes. This poison is a predictable by-product of Agent Orange production. It was a fact known to the military, its scientists, VA chemists, and Presidents Kennedy, Johnson, and Nixon.

The strategy was to defoliate the jungle canopy to better visualize the enemy, destroy the rice to deprive the enemy of food, disrupt the Ho Chi Minh Trail, and drive the population to the cities.

Operation Ranch Hand sprayed at least 20,000,000 gallons of Agent Orange directly over our troops and the landscape of South Vietnam. War planners increased the concentration of the sprayed solution to two parts per million. Five parts per trillion (100,000 times less) causes cancer in laboratory rats.

Monsanto and Dow Chemical deceivingly guaranteed the safety of Agent Orange when coming in contact with humans. There was suspicion that a former CEO of Dow falsified research reports proclaiming the herbicide's safety.

See: https://www.sourcewatch.org/index.php/Paul_F_Oreffice

"After Lyndon Johnson assumed the presidency, he ordered an increase in the use of herbicides. In 1968, Dr. Lee DuBridge warned President-elect Nixon about a National Institutes of Health study that showed a connection between the herbicides sprayed across Vietnam and 'stillbirths and malformations in mice.' Yet by 1970, 200,000 gallons a month of Agent Orange were being used." "Defense Secretary Melvin Laird considered curtailing the use of such herbicides," says historian C.B. Currey, "but General Creighton Abrams, commander in Vietnam, and his boss, Admiral John S. McCain, Jr., Commander-in-Chief, Pacific, as well as Admiral Thomas H. Moorer, acting Chairman of the Joint Chiefs of Staff, reaffirmed the necessity for its use."

See: https://www.theguardian.com/world/2003/mar/29/usa.adrianlevy

"During the war, many people understood some of the dangers and protested the use of Agent Orange. Congressman Robert W. Kastenmeier urged discontinuing the use of herbicides in Vietnam, a demand echoed by an editorial in *The Washington Post*. In 1967, Dr. Arthur W. Galston, often referred to as the man who discovered Dioxin in 1943, joined with other scientists to plead with Washington not to use Agent Orange in Vietnam. The Federation of American Scientists, members of the National Academy of Sciences, seventeen Nobel laureates, the Rand Corporation, and others urged terminating this form of chemical warfare. In fact, in 1969, United Nations Resolution No. 2603-A declared that the use of chemical agents in a manner used by the U.S. in Vietnam was a violation of the 1925 Geneva Protocol, a war crime. The UN General Assembly passed this resolution by a vote of 80 to 3."

See: http://politicalaffairs.net/killing-me-softly-how-agent-orange-murders-vietnam-s-children

The Vietnam War officially ended in 1975. Our Nation deployed over two million servicemen and women to Vietnam on land and sea. All, to varying degrees, were exposed to Agent Orange and other "Rainbow" herbicides that contained Dioxin, Arsenic, and Picloram.

It took a Supreme Court decision in 1984 to force both manufacturers to pay a paltry claim settlement to Agent Orange victims. It necessitated the Agent Orange Act of 1991 to force the Veterans Administration to recognize Agent Orange's disabilities. Until that time, veterans suffered and died from various diseases directly caused by Dioxin. Their children were born with grotesque congenital disabilities. They did not receive the compensation they certainly deserved from an agency representing the country they willingly and honorably served. This evasion of responsibility was a callous decision by our government and its politicians to discard and not help our warriors. Was it done for the nebulous rationalization of the "greater good?"

We at the 85th Evacuation Hospital drank, made ice cubes, and showered with Dioxin-contaminated water. We inhaled the "Rainbow's" aerosolized poisons from the surrounding dust and the grunt's clothing in the ED.

Larry Wright informed me that he was handling stored Agent Orange barrels "next" to the 85th Evac when we were there.

Bernard Downey disclosed the concurrent spraying of the Firebase Bastogne and Camp Eagle with Agent Orange.

The most consequential question about the Vietnam War is, "What does our country owe to those it sends to war? To rehabilitate or discard?"

Yes, all the US government and military leaders did agree, including Presidents Kennedy, Johnson, and Nixon, to utilize multiple herbicides, including Agent Orange. Their decisions' criminal aspect is that they all knew of and ignored Dioxin's presence and potential risk for inducing lethal diseases and congenital malformations.

There still exists a political barrier to rehabilitating our warriors.

When engaging twenty-first-century warriors suffering from "Burn Pit" exposures, the Veterans Administration initially appeared to be reincarnating the old playbook they applied to Agent Orange's disability.

I'm angry that special interests, protecting one's legacy, political inertia, and pet projects pursued for political gain deplete the capital necessary to rehabilitate those who have served this country honorably.

Our great Nation should not discard its veterans!

Never!

IT WASN'T JUST AGENT ORANGE:

The Rainbow Herbicides of the Vietnam War Era

AGENT GREEN
2,4,5-T

USED: 1962
PURPOSE: Defoliation of Jungle Vegetation
IN VIETNAM: 365 drums (20,056 gallons)

AGENT PINK
2,4,5-T

USED: 1961-1963
PURPOSE: Defoliation of Jungle Vegetation
IN VIETNAM: 1,315 drums (72,256 gallons)

AGENT PURPLE
2,4-D; 2,4,5-T

USED: 1962-1965
PURPOSE: Defoliation of Jungle Vegetation
IN VIETNAM: 12,475 drums (685,474 gallons)

AGENT BLUE
Cacodylic Acid

USED: 1966-1972
PURPOSE: Crop Destruction
IN VIETNAM: 29,330 drums (1,611,619 gallons)

AGENT WHITE
2,4-D; Picloram

USED: 1966-1972
PURPOSE: Defoliation of Jungle Vegetation
IN VIETNAM: 104,800 drums (5,758,528 gallons)

AGENT ORANGE
2,4-D; 2,4,5-T

USED: 1965-1970
PURPOSE: Defoliation of Jungle Vegetation
IN VIETNAM: 208,330 drums (11,447,272 gallons)

WWW.VVA.ORG | 1-800-VVA-1316

85th Evacuation Hospital
Excerpts from:
Bob, You Can't Do That
By
Robert F. Jackson, MD

Published in 2021 by Robert F. Jackson, MD. Reprinted with permission from Robert F. Jackson, MD.

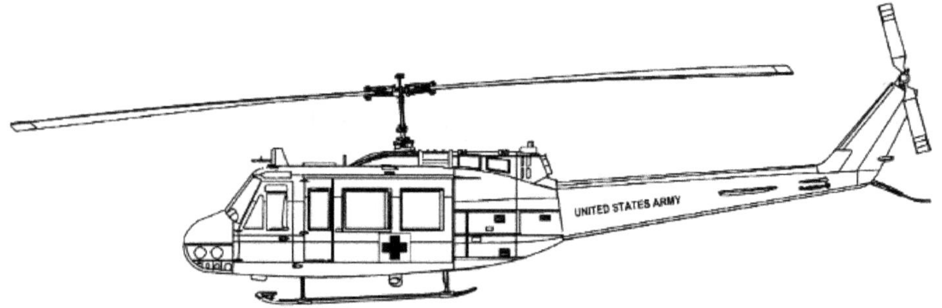

Vietnam

I went through my residency at Miami Valley Hospital in Dayton glibly. Occasionally, I would get something from the Army telling me my rank had changed or some other bit of jargon. In December 1970, many of my colleagues who were finishing their training in June 1971, as I was, began receiving orders as to where they would be going after their training. I received nothing. Though I did not officially finish my residency until June 30th, my duties as chief resident ended on the 28th or 29th. I had received my diploma and was moonlighting in the emergency room. Since I had heard nothing from the Army, I assumed—incorrectly—I would not be going.

I had offers and made plans to enter private practice in Dayton. On the day my residency officially ended, my wife called me while I was working in the emergency room.

"Honey, we just got orders from the Army. We're going to San Francisco," my wife Margie said.

"How do you know?" I asked.

"Well, our new address is APO San Francisco."

Knowing nothing about army lingo, I said, "Take those over to Joe" — our neighbor who spent twenty years in the military— "and see what that really means."

A little later, Margie and I talked again. "This is not good news. He says this means you are being sent to Vietnam," she said.

That was another black day.

There has to be a mistake, I thought. *I'm married and have three children. There's no way I should be sent to Vietnam.*

I actually went to Washington to see if there was some way to get my orders changed, to no avail. At about this point, patriotism kicked in, and I realized if my country needed me to take care of injured soldiers, I had to go.

I remember lying in bed with Margie one night and telling her, "I have to go and serve if my country needs me."

We put our lives on hold and headed for Fort Sam Houston in San Antonio for basic training. Can you imagine trying to indoctrinate 100 or more doctors who were pretty independent? We learned how to march, if you can call it that. I remember marching to the "Mickey Mouse Club March." I'm not sure the sergeants who were teaching us thought it was funny. We also learned how to shoot military weapons, read maps, understand military protocol, and what a gig line was: the fly of the pants and the button seam of the shirt aligned. I still line up my pants and shirt with the gig line straight.

It was my first experience of the segregation of officers and EMSs. We had an Officers' Club, but the soldiers who taught us every day couldn't join us. I didn't understand it. We received our uniforms, which we had to buy. I had to buy another one when I returned from 'Nam because I lost about forty pounds over there.

At Fort Sam, I learned the meaning of *Suck Up*. We had a guy in our class who sucked up to the commanding officer. He was prematurely bald on top with hair around the sides. We referred to him as "General Half Track." He was kind of an a**hole and lorded it over us that he was acting commanding officer. On our final day, we were at Camp Bullis. In the PX, we, meaning the whole class except General Half Track, bought condoms and filled them with water.

When he said, "This unit is disbanded," I think he was struck with about 90 condoms—aqua missiles. While at Camp Bullis, we were taken into the woods at night and given compasses and coordinates, and told to find our way back to camp. We also shot weapons. To emphasize the difference between high-velocity and low-velocity wounds, they had us shoot gallon cans of sauerkraut. Wow, did that leave an unmistakable smell, even though we were a long way from the explosions.

Margie and I didn't want to think about when the five weeks of training were over. We rented an apartment just outside the gates of Fort Sam. The name was Bali Hai Apartments. A doctor going into anesthesia tipped us off to them, and they had a pool, which the kids loved. We lived there for about 4 ½ weeks. Margie had the apartment fumigated three times as she is not a fan of cockroaches.

We stayed busy so we didn't get too depressed over the upcoming separation. San Antonio is a great city with lots of activities. We rented a small car and traveled every weekend. We went to Mexico, Busch Garden, the Astrodome, the Alamo, and spent a lot of time in San Antonio. There was a small amusement park near our quarters. We frequented it many evenings—I think rides were a dime for the military. The boys loved it; Susie enjoyed the noise and the stroller ride. She was only nine months old, and I carried her all the time. After I left for Nam, Margie commented that her arms and back hurt because she wasn't used to having to carry the baby.

It was so hot that August that the boys spent most of the days in the pool. Bob developed the worst cases of otitis externa I have ever seen. We experienced army medicine, and they took very good care of him. While there, all the doctors were drug tested. I rarely take any medicine, including aspirin or acetaminophen, but I had a false positive for drugs. I had to go be retested and meet with a military doctor.

He said, "Your test came back positive. Do you use any drugs?"

"Well, if I thought it would keep me from going to Vietnam, I would say *yes*."

He laughed. "Won't help."

He retested me, and it was fine. It did give me concern all the time I was in country, though—I was afraid I might have another false positive and wouldn't get to come home as soon. However, they tested us many times, and it never happened again.

Margie and the kids returned to Dayton about a week before training camp was over. We kept the boys out the first week of school. We thought I would leave Fort Sam and go directly to Vietnam, so on Margie's last weekend there, we spent a night in Galveston on the beach. I remember it like it was yesterday—after the kids were asleep, walking along the beach, holding her in my arms, and realizing how hard it was going to be without her. I know we both cried a bit as we held each other.

When we came back to Fort Sam, she and the kids left, and I moved in with one of the other doctors who was in the class following ours by about three weeks. He had been one of my interns at Miami Valley, and he and his wife allowed me to stay with them until I went to Camp Bullis. One night he was studying for some test, so his wife and I went to see MASH. It wasn't as funny as when I had seen it before because I knew I was on my way to a unit much like that. It was ironic, or maybe not, that every morning the Fort Sam Band played the theme song from MASH prior to our marching maneuvers.

Our time at Fort Sam was enjoyable. Residency had been so busy, and I had been gone so much that I think it hurt our marriage. One of the rewards of Vietnam was that it reinforced our love for each other and our marriage. In Texas, we had as much fun as possible. We had no money but made do. We ate out a lot, especially after Margie found the cockroaches. All of us living at Bali Hai were transient. Many, like me, had either been in residency or internship programs for a few weeks before arriving at Fort Sam, and we became close. The wives got together during the day, and we had some group cookouts. When we went to the amusement park, many of our neighbors were there as well. During our training, we were invited—or rather, required—to go to a reception at the Officers' Club to meet and greet the commanding officer. My wife refers to it as, "You will go, and you will have a good time." There were some concessions for us who were heading to Nam. We didn't have to buy dress blues but could go in our Class A green. We were also instructed on proper protocol.

Margie and I could not get enough of each other, but it wasn't until I was half a world away from her that I realized how life without her sucked. After Camp Bullis, we got our orders, and I had a few days before deployment. I couldn't imagine not taking the opportunity to spend more time with Margie and the kids, so I flew home to Dayton. It was good to spend more time with the family, but the second goodbye was as hard, or harder, than the first.

Excerpt from Bob, You Can't Do That
by Robert F. Jackson, MD.
Published in 2021 by Robert F. Jackson, MD.

85th Evacuation Hospital (Phu Bai) Officers Club.

The Good, The Bad, The Ugly

I left Dayton on a 747, which was relatively new at the time. Since I was traveling in my military uniform, I was given special privileges and allowed to go on the upper deck where there was a lounge and bar. I tried to read but didn't accomplish much because I couldn't get my mind off the fact I was leaving my wife and kids at home to fend for themselves. I arrived in San Francisco, walked for approximately a block, and found a bus to Travis Air Force Base. At around 8:00 pm, we boarded the bus and traveled the 67 miles in one and a half hours. There I had my shot record evaluated, cleared border control, checked my duffle bag, and met up with another general surgeon, Major Nalder. We had been together at MFSS. (Medical Field Service School – Fort Sam Houston) A nurse from Connecticut joined us, and we went to the cafeteria for coffee. I made a call home to my wife and mother, who came to stay with Margie after my departure.

By this time, many of the other folks who had been at MFSS arrived. I met with a drunken helicopter pilot on his way back to Vietnam for his fourth tour of duty. He was extremely funny and kept offering us some of his birthday Scotch. As soon as we changed into our khakis, they announced, "Clear the building," and we were marched out. It was extremely cold, and after about 40 minutes, they marched us back to the main terminal and said we had a bomb scare. Not the way you want to leave to go to war.

I wrote to my wife, "I guess there is nothing to it since Travis didn't blow up after we left."

At about 3:15 p.m. we were bussed out to the DC-8/Charter flight Q2B3, an airline run by Overseas National Airlines—haven't heard of them before or since. There were 300 of us crammed in like sardines. We flew to Alaska and deplaned in Cold Bay, a good name. The flight to Alaska was the only darkness we had for our entire flight. From Alaska, we flew to Japan. I read half a novel and played Gin Rummy with John Bowman, who I would spend a lot of time with during my tour. John was another general surgeon who ended up stationed at two of the hospitals where I was. The meals were not the greatest, and we made jokes about them either being polar bear meat or water buffalo. I did get to see Mount Fuji, which was very, very pretty. At the PX in Japan, I purchased a cheap watch. Actually, it was 25 jewels; I paid $27 for it. When I went to set it, I realized I lost a whole day crossing the dateline. I remember thinking,

That's good; I get an extra day on the way back. So I gained two days in my favor.

After an hour and a half in Japan, we flew over the South Pacific, Formosa, and many other beautiful islands, and finally landed in Binh Hoa. As usual, we were filed into a large room and filled out more forms. It was hot and raining. We picked up our duffle bags, loaded them onto a truck, and were bussed to the 90th Replacement Battalion in Long Binh. From the bus, I saw what a primitive place Vietnam was at the time. There were shacks with people in rags and streets lined with military convoys. Everyone seemed to have weapons, and reality set in: I was in a war zone.

I've never been able to adequately describe the 90th Replacement Battalion. Red mud everywhere, rain pouring down. There were one or two blacktop-type streets, but filth appeared everywhere. After the bus, we were ushered into a long building for "in processing." A young sergeant instructed us in—yep, you guessed it—how to fill out more forms. Medical personnel were told nothing would be done with us for a few days.

We had an interview at 0830 and received our assignments and billet. I wrote home, "This is no Holiday Inn." I once again learned rank has its privileges. As a major, I was given a room with two bunks. Captains and lower ranks were placed in barrack-type quarters. My room consisted of a squared-off area in a two-story building with plywood floors, two cots, mosquito netting, one lonely lightbulb, and the filthiest, sand-filled sheets I had ever seen. I was so tired I didn't care. I roomed with George Saj, a fellow general surgeon from my class at MFSS. Once we completed our billeting process, I had to get the dirt and slime off my body. I don't think I've ever been that dirty. There was a Vietnamese-run sauna bath with hot and cold showers on the base. I took a cold shower, followed by a hot shower, followed by a hot shower, followed by a cold shower. Even in all the filth around me, I felt refreshed. With the time zone change, anxiety, and uncomfortable surroundings, it was difficult to sleep. I got up at 3:30, shaved, and wrote a letter home at 5:30 a.m.

One night during my time at the 90th Replacement Battalion, I dreamt about the snakes we were told lived in the jungles of Vietnam, which was one of our last lectures at Fort Sam Houston. I woke up out of a deep sleep and saw two beady eyes coming toward me, and it appeared there was a long, tubular body associated with them. Thinking I was being attacked by some sort of viper, I came yelling out of my bunk. I looked up and realized it was actually my mosquito netting rolled up, and the two eyes belonged to a gecko lizard. At about the same time, two officers who had just returned from the Mekong Delta were locked and loaded, standing in our doorway. I'm lucky I didn't get shot. I received a lot of teasing from my colleagues the next morning at breakfast.

At 8:30 a.m., we were taken to a tiny building where we received our fatigues. They were comfortable but not stylish. Around 1:00 p.m. or 1300 hours military time, we went back to processing and were then taken to the 24th Evacuation Hospital to meet medical personnel and again laughingly get interviewed.

During our time at Fort Sam Houston, we were given what were to be our assignments in Vietnam. Unfortunately, they were not accurate. I had been told I would be going to Qui Nahn, but I found out I was going to Phu Bai. Colonel Bruce Raymond was the surgical consultant over surgical personnel and said we didn't need to be there because he had an adequate number of surgeons.

The six of us said in unison, "We will go home."

"Unfortunately, first in, first out, you will be staying," we were told. "Major Jackson and Major Bowman, you will be going to the 85th Evacuation Hospital at Phu Bai."

We went to the map. Our fingers traveled north, and we got to Da Nang. Still no 85th Evacuation Hospital. We went further north and found the Demilitarized Zone (DMZ), and almost within spitting distance was the hospital. I'm not sure I believed Col. Raymond when he told me it would be safer than Qui Nahn. I felt he was honest, though, and later in my tour felt that way even more. He was helpful in realizing the medical facility at Phu Bai should be disbanded. During our interview that day, he told us he needed more nursing personnel and more GMOs.

I remember a young attending surgeon at Miami Valley who returned from Vietnam approximately one year before I finished my residency. He told me, "If you find out you're going to Phu Bai, cry a lot." I found out the 85th Evacuation Hospital was the medical support for the 101st Airborne, and their bases pretty much surrounded the hospital. I received my new address:

Major Robert F. Jackson
85th Evacuation Hospital
APO San Francisco 96308

John Bowman was going there as well, and sometime within the next few days, we were transported to Da Nang and dumped at the airport. Not knowing what to do or how to get to Phu Bai, we went to the hospital in

Da Nang and finally got someone to take us to the 95th Evacuation Hospital. We slept on the ward. They lost us in Da Nang for a couple of days. At the 95th, I ran into Walt Jolly who had been a resident at Indiana University School of Medicine when I was a senior med student. We were told we couldn't fly until after Election Day because President Thu was running unopposed, and they expected some increase in activity from the Viet Cong. However, guess when they decided to fly us by chopper to Phu Bai? Election Day.

When I arrived, I had another surprise. Dick Rau, a classmate from medical school who completed his surgical residency in California, was stationed there as well. When I arrived at Phu Bai, the hospital employed four fully-trained surgeons and two partially-trained surgeons. There was a total of 22 doctors, and the hospital had 200 personnel serving there. We lived in "hooches," wooden, beach hut-like structures raised off the ground because of the monsoons. We used electric blankets to keep our sheets dry and a small electric heater to keep our clothes dry—somewhat unusual in a country that was so hot.

My first day at Phu Bai, I was picked up at the airport and delivered to the 85th Evac, where we were taken to the Officers' Club, and Col. Swanson and Dick Rau met us there. As we sat down, there was a massive explosion.

John and I were ready to crawl under the table, but Col. Swanson said, "Oh, don't worry. They blow up the old ammo dump every Sunday afternoon over at the ammo dump."

It was an exciting welcome for a couple of newbies.

It took a couple of days for us to wade through the paperwork, clear finance, find quarters, etc. I was lucky to take over the hooch of a doctor who was returning to the world. During my first week or so after our arrival, we had the "Hi and Bye" party. After the party, I realized I could be a grunt. I played pinochle with the commander, John Bowman, and a male nurse—probably my first of 500-600 games during my tour of duty at Phu Bai. It seems, at least at that time, it was the Army game.

Finally, after about a week in Phu Bai and almost two months after ending my residency, I was finally back in the operating room. A North Vietnamese soldier was brought in after stepping on a mine. Both his legs had been blown off, and by X-ray, I saw he had frags in his abdomen. We took him to surgery. It was the first time I operated with Cary Conyers, who was a partially-trained surgeon. I let him do the case, and I assisted. I felt like I was a chief resident again. We explored the soldier's abdomen while the orthopods completed his amputations. Once he was stabilized, he was sent to the POW camp in Saigon. The OR was very workable for what we were doing. But more importantly, I learned the OR techs were good. The nurses, both in the OR and the hospital, were great.

A few days later, I was playing volleyball. We did anything we could to make the time go faster. One of the Ems came and told me there was a phone call for me in the hospital.

"Who is this?" I asked.

"Captain Rugsegger."

He was one of my interns from the Valley who followed me a few weeks later at Fort Sam and was now at the airport in Phu Bai. I obtained a Jeep and picked him up along with other medical personnel who were stationed near Phu Bai. It was a neat surprise. Our wives were both in Dayton, and we attended the same church, so it was kind of like having family there. It just so happened that night at the Officers' Club, we had a USO troop of Korean singers and band. Mike and the other officers with him stayed for the show. The 101st chopper pilots attended, as well as others. After the show, when it was just hospital doctors and nurses. We conned the cook at the club into fixing bacon and eggs.

Excerpt from Bob, You Can't Do That
by Robert F. Jackson, MD.
Published in 2021 by Robert F. Jackson, MD.

90th Replacement Battalion – Long Binh.

October

October 16th. I'll never forget it. A young soldier named Robert Nugent Brown was brought into the ER. He was a year out of West Point and one of the bravest men I ever met. He was leading his men, as many of these courageous young officers chose to do, taking the point instead of delegating it. I was on call when they brought him in critically injured. We called for help, and I think there were three orthopods and three surgeons working on him. I explored his abdomen, debrided his scrotum and penis, and repaired his urethra. He lost one leg at the hip and had a fractured ankle on the other leg. We had to remove the radius from one of his arms, and he lost four fingers on that arm as well. We gave him 45 units of blood. Believe it or not, we got him stabilized. He had an eye injury, too, but we didn't have an ophthalmologist in Phu Bai, so we planned to send him to the 95th Evac. The next morning, he was somewhat conscious. I was making rounds and walked up to his bed in the ICU. With his good arm, he pulled out the endotracheal tube.

He looked at me and saluted. "I am sorry, Sir, I just couldn't stand that thing."

The amazing thing is he probably didn't initially end up on a casualty list because injuries from land mines were not listed as being from hostile fire. We transferred him to the 95th when he was stable. A day or so later, they had to change his hip dressing because he began bleeding. Because of the blood we gave him, plus the blood they gave him in Da Nang, he developed DIC, a clotting abnormality that occurs sometimes after blood transfusions. The blood couldn't clot.

He died in Da Nang.

What a waste. Those of us who took care of him were depressed and angry for days, and I wrote about him to my wife. I didn't realize he was the son of an assistant football coach at Indiana University. Margie was watching the Indiana/Ohio State game a few weeks later when she saw Coach Woody Hayes walk across the field and hug one of the coaches.

The announcer stated, "Coach Hayes went over to offer his condolences to Coach Brown, who lost his son in Vietnam."

I didn't even know he died until I received a clipping from Margie and the story about the game. She wrote, "Honey, that was your patient." Unfortunately, that was the case. Ironically, he had spent time in Dayton as well. I called the doctors in Da Nang to find out what happened after her letter. I have since been to the Wall to find his name, something I had to do! What a brave young man.

***

Later that same day, another soldier lost his leg. I wrote to Margie about how good it felt to do an appendectomy on a GI who came with appendicitis. It was good to do a clean, trauma-free surgery. Even that soon, I developed some anger because we realized they were deescalating the war but were still sending these kids out on what we felt were unnecessary missions. It seemed such a waste of young lives.

At some point, I wrote Margie that people came into the ER who were hysterical, drunk, or drunk *and* hysterical. A couple were drug addicts. However, we also had things you would see in any city of 40,000 or so, which is what we served: kidney stones, fractures, appendicitis, etc.

We operated on a lot of Army of the Republic of Vietnam soldiers, too. One afternoon, a couple of ARVN soldiers were brought in. I operated on one of them who required a knee disarticulation on one leg, an above-knee amputation of the other leg, a left arm amputation, and an orchiectomy. The mines that both our soldiers and the Vietnamese stepped on sent explosives and fragmented metal up under any flak jacket. In other wars, jackets were not worn, chest and body wounds often resulted in death. In Vietnam, we were able to save many, but often with the loss of limbs and other debilitating injuries.

During my months at Phu Bai, my family asked me to describe what my living quarters were like. My hooch was made of a hodgepodge of materials. The walls were made of brown, hard board, and the ceiling was 1/8-inch plywood painted a dirty gray by one of the former occupants. The floor was green-painted plywood. I had a couple of fans, a bed, an old ammo box, a small refrigerator, a shelf that served as a desk, and a wall locker for clothes. I slept a lot in that hooch. The saying was, "If you slept twelve hours a day, you cut your tour of duty in half." Another saying was, "The wind doesn't blow in Phu Bai, it sucks." The officers' hooches were lined on either side of a metal walkway to try to keep us out of the mud. There was a common "shower" on the back of the hooch next to mine. The water was usually cold. It was not uncommon to be showering and have mamasans come in to rinse clothes or empty a bucket.

Bill Harmon, a partially-trained orthopod from Alabama, told me one day, "Hey, Jacks, I don't mind so much when a mamasan comes into the shower, and I don't mind when she gets some other mamasans, and they come back, but, man, I hate it when they sit there and laugh."

He had a sense of humor.

One of the things I learned quickly was my training at the Valley prepared me well, and I found I was a competent surgeon. I say that not boastfully, but humbly; I was so appreciative of my training program and especially my program director, Dr. Finley.

He told us, "There is no way I can have you do every procedure. I believe, however, I can train you so you can operate on most anything."

I found that to be true in Vietnam. In one day, I explored a soldier's neck and removed frags and took care of an RVN colonel involved in a truck accident. He had practically scalped himself with loss of tissue, but I was able to repair it. He also had a basilar skull fracture and a fractured clavicle. I ended the day taking care of a GI with a thrombosed hemorrhoid.

A recurring theme to my tour was how important Margie was to my life. The overwhelming thing I remember is how much I missed my wife and the realization of how much I loved her. Our letters gave us a closeness we never experienced before. I knew I loved her but didn't realize the depth until I couldn't touch her, call her, and talk to her. It was like I was only half there. I constantly prayed for a drop. I dreamt of her and woke up to realize I was alone. It was terrible not being there to help raise our kids, but I didn't need to be concerned. She was doing a fabulous job at home keeping everything in order.

I missed the kids so much. I wasn't there to watch and encourage Bob in his sports, wasn't there for Tom's elementary school moments or activities, and, of course, it was hard not to see Susie's first steps. Margie kept me updated with letters as best she could, but it didn't change how much I longed for my family.

***

I became friends with the nurses at our hospital. They were very dedicated. One of them, Marilyn, was married to a chopper pilot, John Tarnosky, and we spent a lot of time together. Marilyn became my favorite pinochle partner. John wanted to stay—he loved the Army and flying helicopters—and was on his second tour. In October, he found out he was going to be RIFT. I was angry that after all those years of putting his life on the line, the Army was kicking him out. The chopper pilots reminded me of what I believe our WWII Air Corps must have been like.

At one point, Margie wrote there was nothing in the papers about Vietnam. It didn't surprise me; I knew the politicians were trying to soft-pedal the fact that we were still in Vietnam. But for the 200,000 of us there, separated from our families, and for those kids out in the field on patrol or the kids we treated with multiple injuries, it was very real. At that point in the war, the Army no longer received good equipment. The new equipment went to the Vietnamese, and much of our equipment and weapons ended up in the hands of the Viet Cong and North Vietnamese. I think it was similar to what is happening today, where our military is working with antiquated weapons and equipment while we furnish our "allies," and our weapons and equipment are taken by the radical Islamic terrorists. However, President Trump replenished our military during his presidency.

***

After a while, things settled into a routine. Some days we weren't busy, and we found ways to fill the time. We read, studied, slept, played volleyball or baseball, played Ping-Pong or pinochle, watched movies (if one got sent up), and prayed for a drop. During those times, the morale of the hospital bottomed out. Then there were days when we were inundated with mass casualties. Even though we were angered at the waste of young lives, the morale of the hospital went up because we felt needed and could practice our God-given talents.

We also experienced Typhoon Hester. We spent two days sandbagging the roof of the hospital and our hooches and tried not to blow away. The rain came down horizontally and felt like sand stinging our skin. It was actually kind of fun to battle the elements. We protected our patients in the safest places possible, making sure we had personnel to watch over them. After Hester had done all her damage, there was a lull the next day. It was cool with not much humidity, unusual in Phu Bai. My buddy Mike had brought some specimens down to the hospital lab and was trapped there until the storm was over. When we shored up the hospital, he lost his wedding ring. The next day, probably twelve hours after he lost it when Hester was at her worst, we went outside searching for it, wandering and looking at the damage and sandbags we filled the day before. We found the ring lying totally exposed on top of the sand.

One day I was in the mess hall, and an EM came in, yelling, "Are there any surgeons here?"

I ran to the ER and found a young GI who had been flown in from up north. (It couldn't have been too far north since we were only ten or twelve klicks from the DMZ.) He had stepped on a booby trap and was in severe shock. As I evaluated him, the commanding officer of the 101st came in.

The general asked, "Major, is there anything I can do?"

"This boy needs blood."

Literally, a few moments later, we got these guys on the OR table. The 85th Evac worked as a fantastic machine.

A corpsman came in. "Dr. Jackson, there are 20 or 30 guys lined up at the lab donating blood."

I took out the GI's spleen and debrided the multiple wounds, and the orthopods took care of his many orthopedic injuries. We gave him about 30 units of blood. After we had him stabilized, I came out of surgery. The general was waiting to check on the boy's status.

"Did you order those GIs with that blood type to come and give blood?" I asked.

"No! All I did was make an announcement that 'One of your comrades needs blood of this type.' These are all volunteers."

Later, I put a letter in the GI's Purple Heart case, telling him what his buddies and fellow soldiers had done for him. His name was Chuck Ayers. About three months later, I received a letter from Chuck, thanking me for letting him know and telling me he was on the mend. He was brave and in a lot of pain when he was with us, but he didn't complain. He was pretty much in a coma when we medevaced him to Okinawa, so he remembered very little about the whole episode. I complained at the time that the politicians and congressmen should see these kids. We felt like we were ignored stateside.

***

I missed Margie and the kids so much at times it was a physical pain. There was a period of ten days I received no mail from anyone, and I was sure something was wrong. I remember the relief when letters that had been held up finally arrived, and everything was okay at home. Skype and email would have been nice, but it might have made us even more homesick.

We often played basketball. Someone had taken the end of an old hangar and converted it into a makeshift basketball court. It probably looked funny: eight or ten shirtless guys in fatigue pants and combat boots playing basketball. We did everything we could to pass the time. John Bowman decided to learn Vietnamese. He had a real language aptitude, and the hospital interpreter taught him. He learned so well he developed an accent of the area around Huế. Later, when he and I were moved to Long Binh, the Vietnamese workers asked if he was from North Vietnam. I don't have that kind of language capability, so I learned slang, like, "You number one GI" or "You number ten GI."

When I first arrived, one of the mamasans asked, "Bác sĩ?"

I wasn't sure what she was asking and thought I was being propositioned. One of the docs who had been in country informed me, "Don't be flattered. She wants to know if you are a doctor."

During this time, Dick Rau and I went to Huế and toured the ARVN hospital, which sent two drivers down to take us up there. We visited the old imperial city of Huế and were invited for tea with the commander. We were hoping to operate since the hospital was overcrowded. The hospital commander told us there were 1000 beds, but the usual patient load was 900 to 1300. They often had two patients in a bed.

One evening, when I was on call, two soldiers were shot by another soldier who had been court-martialed. One was shot in the chest, so I inserted a chest tube. The other had a small bowel injury, and I helped Dick do a small bowel resection. Another memorable case was a chopper pilot who was shot by enemy fire with an AK-47. The bullet went in one arm, traversed the chest, and came out the other arm. He had a pneumothorax on one side and hemopneumothorax on the other side. I placed two chest tubes. The sad thing was, he was paralyzed from the waist down. I called a neurosurgeon at the 95th in Da Nang and transferred the soldier down.

We did operate on civilians in emergency situations. Since they were supposedly deescalating our involvement, to our dismay, they made us quit doing elective surgery on civilians. One day, when I was on call, a civilian was brought in. He had a dislocated hip, perforated bladder, separated symphysis, and multiple serosal rents of his colon.

I laughingly wrote to my wife, "Luckily he came to me, ha-ha."

After a bladder repair, colon repair, wiring of his symphysis, relocation of his hip, skeletal traction, and three units of blood, he did well. He survived and was given great post-op care. One night, an EM who was leaving threw a going away party. He was the one leaving, and that was a good reason to have a party. That same night, the USO had an all-girl Korean band at the club. They were pretty and quite good. Any diversion was welcome.

The nurses were dedicated. Military wartime nursing was so different from stateside, and women were in the most unbelievable minority, so they had to toughen quickly. They saw the ravages of war first.

I remember being in the ER one night while reading or writing a letter and heard a cute little mild-mannered nurse say to a GI, "You have the Clap. I am going to give you a shot of penicillin, then bring that manasan you've been screwing in. I'm going to give her a shot of penicillin, and then you go get all your buddies that have been banging her and send them in, and I will give them shots as well."

I am still impressed with the surgery we were able to perform. One night, Jim Woodburne had a soldier come in who had been stabbed in the heart. Jim cracked his chest and sutured the hole in the heart. The patient did just fine. I remember being envious that I hadn't gotten to do the case. We were all just out of our residencies and wanted to operate.

One of the insufficiencies of the hospital was record keeping. We had to write everything: history and physicals, operative reports, discharge summaries, and, of course, notes and orders. During slow times, it was okay, but in periods of mass casualties, the paperwork backed up. I am sure we gave the essentials, but we weren't long-winded.

When we were in Phu Bai in the last few months of 1971, the people at home were told there were no Marines left in Vietnam. However, there was at least one unit on TanMai Island. They came to the hospital periodically, brought fantail shrimp, and traded for penicillin. We never asked why they needed the penicillin. Mai, the gal that pretty much ran the club, cooked the shrimp for us.

Excerpt from Bob, You Can't Do That
by Robert F. Jackson, MD.
Published in 2021 by Robert F. Jackson, MD.

My quarters at the 85th Evac (Phu Bai) Robert Jackson, MD.

Christmas in Vietnam

In November, a comatose Vietnamese man was brought in. Evidently, he was a builder and was constructing a Christian school in Huế for a missionary, Reverend Josephson, who came to the hospital. I met him and his wife, and he invited me to a meeting of some pastors. I also met the patient's son, Shay. He was a young medical student at the school in Huế. At the meeting, I was offered the head of a chicken in some sort of broth. I later learned that was a high compliment, but I picked at it. I had hoped to work with Reverend Josephson in some sort of ministry. The Army at that time somewhat restricted travel, so I was never able to accomplish that plan, but I was able to maintain contact with Shay. His sister worked at the hospital. When I closed the hospital, I asked command what to do with the library since there were approximately one hundred medical and surgical texts. They said, "Probably nothing." I had Shay's sister get him to come down, and before I left, I gave him the library. He stood there and cried as he thanked me. I felt it was a waste not to have the books used, and Shay likely had the best medical library of any Vietnamese physician.

I went to Da Nang a couple of times, once by chopper and once in a Deuce and a Half, and visited the doctors with whom I had come into the country. Once of those visits, I went to a surgeon at the 95th Evac, and someone told me where his quarters were. I didn't know he was gone with a patient for a few days and had loaned his room to another man while he was gone. I opened his door and interrupted a couple involved in a noontime sexual repast. I quickly closed the door and apologized.

The time I went down in a Deuce and a Half, as we went through the Hải Vân Pass, we locked and loaded. The Hải Vân Pass goes through a mountain range and is 21 kilometers long on Highway 1A. It was reported to be inundated with VC. This incident reaffirmed we were at war. In Da Nang, we picked up a radiologist. We had been without a radiologist for about a month. He expressed wide-eyed fear when we locked and loaded in the Hải Vân Pass.

Around this time, five of us went to Long Binh to take surgery boards, and we were assured they would transport us there. However, we had to make our own arrangements, and it was quite a hassle to get there. We arrived too late to get to the 24th Evac, so they let us stay in some barracks that were only a step up from the 90th Replacement Battalion.

The next day, we went to the 24th Evac. We learned quickly the living conditions were much better than Phu Bai. After the test, I went with John

Bowman to Saigon and visited a couple of guys with whom I came in country. The guys ran a dispensary where they also lived. They had a really good cook, and we wanted to chard a great meal with them. Believe it or not, though, I really wanted to get back to Phu Bai and read my mail from home.

On our return, rumors flew that the 85th was going to close in the not-to-distant future. I was given the title CPS, Chief of Professional Services, sometime in November. With the rumors came a lot of anxiety. We knew some were definitely going to be reassigned. I wrote to Margie that I hoped I would get to stay in Phu Bai. Rumor had it that the 101st was going to stand down their colors sometime in March. I thought by then there would be enough reduction in force and the other hospitals full of surgeons, so maybe I would get a drop. In spite of the rumors, we continued to get wounded soldiers as patients. One day in December, I treated five soldiers with frag wounds. It became clear the hospital was going to close, and Col. Swanson informed me I would be staying to provide surgical care. I would have a partially-trained surgeon, an anesthetist, a couple of male nurses, and some corpsmen. We would have 25-50 beds and only offer stabilizing care. However, he indicated the picture could change.

During that time, Mike's company stood down. He requested and was granted reassignment to the drug treatment center in Phu Bai. Not long before Christmas, our Filipino radiologist received his first letter from his wife. He had joined the Army to obtain citizenship, never thinking he would end up in Vietnam. We were sitting, talking, when the letter arrived. He began to sob and got up and left. Home sickness was real.

Once the hospital planned to close, we grew much busier, treating wounds, cellulitis, and massive abscesses. I think Margie and I started counting the days until our R&R the day I arrived in Vietnam, and with each letter, I counted off the days until I would see her again. We determined to do our R&R in Hawaii. It was my consuming thought, and much of the time I wasn't working was spent planning and dreaming of our time together.

Around the middle of December, many of the docs got reassigned to hospitals throughout Vietnam. At this point, I realized the 85th Evac was really going to close, and it looked like I would be the one to close it. A few days before Christmas, a mass casualty was brought in. The casualties consisted of multiple frag wounds. The medic assigned a young corpsman to take care of them, and he dressed their wounds, called in a chopper, and medevaced them to us. He was wounded himself but took care of the others before thinking of himself. He arrived about an hour later and was the worst injured of the five, with a hole through his colon, and we had to do a colon resection. I recommended him for the Silver Star.

During this time, I was the CO of the hospital. On the 24th of December, a Vietnamese general came and handed out some awards. That afternoon, I appropriated four Deuce and a Half trucks and emptied the hospital. We took all the patients, even some on stretchers, and most of the hospital personnel to Camp Eagle for a very special show. Bob Hope will forever be a hero in my mind. What he did for the morale of the troops can't be measured. One of my patients, Dave Swartz, would occasionally hold up his crutch with a sign on it. I asked my wife to look for it since I was standing beside him. When Jim Nabors sang "The Impossible Dream," he received a standing ovation. I guess I wasn't lucky; I didn't get a kiss from the Deb Stars or Miss World USA.

When we returned from the Bob Hope show, we put our patients back in their beds, and that evening, we had a good floor show. I'm not sure if it was coincidental or if someone realized we needed something to take our minds off the fact that it was Christmas and we weren't home.

On the 24th, I was informed I was to meet and round with General Rossen, Commander of the U.S. Army, Pacific. I met him at 0650 in the ER. The show the night before and all the activities caused me to oversleep. I got a call that General Rossen and his helicopter had arrived. Fortunately, my mamasan had a clean set of fatigues for me. I ran to the ER and led General Rossen around the wards. He is one of the most impressive men I've ever met, with steel-gray eyes and a demeanor that demanded respect. He sat with each man in the hospital, spending probably no more than two or three minutes with each patient, but for that period of time, the soldier knew he had General Rossen's full attention. The 101st had planned a big celebration with the 101st band and special quarters.

General Rossen said, "I believe we still have firebases. I will spend part of the night at Camp Eagle and part of the night at Camp Evans." So he arrived at the hospital after being on firebases all night long.

On the 24th, I did get an early Christmas present: I received a letter from Chuck Ayers, the patient I'd sent to Okinawa, and included a letter in his Purple Heart. I had expressed my faith in Christ to him. He informed me of his progress and told me he was being moved to Walter Reed.

The last day of December, we transferred most of our patients or discharged the ones who were able. I became commander of the 616th K A surgical team attached to the 48th Medical Detachment. The 326th Medical Unit was also on the compound, and I was the commander over all three units. On January 2nd, I appropriated a medevac chopper and went to Da Nang. I got my orders and was briefed as to what our mission would be in Phu Bai. We were to do emergency surgery only, stabilize the patient, and keep them in the hospital for no more than 72 hours. I had a couple of vehicles at my disposal and was also instructed to move into the house trailer that the commander lived in. Marv Wheeler, an anesthetist, moved in with me since the trailer had two bedrooms. We had a stand-down ceremony for the 85th Evacuation Hospital. On my way back from Da Nang, I was in the helicopter with a case of Coke I bought in the PX under my feet. Suddenly, an automatic weapon fired. The helicopter swooped and dodged and flew in a zigzag pattern. I checked, and I was still intact. We flew on to Phu Bai, and the pilot dropped me off at the heliport.

I didn't see him for a few days, but in the mess hall, he came over and said, "Major, I am sorry about your flight back from Da Nang, but we were taking fire, and I had to take evasive action."

Excerpt from Bob, You Can't Do That
by Robert F. Jackson, MD.
Published in 2021 by Robert F. Jackson, MD.

Christmas at Phu Bai.

1972

Being commander of the compound was kind of a headache. Once the two medical companies occupied the compound clinic, work picked up. We probably treated a hundred-plus guys with the Clap. On January 4th, Marilyn and John Tarnosky left to go home. They were a couple of my best friends, good people, and I hated to see them leave. Surgery clinic became a drag. We had patients in droves, but we couldn't do anything because most of them weren't emergency situations or were things we could ship elsewhere. Mostly, we saw orthopedic problems. My anesthetist was transferred to Qui Nhơn, and Cary Conyers was on R&R, so I was the only surgeon on the compound for a while.

At about this time, I was reading my devotions, and a verse seemed to fly off the page: "I will not die but live, and will proclaim what the LORD has done." (Psalm 118:17).

From that time, I don't think I worried about dying in Vietnam.

***

One evening around the middle of January, I took a bunch of my corpsmen and a couple of other docs to the MACV compound because they had appropriated some steaks and large charcoal grills. On the way back, I rode on the back of a Deuce and a Half. They wouldn't let Spc. Davis, the driver, back on our compound. The guard at the gate said the compound was closed, and Spc Davis asked, "By whose order?"

"The CO's."

"Well, you better ask him because the CO is sitting on the back of this truck," Spc. Davis said.

Up went the gate. That was the day the 326th got stand-down orders.

On January 20th, I found out the 326th was leaving and the mess hall would be closing. I appropriated a chopper and flew to Da Nang. I talked to Col. Wells, the commander over medical units in Military Region II. I told him we no longer needed a surgical team in Phu Bai, and we were actually obstructive since we couldn't take care of patients. In the time it took us to stabilize them, they could be at the 95th Evac Hospital and receive adequate care. Maybe my convincing argument was that the med command was going to be stuck with the compound. He stated he would be up the next day to evaluate the situation.

I think God helped me prove my point. That night, we received five casualties. It took us over 40 minutes to stabilize them and send them on their way to Da Nang—40 minutes that would have had them where they could receive definitive care. I pointed that out the next day when the higher-ups came, which was somewhat interesting. I ran around throughout Phu Bai with those in command over the region, and we ended at the 8th R&R and planned a dispensary. The colonel seemed to think they were going to be there forever—there were a couple of nice buildings to put the dispensary in, but he wanted them to go into temporary quarters until they could rebuild and remodel for a fancy dispensary. In the Army, there is a saying that nothing is more permanent than temporary quarters. At least I got permission to disband the 48th Medical Detachment.

I called Col. Richards at Med Command. "Since we are closing this unit, how about sending me home?"

He said, "What's your second choice?"

"Either 3rd Field or the 24th Evac."

Once I knew that, I quickly made plans to clear finance and get to Long Binh as soon as possible. I wanted to leave before they could change their minds.

The following day, since the mess hall had closed and my mother had sent a couple of hams, I baked them in the trailer oven. All of us who were left had a great feast. When I first became CO, I told my master sergeant I needed something I could cook in the trailer. He was kind of like Radar on *MASH.* At about 3:00 a.m. one morning there was a knock on my door. Sarge was a little inebriated, but he slid in a case of steaks.

He said, "Major, tomorrow I'll get you potatoes to go with them."

Needless to say, we ate pretty well and didn't have to stomach C-rations. I did try one. I hope they have improved since the 70s.

On January 24th, I flew to Da Nang. I went over to the 95th Evac and found Jim Woodburne had taken the five casualties we sent down a few days ago to Japan. I saw Kathy Moody, one of the nurses who served with us at the 85th. I cleared finance and personnel and was able to get a chopper back to Phu Bai. The last day in Phu Bai, I drove over to the PX. While there, a young EM from our compound needed a ride to the Red Cross. His unit leader told me they were going to inform him his father had passed away. I went with him and waited until he got the news. I hope I was a comfort. I shared my faith with him.

Two days later, I left the 85th for the last time. We flew to Saigon. I was traveling with Flint Gullet, my male nurse. It was a real hassle. The flight was supposed to leave at noon to Saigon, but it didn't leave until 5:00 p.m.

We arrived at Tan Son Nhut airport about 7:45 p.m. We went to the Air Force Officers' Club and had supper, and I had my first trip in a cyclo cab. Flint was a Seventh-Day Adventist and knew where the Seventh-Day Adventist servicemen's center was located. One of the missionaries brought us back to the airport, and we picked up our gear.

I went over to 3rd Field with Flint and visited with Udi Gahimi, the radiologist who had been at Phu Bai. I also saw Mary Pumphrey, Di Dupont, and McKinney, all of whom were now working at the 3rd Field Hospital. One of the missionaries from the Seventh-Day Adventist Mission took me out to the 24th Evacuation Hospital. Soon, I was much busier than I had been the last few days with the 616th K A surgical team. I did two cases on my first day at the 24th. One of the patients was from Anderson, Indiana. He had multiple frag wounds and an injured radial nerve. The other patient had a large flank wound and, by the Vietnamese language, *tee tee* other wounds.

We went into Saigon two days after I arrived in Long Binh. We had dinner with Bill Harmon and Dave McKinley. The Jeep we drove kept stopping, and we'd get out and bang on the carburetor with a pipe so it would run again.

Excerpt from Bob, You Can't Do That
by Robert F. Jackson, MD.
Published in 2021 by Robert F. Jackson, MD.

85th Evacuation Hospital Helipad (background–helicopters at the ready).

One Man's Story:
Memories of a Vietnam Vet
By Michael Clark

Published in 2014 by Michael Clark and Lulu Publishing Services.
Excerpt reprinted with permission from Michael Clark.

My reporting date was 9 August 1970. My flight was from Detroit to Tacoma, Washington, with a ten-mile ride to Fort Lewis. I was glad I was processing through Fort Lewis instead of San Francisco because of the riots there. Soldiers traveling to and from Vietnam through San Francisco had to be escorted and protected from rioters by police and MPs. Objects were thrown at them, and some minor injuries occurred. This was the typical thank-you Vietnam veterans got from their country for serving.

I was assigned to a transient barracks while the processing was completed. To make certain we had something to do, we were assigned various details. I was assigned to the mail room. I don't remember what my detail was supposed to be. I only remember sitting around all day. The army didn't allow the delivery of pornography on-base, and it was confiscated in the mail room. That doesn't mean it was thrown away. The mail room had one of the best pornographic libraries there ever has been. Anything and everything was there. Men, women, and even animals were involved. It was so disgusting, I couldn't stop looking!

Orders came through on 11 August for travel. We flew on Flying Tiger Airlines. The first stop was in Anchorage, Alaska. We had a one-hour layover there. Visiting Alaska had always been a dream of mine, but not under these circumstances. I walked outside the airport, taking in as much as I could.

The next stop was Tokyo. We had a five-hour layover there. We were restricted to the terminal, and I played video games the whole time.

The next stop was Cam Ranh Bay, Vietnam. Total flying time was sixteen hours. I attempted to sleep on the plane with little success. We arrived after dark and stepped off the plane into an oven. There was some initial processing, and we were assigned a place to sleep depending on where we were going. I did not yet know what unit I was being assigned to.

On the way to the barracks, I passed a large pile of puke. I would learn the significance of this later. On the puke were about a hundred cockroaches enjoying dinner, some of them four inches long. They made a clicking sound much like pebbles would sound if they were in a plastic tube that was being rotated. They scattered as I approached but did not go far. By the time I was ten feet away, they had re-congregated.

There were only three or four of us assigned to the barracks. Mattresses were rolled up in an attempt to keep sand from getting on them. It didn't work. Lying on them was like lying on a beach without a towel. Brushing it off made no difference. We did not have sheets or pillows. It was hot with little air movement. There were no fans and no air conditioning. Again, I attempted to sleep.

I received orders for the 101st Airborne Replacement detachment in Phu Bai. There were shops in the airport at Cam Ranh, and I bought a silver necklace with a heart-shaped pendant that had a diamond chip in the center for $20. I was able to ship it home to Connie before we flew out.

The transportation was a C-130 transport plane; the distance was about three hundred miles. Seating was nylon cargo straps fashioned into a seat. It was hot and noisy, and there was no ventilation. We were packed into the plane shoulder to shoulder for the uncomfortable ride, each man with his gear.

We arrived in Phu Bai midafternoon. It is said the Marines filled a million sandbags at Phu Bai in 1965, and it was known as the "sandbag capital of Vietnam." Getting off the plane, we were assembled in loose formation. The sun was bright, and the sand was white. I couldn't look up without sunglasses because it was so bright. Temperatures at that time of the year were upwards of 118 degrees, and the humidity was a constant 100 percent. We were directed to our temporary quarters to wait for transport to Camp Evans for in-country training.

Somewhere along the line, we were issued jungle fatigues and jungle boots. Jungle fatigues were green, loose-fitting jackets, long-sleeved with side pockets as well as breast pockets. The pants had the customary four pockets, with large pockets on each leg, like cargo pants. There were laces at the bottom of the pant legs so they could be tied at the tops of your boots. Jungle boots were fabric uppers with leather lowers. The soles looked like a knobby motorcycle tire and had a steel plate in them. At that time, the steel plates were relatively new, and they were there to prevent bungee sticks from entering the boot and piercing the foot.

We were issued steel pots (helmets) with pot liners, flak jackets, and a heavy-duty raincoat. American currency (greenbacks) was not allowed and was exchanged for MPC, or military payment certificates. This was paper money issued in denominations of a nickel, dime, quarter, and from a dollar to twenty dollars. This was done to prevent anyone from making a large amount of money on the black market. The MPC were exchanged for a new series every two years. Accumulating too much MPC required a good explanation for where it came from. Having a greenback in your possession carried a stiff penalty.

***

The trip to Camp Evans was twenty to thirty miles north on Highway One. Phu Bai was in the Thua Thien province in northern Vietnam. Militarily, this was known as the I Corps, the northernmost combat zone. We weren't far from the DMZ as it was; moving farther north made me even more uncomfortable. This area was particularly vulnerable because it was relatively narrow east-to-west, and the Ho Chi Minh Trail kept the North Vietnamese Army (NVA) well-supplied.

Laos was not far away. The NVA could move in quickly, strike, and retreat back to Laos, which US forces were not allowed to enter. The convoy had jeeps front and back with a .50 caliber machine gun mounted on a turret in each jeep. We were loaded in deuce-and-a-halfs for the trip. We hadn't gone far when we saw F-4 Phantom fighter jets attacking a hillside less than a half mile away. They were dropping napalm. There was a bright red flash of flames followed by black plumes of smoke as the napalm bomb struck the ground.

We didn't see any ground action in the area. I had been in-country four days, and I remember asking myself, *What the fuck am I doing here?* The rest of the trip went without incident. Highway One was relatively paved, and there was no concern for mines.

In-country training was one week long. I ran into a high-school classmate there, but he was in a hurry and not interested in talking. We were taught about the heat and the importance of keeping ourselves hydrated. The line that was recited often was: *When you feel exhausted and think you can't continue, take two salt tablets and drive on.*

There were classes on booby-trap identification. These consisted of trails cut through heavily wooded areas with several types of booby traps along the way. We would walk the trails looking for the different hazards we would encounter. Clear nylon trip wires were strung across the trail attached to a concealed hand grenade. Holes were dug in the ground with bungee sticks stuck in the bottom. Bungee sticks are sharpened bamboo sticks that will easily penetrate the sole of a boot. The holes were then concealed with vegetation. A one-by-one-by-four-inch wooden block would have holes drilled in it the correct diameter to hold a rifle cartridge.

A nail was driven into the bottom of each hole. A rifle cartridge was placed in each hole, and the unit would be placed in a small, concealable hole. Stepping on the cartridge would put enough pressure on the primer to cause it to fire, shooting it through the foot and into the body. We had to assume that anything, anywhere, was booby-trapped.

We were issued gas masks in a case. In the case was an atropine syrette. This is a device the same as an EpiPen, but it contained atropine. The reason for this was the step-and-a-half, also known as the bamboo pit viper. The actual name for this snake is the Many-Banded Krait. The snake is native to India and Southeast Asia. This is one of the most potent snakes in the world. One bite contains enough toxin to kill twenty adult males. The story was that if you were bitten, you had a step and a half to inject the atropine and save your life. This was an exaggeration, but it stressed the importance of carrying the syrette. Everywhere else I have looked, the snake is referred to as the two-step. I assume the army snake was a little bit faster.

There were foxholes about every fifty yards around the entire camp. They were four feet deep, two feet wide, and five feet long. Every foxhole was occupied by two soldiers pulling guard duty. Every other foxhole was assigned an M-79 grenade launcher and the other half an M-60 machine gun. We had to qualify with both in preparation for this detail. I tended to shoot low with the M-60 and had to compensate. My assigned foxhole had an M-60.

With steel pots, M-16s, and flak jackets, we assembled at the ammo bunker. We each had a bandolier that held six magazines of ammunition for our M-16s, each holding twenty rounds. It took four trips to the foxhole to carry all the munitions for the night. The foxhole was a couple hundred yards from the ammo bunker. It took both of us to carry a case of ammunition for the M-60 and the rifle, a case of grenades, a case of M-16 ammunition, and a case with claymore mines in it. We carried our M-16 and the bandolier of ammo with us at all times. There were thirty hand grenades, each in a separate container—1,000 rounds for the M-60 and M-16 and six claymores.

After everything was in the foxhole, we set our claymore mines. A claymore is slightly curved, with the front of the curve facing forward. Each one was about four by six by one and a half inches. There were two pegs on the bottom that swung down so they could be pushed into the ground, holding it upright. It was filled with an explosive and ball bearings. Claymores had to be hardwired, with the wires attached to a switch and strung through the concertina wire to the foxhole. The first click of the switch armed it; the second fired it. The back blast of a claymore was deadly at thirty feet, so they had to be angled away from the foxhole when positioned.

With everything set for the night, the routine was that one guy would watch for an hour while the other slept. We were to rotate back and forth all night. *Riiiight!* We may have gotten an hour each all night.

Every few hundred yards, there was a guard tower. These were equipped with a newfangled contraption called a *starlight scope,* which allowed the guards to see in the dark. It was just after midnight when word came down the line that a company of NVA had been spotted about two hundred yards in front of our position, and that Cobras had been called in to help. A Cobra is the precursor of a Blackhawk. The body was thirty-six inches wide with the pilot and copilot stacked, the pilot being above the copilot. There was a seven and a ten-pound rocket pod mounted on each side. On the front was a minigun, a machine gun that fired 1,200 rounds a minute. It was also equipped with a grenade launcher. The maximum speed of a Cobra in a dive was 190 knots, or 219 miles an hour.

I was too new in-country to be able to identify different helicopters by the sound of their rotors, but there was no doubt about them coming. They flew lights-out for obvious reasons. I couldn't see anything, but I could hear the rhythmic sound as they approached. The sound of the rotors got slower and slower as they climbed to their peak, until it sounded like they might stop. The sound then increased rapidly in frequency as they went into a dive, and then all hell broke loose! The rockets gave off a swishing sound when in flight. They left a trail of sparks behind them all the way to the ground, followed by the explosion and a burst of light. The back blast was several feet long, with an eddy developing that caused the sparks to swirl in the air.

The rockets were fired less than a second apart, and the sparks lit up the night. The minigun was firing at the same time, every fifth round being a tracer. Every once in a while, a tracer wouldn't light up, and there would be a break in the beam of bullets. Otherwise, it looked like a laser beam leading down to the ground and sounded like a buzz saw. The sight was as good as any fireworks display I have ever seen. As soon as the first one finished its dive, the second one followed. Then they went around and did it again. I was in awe. All I could think was, *Holy shit! I'm glad they're on our side!*

There was brush between us and the site that the rockets hit, and I could not see what was happening on the ground. The concern now turned to Sappers. Sappers were NVA special forces trained in stealth. They would crawl through the concertina, do whatever their deed was, and leave the same way, undetected. The rest of this night was uneventful. With daylight, we had to return all munitions to the ammo bunker. Getting allowed time to sleep during the night meant we had a full day of training ahead of us. I had one other day of guard duty at Camp Evans, but that night we did not see any action.

Michael Clark while with the 101st Airborne Division.

We would march to sites off-base for training during the day. We were seated in bleachers for a demonstration one afternoon, and a mission was called in to a naval ship in the South China Sea. There was a fifty-five-gallon drum in the field in front of us, and a single artillery shell dropped from the sky from twenty miles away, landing within six feet of the drum. Impressive, but they weren't done. A couple of adjustments and the barrel was struck, flying several feet into the air.

Lunch was C-rations, surplus from the Korean War. There was an entrée in a four-ounce can, a chocolate dessert, and a pack of three cigarettes in each box. Everyone carried a P-38 can opener to open the cans. My favorite entrée was lima beans and ham, best if it could be warmed. Use your own judgment about how the others tasted if lima beans and ham was my favorite.

Camp Evans was the training site for Kit Carson scouts—NVA deserters accompanying and scouting for American troops. I felt like I was being watched every time I was around one. There was a great deal of skepticism about this program.

We went out on a patrol one afternoon looking for any evidence of enemy activity. Everyone was carrying all the equipment he could carry, even though it was a day patrol, and we were expected back before dark. I had my pack, steel pot, flak jacket, medics bag, M-16, and a bandolier—and then they put a radio on my back and made me the RTO (radio telegraph operator). I was supposed to remain with the CO as an RTO. What happened if someone needed a medic? Did the CO accompany me to the site of the injury? I didn't think so. He was going to stay in the back. It didn't make sense for me to carry the radio. But what did I know. I was an enlisted man.

Carrying all this equipment made me about two and a half times my body size. I was the last person to board the Huey, and space was cramped with seven other guys inside. I had previously noticed several guys riding in Hueys sitting in the door with their feet on the skids since arriving in-country, and I decided to take this position. I estimate that we were flying at a thousand feet.

Looking down, I noticed the number of bomb craters in the ground. It looked like the entire surface was pocked with craters with a little undisturbed ground sprinkled in here and there. I was impressed by the degree to which the earth had been defaced.

The pilot knew he had a cherry at his mercy, and he took advantage of the opportunity. He made a hard right turn that banked the helicopter so hard the right side was parallel to the ground. I was sitting on the right side. This put him in a position so that I was looking straight down at the ground a thousand feet below. There was nothing between me and the ground but air. I was not strapped in and had nothing to hang on to. I tried to sink my fingernails into the steel floor of the Huey, but good luck with that. The only thing holding me in the helicopter was centrifugal force. Point made! When the Huey leveled out, I scrambled into the middle of the helicopter. I didn't care whose lap I had to sit in. He got me and got me good. Lesson learned, and I never sat in the doorway again. I'm certain he still laughs about that day.

We made a sweep around the perimeter of the compound a mile or two out. A squad would be sent in to sweep wooded areas, while others would set up positions around them, watching for any activity. Thankfully, the day was uneventful. We were late heading back to camp, and darkness set it. I can't begin to tell you what it is like moving in the open after dark. I was white-knuckled, hanging on to my M-16, my thumb on the safety and my trigger finger alongside the trigger guard. I just knew someone was going to jump up and open fire any second.

It was impossible for sixty guys to move and not make noise. Something was tapping on one guy's pack. Something was jingling on another's. The sound of feet on the ground made enough noise to be heard a hundred yards away. I was acutely aware that we were making too much noise. My adrenaline was flowing, the hair on the back of my neck was standing up, and I was on high alert. The thought of NVA moving two hundred yards from the perimeter while on guard duty the night before entered my mind. I was beyond relieved to enter the confines of the compound without anyone getting hurt.

***

With the completion of in-country training, I was assigned to my unit with the 101st. I reported to Company A, 326th Medical Battalion, Headquarters Brigade at Camp Eagle. Upon arriving, I found that Doug had been assigned to the same company and was working in the Battalion Aid Station. I was led to my hooch to drop off my gear.

Hooches were about fifteen feet wide and thirty feet long. They were built on stilts two feet off the ground so the floor would stay dry during monsoon season. There was a gable roof with a six-twelve pitch made of corrugated steel. The side walls were six feet tall; the top eighteen inches was a screen to allow for ventilation. A lateral wooden shutter made of plywood could be closed when needed to keep the rain out. The floor was made of plywood. There was a door on each end with a walkway between them.

There were two half-walls four feet tall running from the side walls upward toward the middle, dividing each hooch into six areas, approximately six by eight feet. Each of these areas was home for a GI, unless the beds were bunked. Then it was home for two. Each area had an electrical outlet. It would make hot nights much more comfortable for someone if he was lucky enough to have a fan. Being a cherry, or FNG (fucking new guy), I was put in an area that was bunked.

Vietnam had its own slang made up of a medley of English, French, and Vietnamese. One of the first questions asked of someone was always, "Where are you from back in the world?" *Ti ti* meant little bit, *beaucoup* was a lot. *Took fin* was marijuana, and *round eyes* were Anglo women. *Number one* was very good, and *number ten*, very bad. There was *beaucoup number one* and *beaucoup number ten*. *Dinky donk* was crazy, but you could be *beaucoup dinky donk*. *Bac si* (bock see) was the doctor. *Bac si no dow* was broken English and Vietnamese for "don't hurt me." *Bac si com dow* was Vietnamese. *No bic* meant "I don't understand." To *souvenir* someone was to give them a gift. *There it is* was used to agree with someone.

Reporting for duty at the orderly room brought the news that there wasn't a position for me as a 91D20. There were two slots in the company, and they were both filled. I was given different jobs in the company but worked mostly in the motor pool. Now, let's review. When I entered the army, I was asked what job I would like to do. My response was to be a light vehicle mechanic, and I didn't want to be a cook or an MP. The army just sent me through six months of training to be an operating-room technician. Now I am in Vietnam with no slot in the company for me, and I am working in the motor pool as a light vehicle mechanic. Is there any doubt in your mind as to why *military intelligence* is considered an oxymoron? There were a couple of days that I was sent out on day patrols or rode on a convoy as a medic.

About three days after arriving, I was sitting outside the hooch in the evening with about a half dozen other guys, and a joint was lit. I had never smoked marijuana before and really didn't intend to. When it was passed to me, I took a hit like everyone else and passed it on. This continued on until the joint was consumed. I thought it strange that I never got a buzz from it. The next night, we did the same; there was nothing else to do, and it helped pass the time. I can't say I didn't get a buzz then. I found out that potted meat on a Ritz and Vienna sausages were considered a delicacy. I had the munchies!

It was getting late into the evening when I lay back on my bunk and dozed. I awoke startled, on high alert, and the hair standing up on the back of my neck, but nothing happened. It was about ten seconds before the first 122 rocket slammed into the compound. It makes a sound like *shooo* in a crescendo for about two seconds before it hits. I wasn't sure if I should run for the bunker or just hit the ground. Running made a bigger target, but the bunker was a safe haven. I ran like hell for the bunker.

There was about an inch of stale water covering the floor of the bunker, and it smelled like a sewer. It was a steel box buried in a hillside with only the door exposed. There were all kinds of creepy crawlies in the bunker, but there was no place I'd rather have been at that moment. I was scared to the point that I was giddy. Anything said drew a nervous laugh. The attack went on for several minutes, and we got pounded. The compound took several rockets, but there was only moderate damage to several buildings, and no one was injured.

This attack made me realize why it is said that the most dangerous times in-country were the first three months and the last two—the first three because you got scared and couldn't think, the last two because you were distracted and thought too much. I understood that controlling my emotions could make the difference between living and dying, for myself and others.

Days were spent in the motor pool working on trucks and listening to AFVN (Armed Forces Vietnam) radio. This was the only station available. They played contemporary hits, gave some news from home and played reruns of the superhero (*bawk bawk bawk bawk*) Chicken Man! We were able to listen to the Muhammad Ali fight while I was in-country.

I was listening to "War: What is it good for?" (they actually played that song) and mulling over the last two weeks. I was convinced that the only qualification necessary to do any job in the 101st was a pulse. I talked to the company clerk and put in for a transfer—91D20 was a critical MOS, meaning there was a serious shortage, and I could be at the 85th Evacuation Hospital doing some good. A week later, the clerk told me my paperwork was in the CO's drawer, and he intended to do nothing with it. The clerk suggested I see the IG (Inspector General) when he came through in the next couple of days.

When the time came, I walked into the room, not knowing how to address the IG—this had not been taught in basic. The army didn't want us to know about this office because it was there to settle injustices to any army personnel. Basic would have been much different if a couple of visits had been made by the IG. As I approached him, he snapped to attention and initiated a salute, clearly indicating that this was protocol. Though it is generally not required to salute indoors, I returned the salute and held it until he dropped his, as per protocol (although I was supposed to initiate the salute). I explained my situation, and he assured me he would look into it. An appointment was set up to see him again to follow up on the progress. My transfer cleared company and battalion that day and was sent to division.

Minesweepers would sweep the roads every morning before anyone was allowed to travel on the roads on and off compound. A minesweeper was a deuce-and-a-half with a steel snow blade on the front. In front of the blade was a horizontal pipe about four inches in diameter. Several chains were welded to the pipe. When the pipe spun, the chains would spank nearly every square inch of the ground. This caused enough pressure to detonate a mine if one had been planted during the night. The snow blade was heavy-duty enough to protect the driver.

There was artillery from Camp Eagle, and it fired frequently. Most of the time it didn't draw much attention. But there was one eight-inch gun located close to a mile from our compound. That drew attention every time it fired.

The first thing I had to do was decide if it was incoming or outgoing. After deciding it was ours, I knew to stand clear of anything that might fall on me. The hooches would literally shake two inches from side to side when it fired. It was the cause for a couple of unnecessary trips to the bunker in the middle of the night. Better safe than dead.

The first Monday in September, I was assigned to accompany one of the doctors on MEDCAP (Medical Civilian Assistance Program). This was a program where we would go to various sites in that area to pull sick call. Everyone would line up to be evaluated. Many would not have a medical condition, but all would receive medication. Those who were not ill received a medication that had to be taken once daily (vitamins). Others would receive antibiotics or any other medication that would help their condition.

One guy had a huge cancerous growth on his left cheek. Another had a hernia so severe his intestines pushed out, and he carried them around in a bag (his skin was intact). A very ill child less than a year old had a thick white pus draining from his ear. Penicillin was given, and the interpreter was told to impress upon the mother the importance of the child receiving the medication. The child might die if the medication wasn't given.

Many times, the medications given out would be sold on the black market for much-needed cash. Did the mother give the child the medication, or did she sell it to feed her other children who might have been starving? Was she forced to choose between sacrificing one child or starving the others? Such was the life of many mothers in Vietnam.

I went with a bunch of guys to the EM (enlisted men's) club a couple of times. We could not have anything but beer in the hooches, and no one had a refrigerator, so we went to the club. There were some raucous times and interesting rides in a jeep returning to the compound.

One night in the club, there was a confrontation between some blacks and whites. I had no trouble being around blacks and tried to help defuse the situation. That was the first time I was told to watch my back; they would not trouble shooting me because I was white, and they hated whites.

I was told this on three occasions by four black soldiers while in Vietnam. It made you nervous having guys carrying M-16s and threatening to kill you.

It was a couple of months later those two black soldiers threw a hand grenade in each door of the EM club. We treated the wounded at the 85th; a couple were dead. That was known as fragging, and it was not uncommon.

***

It was assumed that my transfer would go through, and I was sent TDY (temporary duty) to the 85th toward the end of September. Passing through the gate of the 85th, I noticed a football game in the field to my right and wondered what that was about. I found out that it was the 85th Evac football team practicing for their game against the 95th Evac in Da Nang. I wondered if they might need another player, but it was not to be. I no sooner arrived than I developed abdominal pain and spent a week as a patient. While I was a patient, the football team flew in helicopters to Da Nang. They returned victorious.

Whatever caused my pain resolved—it was not my appendix—and I reported for duty. Lieutenant Colonel Arola was in charge of nursing, and she was hardcore army. She was married to an enlisted man and would not live with him; he had to stay in enlisted-men's quarters. Officers were not allowed to fraternize with enlisted men.

I was assigned a hooch and a bunk. There was one room in the hooch; otherwise, it was an open room without dividers. There were hooches on each side of a cement sidewalk with cement walkways leading to the steps of each hooch. They were otherwise the same as at Camp Eagle.

The shower was a few buildings down, and sometimes there was even hot water. The moss was an inch thick on the cement floor, and green mold grew on the walls. Sometimes, I felt dirtier leaving the shower.

There were also *flush toilets*! It had been less than two months, but this was already a big deal. They were supposed to be for patients only, but everyone used them. The walls were plywood, and artists had left their messages freely. "Flush hard, it's a long way to the kitchen" was one of my favorites. "When I die I'll go to heaven, because I've spent my time in hell" adorned every wall that could be written on.

One of my hooch mates was named Dave. He was a big Procol Harum fan, and their music was often playing. Once a month, he would receive a letter from his brother. It would be written on linen paper that was yellow in color. It was white when it was purchased but turned yellow after it was soaked in LSD. Dave would tear off a corner and go tripping. He would frequently try to get me to participate, but I always refused. He hated the army and eventually accepted an undesirable discharge and went home.

I was walking into my hooch one evening after working a twelve-hours shift and found a line of guys leading up the stairs and to the door of the only room in the hooch. The occupier of that room had smuggled a prostitute on-compound, and the fee was five dollars. Thirty-nine guys went in and out of that room over the course of a couple of hours. When there were no other customers, he came out and apologized for the inconvenience and offered me my turn for free. He had the option of splitting the money or having her spend the night with him, and he was going to have her stay the night. I politely declined but felt ill inside. I didn't want to be second, let alone number forty! Being married, I wouldn't have considered it anyway.

I was not in-country long before I understood the piles of vomit on the sand. Heroin was the easiest drug to get in Vietnam. It came in a small vial and sold for five dollars. Heroin was cut with strychnine. About thirty minutes after the heroin was snorted, the strychnine would cause vomiting. After vomiting, the person would enjoy the buzz. I would hear guys vomiting outside the hooches every night. Cockroaches ate well in Vietnam.

***

Overall, life at the 85th Evac was pretty good for a war zone. I hated being there, but I was glad to be there. We were located near the base camp at Phu Bai. Highway One ran through the middle of the camp for over a mile. We were located at the northern end of the camp on the east side of the road. Concertina wire surrounded the hospital on all sides. There was a field on the north side that was about two hundred yards wide. There was an ARVN camp on the other side of the field, and we could watch their daily activities. They had a roof with hammocks strung underneath for sleeping quarters.

On the east side, there was an airstrip with the terminal about a half mile south. There was concertina wire between the hospital and the airstrip. There was never a minute that there weren't a half dozen choppers in the air during the day. It didn't take long before I could recognize the type of helicopter by the sound of the rotors, and, yes, you can tell a helicopter is coming and what type it is before you can hear it. We had Hueys, Cobras, Chinooks, Sikorsky Sky Cranes, and Loaches.

F-4 Phantom jets used the airstrip on a regular basis. My hooch was a hundred yards from the end of the airstrip. They would take off with their afterburners going, and the noise was painful to my ears. It would wake me from a sound sleep, and I would have to cover my ears with my hands. I can still envision the two red circles taking off into the night sky. The army assures me my hearing problem is not service-related.

About a quarter mile to our south, there was a fuel dump. Across the street on the west side was a communications center. So, let's review: an ARVN camp on the north side, an airstrip on the east, a fuel dump on the south, and a communications center on the west—four of the biggest targets for rockets and mortars. What would make someone think it would be a good idea to put a hospital in the middle of all this? Did they think it would deter the enemy from firing rockets into the area? I didn't think so, but what did I know? I was an enlisted man. Again. Military intelligence.

There was a guard shack with a gate at the entrance to the 85th. There was only one way on or off the compound. Entering through the gate, the enlisted men's quarters were located on the left. The nurses' quarters were immediately to the right and were secured with concertina and gates. Next, there was an open area on the right that served as a softball diamond. On the other side of the field was the officer's club, orderly room, and officer's quarters. The road curved around the east end of the field and the wards. ER, OR, ICU, and radiology were on the left. The mess hall was beyond that. On the right was the motor pool, supply, and lab. Headquarters was at the end of the road on the left, with the EM club between the ER and headquarters.

The helipad was on the east side of the ER next to the airstrip. It was made up of PSP—steel plates that fastened together to form a platform. A sidewalk led from the helipad to the ER. There were several stands in the ER to accommodate litters—canvas stretchers. There was a tunnel between the ER and OR with radiology located on the left. There were double swinging doors on both sides of the tunnel next to the OR. The mess hall was out the door to the left, and CMS was to the right. Walking straight through another set of swinging double doors took you into the OR.

The OR had two rooms on the left and two rooms on the right. One of these rooms was used to store sterile instrument sets and drape packs along with other sterile supplies. The two rooms on the left were used routinely, and the third only when necessary. The floors were bare cement with a drain in the middle of each room. There were plywood walls painted a light green and an air-conditioner stuck in one wall in each room. The rooms smelled of mildew, and a supply of methyl salicylate (wintergreen) was kept in the cabinets in each room as an air freshener. Cleaning the room between patients consisted of spraying the floor with a hose and scrubbing it with a cane broom.

Attire in the OR was a light blue sleeveless scrub top, hat, and mask with jungle fatigue pants and air-issue jungle boots. Occasionally, an FNG (fucking new guy) chopper pilot would fly over from the west to get to the helipad. The wind from the rotors would blow the double doors open to the OR, and everyone who was scrubbed in would dive over the patient to keep dust from blowing into the wound. The message would be immediately delivered to the pilot that he was to approach from the east.

Power to the OR was also a problem at times. We had backup generators that worked some of the time, but several times we operated by flashlight. There were also times when we would be in the OR during a rocket or mortar attack. There was no such thing as running for cover; we stayed the course and did our job. Fortunately, we were never hit.

Twice when I was at the 85th, we had guys come in with live rounds embedded in them. The OR would be cleared of everyone possible, and a munitions expert would be in the room to help guide the removal. This act had carried a Silver Star for bravery at one time, but that award had been dropped. Although it was only a detonator, if it exploded, it would have caused significant injury to anyone in close proximity.

A file was kept in the department of the names of the guys anywhere on Phu Bai with rare blood types and when the last donated. When blood was needed, the MPs would be sent to get them to "donate" blood. Forty units of blood were given to one patient during surgery.

CMS (central material section) was out the north swinging doors on the left. There was a cement sidewalk leading to the entrance. As OR techs, we were responsible for sterile supplies for the entire hospital. Any reusable item was returned to CMS for cleaning and sterilization. We had two autoclaves for this—one inside and one outside. We had to manually add water to the jacket and seal the sterilization chamber.

Sterile items were considered sterile for one month. Anything on the shelf over a month had to be rewrapped and sterilized. Instrument sets from the OR were placed in a sink and hand-washed. They were arranged in the proper order and autoclaved. Autoclave tape and diacs were used to indicate proper temperature had been achieved. Diacs were small glass tubs with a chemical in them that would turn from red to black when the proper temperature had been attained. This indicated temperature, not sterilization.

There was a radio in CMS, and we listened to AFVN (Armed Forces Vietnam Network) twenty-four hours a day. Some songs still take me back to CMS in the middle of the night.

Cockroaches were everywhere, and CMS was no exception. I was sitting at a table one night and saw a four-inch-diameter spider walking down the aisle. The body was only a half inch in diameter, but it had long legs. It was disposed of and removed.

It didn't take me long to recognize that a lot of work was being done for no good reason. We were pulling outdates on a regular basis. There were too many of several items and not enough of others. I took it on myself to create an inventory of all items with appropriate numbers on each. Each shelf in every cabinet was itemized, and the list was kept with the cabinets. The list was checked daily, and levels were maintained. This ensured that items were always available, we had fewer outdates, and we knew where the items were located without having to look for them. Bulldogs were spring-loaded vascular clamps that opened by pinching the tabs together on one end. They closed on the vessel by releasing the tabs. We had trouble keeping bulldogs because they made excellent roach clips.

The supply chain was simple: south to north. Supplies came into the southern hospitals, they took what they needed, and they sent the rest to the next hospital to the north. Only the 18th Surgical Hospital was north of us. That means we continually got leftovers. There was a lot of what we didn't need and little of what we did. Many items were burned because there were too many of them, and we had no place to put them.

Sham Palace was directly in front of CMS. This was a shed, built like a hooch, where linens were stored. The items would have to be folded and stored. There were wrappers, gowns, drape towels, sheets, fenestrated drapes, or anything that was needed for the hospital. Doc Holiday used this as a hideout. He was a jovial guy and fun to be around, but he spent more energy trying to get out of work than it would have taken to get the job done.

We typically worked twelve-hour shifts, 0700 to 1900. On busy days, it was more; on light days, it was less. We were happy with light days, because it meant guys in the field would live to see another day. Night shift was covered by two techs, 1900 to 0700. We would work in CMS but cover the OR if anything came in. When we took mass casualties, the call would go out for all available to come to the OR, day or night. We would return to our hooch when the work was done.

The longest shift I had to work was eighteen hours. There were days when I worked longer, but it was split up, with some time off in the afternoon. Because people worked twenty-four hours a day, the mess hall was open between midnight and two in the morning. We referred to this as midnight chow. Breakfast was served every night for anyone who was up and hungry. We took advantage of this often when we had the munchies.

Sleeping after a night shift was a challenge. There was no AC, and I would wake in a pool of sweat in the 100-plus-degree temperatures. I had a fan, but it was little help. Often, we would sleep on the floor of the officer's changing room next to the OR.

During monsoon season, it was too cold. There were no heaters in the hooch, and it got as low as 52 degrees one night. It would occasionally snow in the highest elevations, but not where we were. The bed was damp and cold. It took several minutes to warm it up enough with body temperature to be able to sleep. If I changed positions, I would wake up and quickly return to a warm place in the bed.

Some time during my tour, I paid ten dollars for an electric blanket from a guy who was going home. What a life changer! I was always grateful for a bed and roof over my head. I never took this for granted. At least I wasn't sleeping out in the rain.

I would take my boots off at night and place them under my bed. When I woke in the mornings, they would be covered with mildew, and I would have to use a shoe brush to buff them, every morning. Foot powder was a necessity.

***

I was TDY at the 85th from the end of September to mid-November. During this time, I visited the IG at Camp Eagle six times, checking on my transfer. This required me to hitchhike to Camp Eagle for every visit. I was in the back of a three-quarter-ton pickup one day to make the trip. A three-quarter-ton has a canvas covering the bed of the truck. As we traveled down the road, automatic weapon fire opened up on both sides of the road. Being in the bed of the truck, I couldn't see what was going on, and canvas does not provide good protection from a bullet. I lay as flat on the steel bed as I could get.

We made it through all right, and I still don't know exactly what the shooting was about or who they were shooting at. On one of my visits to the IG, I was told in no uncertain terms that if he was to help me, I had to report to him with a proper haircut and a mustache that met Army regulations. I visited the barber before subsequent visits.

Nearly two months passed, and my transfer had not come through. I was summoned back to Camp Eagle. Upon arriving, I learned the Red Cross was trying to contact me. I had an emergency call from home. The only way to reach home was by mail or by a MARS call. A MARS call was a series of ham radio operators around the world, holding their mikes open to create a line of communications. Conne was trying to reach me to tell me her father, Nick, had died on Friday, November 13. Each statement had to be concluded with "over" to tell the ham operator to reverse their mikes so the other person could talk. She assured me she was okay, but I was not allowed emergency leave because Nick was not a blood relative.

I was back at Camp Eagle for two days when my transfer came through. The orders were dated 16 November 1970. I processed out of the 101st on the seventeenth and flew to Da Nang to process into the medical group for assignment to the 85th Evacuation Hospital for permanent duty. I spent two days in Da Nang before returning to the 85th. I was assigned a new hooch at that time, the one by the airstrip. There were no rooms built into the hooch, and six guys occupied the open space.

In the army, if you could get supplies back to your hooch, they belonged to you. We were able to accumulate enough plywood and two-by-fours to build rooms for Tree and me. The rooms were about five feet wide and ten feet long. Since we built in the corner, only two walls were required. A space was left at the top and bottom of the walls for ventilation.

This was the first time I'd had any privacy in months. Not long after building the rooms, we were able to buy a refrigerator from a guy going home for ten dollars. We had nearly all the comforts of home.

The shit burner was located not far from the back door of our hooch. This is the place where the drums from the latrines would be taken every day for disposal. Diesel fuel was poured into the drums, and the contents were burned. The odor often woke me from sleep. *Nuok mam* was a sauce made from fermented fish and added to food by the Vietnamese for flavoring. This smelled far worse than the shit burner, and when lunch was served in our hooch, the odor was unbearable. I would wake up and kick them out of the hooch to dine elsewhere.

***

Monsoon season started in October in northern Vietnam and ran into April. The rain started, and it didn't stop for months. PSP steel plates were strung on ammo boxes, providing sidewalks from place to place; otherwise, you were walking in the mud. Monsoons have a big impact on mail call, and mail was sometimes undeliverable for a week. A walk to the mail room was often futile. It was only recently that I considered the stress of loved ones at home not receiving mail for a week. I knew I was okay, but they didn't. What was going through their minds? Were they expecting a letter from Western Union?

Mail was free for us. We only had to put an APO return address on the envelope and write "free" in the upper right-hand corner of the envelope. I wrote home every day.

I had been back at the 85th for a week when Typhoon Patty hit. Winds reached 155 miles per hour over the South China Sea, but it was a tropical storm when it hit land just to our north. Roofs were blown off hooches, and the buildings were blown off their stilts. I climbed onto the roof of our hooch wearing my flak jacket, raincoat, and steel pot to tie sandbags to ropes and suspend them on the steel roof to provide weight on the roof. The rain was blowing so hard it felt like needles when the drops hit my skin. I don't know with any certainty if anything I did made a difference, but our hooch was not damaged in the storm.

Guard duty was required at the 85th, but it was much different from Camp Evans. Our perimeter was surrounded by other secured areas. There were different sites to be patrolled, and we would switch areas every couple of hours. Guard duty could be sold to the right person for one Preludin, a type of speed. I always pulled my duty. I was in the guard tower on the northeast corner of the compound one night when mortars started coming in. I can't say I'm fond of rockets, but hated mortars more. Rockets make a noise before they strike; mortars are silent. They could be heard when they detonated in the tubes. The noise sounded like saying the word *tube*. The mortars were worked in pairs, one walking east and west, the other north and south. I could hear *tube, tube, tube* several times, a few seconds apart. The silence was eerie. Several seconds would go by before the first shell hit. They then landed continuously for minutes.

I decided I preferred to be in the bunker on the ground rather than in the air, even though the tower was reinforced with sandbags. I was about two steps down a fifteen ladder when a mortar exploded behind me. I jumped to the ground, thinking about how stupid it was to leave myself in the open during a mortar attack. Fortunately, their aim was good, and the 85th did not experience any damage. The target that night was the airstrip right next to the guard tower.

When pulling guard duty at the 85th, we carried an M-16, a bandolier of ammunition, and three flares. Flares looked like a road flare but in an aluminum cover. The top could be pulled off and slid onto the bottom.

Striking the bottom with an open hand made the flare fire about 100 yards into the air. It would ignite, and a parachute would open, allowing it to float slowly to the ground. This provided light to a large area for over a minute.

I had flares in the right-hand pocket of my jungle pants as I approached the helipad one night. I heard someone calling to me, "*Hey!*" As I looked out, I could make out a dim figure in the middle of the concertina wire. No one belonged in the wire at night. The guy spoke with a Southern accent or spoke in perfect second-language English. I would not have hesitated to fire. But no one learns to speak English with a Southern accent; he had to be an American from the South.

I directed him to a weak spot in the wire and guided him through. I then escorted him at gunpoint to the ER and called for the sergeant of the guard. According to his military ID, he was from Kentucky, and his name was Bubbles. True story. He was a walk-away from a psychiatric unit at another hospital and was supposed to be going home. He'd hitched a ride on a chopper to Phu Bai and was trying to get to the local hospital. On that night, Bubbles was a lucky man.

The first Monday of every month would find us outside the back of my hooch. The ARVN compound would take three rockets just after dark. The standing joke was that *papa-san* got his paycheck from the US government and could afford three rockets. We would sit outside and watch for the rockets to arrive. We would bet on what time they would strike. The person farthest off would lose the bet. The bet was never about money; it was always a consequence, like a thirty-second shotgun or chugging a sixteen-ounce boilermaker.

***

Monsoon season made it nearly impossible to do anything outdoors. There were several activities scheduled to entertain and occupy the troops. A warehouse was cleared out at the motor pool, nets were put up, and a basketball league was started. There was a movie theater on the compound, but it was outdoors, and only a small area was covered with a tarp. Sixteen-mm movies were circulated from camp to camp and shown over and over. Many of the movies were missing lengths of films, making it difficult to follow the story at times. It was something to do, and beer was allowed.

Floor shows came through once a month. These were bands from different countries touring and entertaining the troops. There was a stage in the EM club, and all seats were always occupied. There were favorite songs sung by all the bands. “I Left My Heart In San Francisco” was one, but our anthem was “We Gotta Get Out of This Place” by Eric Burdon and the Animals.

I was leaving the EM club after a floor show one night, walking toward the ER, when a chopper came in and landed on the helipad. As I continued to walk, there was a second chopper hovering, waiting to land. Then there was a third, and a fourth, fifth, and sixth. Someone was in the shit. The word went out, and all available reported to the ER and OR.

Typically, I helped in the ER until the wounded moved into X-ray on their way to the OR. I then went to the OR to scrub in and set up for the case. Sometimes I scrubbed, and sometimes it was a light wash. There were times when the patient was in the OR minutes after arriving, leaving little time to prepare. There were times when I was still opening instrument sets when the operation began. The scene was often hectic, and the pace was furiously fast. Time flew by, and hours would pass seeming like minutes.

Gus, one of the trauma surgeons, had his back to me once and asked for an instrument. I couldn’t understand what he asked for, so I slapped a hemostat into his hand. He quickly pulled his hand back, shaking it, and looked at me with a shocked look on his face. He looked at his hand, then me, and said, “I asked for a knife.”

I did fine during a long, maybe twelve-hour case, until we started to close. Fatigue then set in, and I sometimes felt like I couldn’t finish. It was also at that point that I realized how bad I had to go to the bathroom; my eyes were floating. There were times we worked for hours on a soldier only to have him die. I had trouble dealing with this, and my emotions came out as anger. “You son of a bitch, you have the nerve to die on us after we worked so hard to save you!”

It really wasn’t anger, and I really wasn’t calling him names. It was a way to vent my frustration, trying to maintain my own sanity in an insane environment. There were nineteen- and twenty-year-old guys too young to die, and it was always difficult. I, myself, was only twenty years old, witnessing the horrors that no human should be exposed to. About once a month something would come into the OR that would horrify me. It would send me to the depths of depression. The back steps of Sham Palace were about the most private place on the compound. That is where I would go to cry.

The depression would last about a week, but Deeg, Dew, and Tree were always there to help. We became brothers there. It seemed like it was one of us affected one week, then another, then another. We would always pull together to support one another.

Every time I came out of a depression, I became harder and harder. I would feel like nothing could ever bother me again. But there was always a next time. The destruction that occurs to the human body in a war zone is unimaginable. Explosives are equal opportunity, any person, any time, any body part. Body parts become unidentifiable. We dealt with it every day in Vietnam, and we are still dealing with it. No one comes home the same person he or she was before.

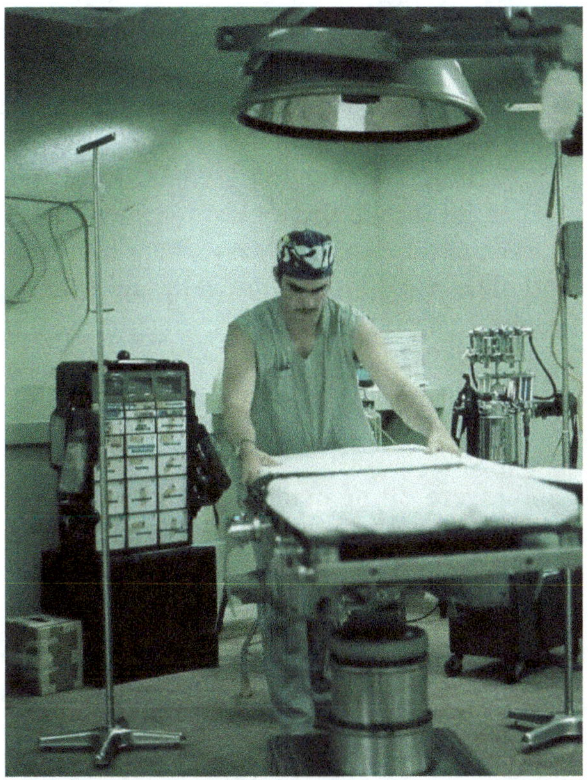

Michael Clark in the OR at the 85th Evac.

The call name for the 85th was "Plasma Hotel." A call came into the Plasma Hotel on the evening of December 24, 1970. Christmas Eve. The 101st was in the shit in the A Shau Valley. It turned out it was friendly fire. There are two theories about what happened that night, and the investigation continues to this day. One theory is that an FNG lieutenant called in his own coordinates, and the 2/320 artillery sent a round from Firebase Birmingham right on target. This was the story we were told and clung to until recently. A second theory has evolved after investigation. There were two companies too close in proximity. One company called in coordinates for their night defense target at the same time the lieutenant called in his coordinates, and they were confused somewhere along the line. Whatever happened, twelve soldiers died that night, and six others were wounded.

We worked all night that night. It is still a topic of conversation at our reunions. The nights run together after a time, and I can't say specifically exactly what I did in the OR that night. I do remember Mike singing "Oh Holy Night" at church services that night.

CMS was hosting the Christmas party that year. Every department would take turns hosting a holiday party. I was up at 0800 behind the lab building to roast the pig. Since it was monsoon season, the weather was predictable, and it didn't disappoint the weatherman. It was pouring down rain all morning. Somehow, I got the fire going and the pig situated on the spit. I built a small shelter for the fire by leaning sheets of corrugated steel together, keeping most of the rain off. I sat for four hours with my raincoat on, turning the spit. The party turned out well, and everyone was able to let off some of their frustrations. I got sick on the eggnog and haven't drunk it since.

***

Chuck, Tree, and I were sitting in my room one night relaxing when we heard an explosion right next to us. We cautiously went out the front door of the hooch and began looking for the source of the explosion. Using flashlights, we were able to see a liquid running from the floor of the hooch next to us on the opposite end. The dirt was disturbed under the hooch, and it became obvious what happened; someone had thrown a grenade under the hooch.

The MPs were called, and the spoon was found intact. Fortunately, we were sitting in the southeast corner of our hooch, and the damage was to the northeast corner of the hooch next to us and the northwest corner of our hooch. They caught the guy who threw the grenade. He was a black soldier who got into an argument with his white sergeant on the ward that day. The sergeant happened to be in the shower when the grenade was thrown. Jim from our hooch was at work. No one was injured. The liquid running through the floor was a bottle of wine in his refrigerator that had been burst by a fragment.

Racial tensions were high. Essentially, the blacks stuck with blacks and whites stuck with whites. I never had a problem with anyone because of his color, but there were plenty of guys who did, black and white. I was told by two soldiers at the 85th on separate occasions that they would be happy to kill me because I was white. In total, there were four soldiers on three occasions who threatened my life simply because I was white, and I really didn't know any of them. Racism is racism, no matter what color your skin is. I don't care about the color of your skin. I only care about the kind of person you are.

We had several black friends we chummed with on a daily basis: Scotty, Doc Holiday, Tucker, Marshall, and several others. The NCOIC in CMS was Staff Sergeant Russell, a black sergeant I had great respect for. He and Staff Sergeant Johnson, a black sergeant, were always working with us to do whatever job needed done. We all partied together when we could.

The brothers had a celebration when greeting each other. It was referred to as the DAP. It was a series of handshakes, finger snaps, claps, and arm raising that is hard to describe. I don't intend to demean it, but it was like patty-cake on steroids. I don't know how else to describe it, but it was specific to blacks. I saw a white soldier doing the DAP with a black soldier perhaps three or four times in a year.

***

I was working a night shift, and we were caught up in CMS, so were helping in the ER. A drunk soldier came in after getting in a fight and getting the worst of it. His face was beaten pretty good, and he had lacerations that needed closing. Many lacerations were closed by us, the medics, but Bob (MD) decided he would close these. The soldier was abusive, obnoxious, combative, belligerent, and resisting any attempt to help him. Bob took a #2 silk suture and sewed both his earlobes to the canvas litter to keep him still, and it worked.

I was working at the counter wrapping supplies on another night shift, early in the morning. A guy came into CMS and asked where the ER was. I started giving him directions but then asked if he had a problem. He stated that he was driving, and his truck broke down. He'd started walking for help, but he was shot as he was walking. He opened his shirt, and there were two gunshot wounds in his right upper chest. The guy had just walked a mile to get to the hospital! I had him lie on the counter while I ran to the ER to get a litter and help. He required a chest tube but didn't have to go to surgery that night.

The med-evac unit at Phu Bai was Eagle Dust Off. They flew the Hueys into some serious shit to get guys out. As a result, they took heavy casualties and had about a 50 percent turnover rate each month. They made a monthly trip to the 85th to try to get guys to sign on. I didn't consider it. I wanted to do what I could to help, but I didn't want to come home in a body bag.

***

On the hooch kitty-corner to the left of ours, there was a ten-by-twelve lean-to addition. No one lived in this addition. Rich turned it into "the room." The room had one entrance. Inside, there was a Pioneer turntable, a Kenwood amplifier, and four Sansui speakers, three feet by two feet and 200 watts each. There were about two hundred albums contributed by everyone who could find one at the PX.

Think about the classic music of the time: Led Zeppelin, CSNY, Iron Butterfly, Steppenwolf, Jimi, Janis, the Doors, the Woodstock soundtrack, Steven Miller, the Moody Blues, Three Dog Night, and the list goes on and on. The music was always playing as guys were lying on mattresses on the floor, looking at posters on the wall illuminated by black lights on the ceiling. This was an escape to another world, a way to forget what you saw or did that day. *Took fin* was the substance of choice in the room. It was all about trying to escape.

One of the career sergeants got a strip show on-compound. There were a half dozen girls on stage in sheer covers and an emcee, all Vietnamese. They would do different dances and skits, and even their sheer covers would come off. Guys were called from the audience to participate in the different acts.

One of the girls was making eyes at me during the show and called me up on stage. My thought was that a picture of me with a naked lady plus a letter to my wife equaled divorce court. I didn't go up on stage. To my knowledge, these were dancers, not prostitutes.

***

As a medic at the 85th, I was required to get a license to drive a deuce-and-a-half. There were times when we had to be the medic on convoys to Da Nang (which *always* took enemy fire). The 85th also had an aid station on Eagle Beach, and we were required to drive supplies there. The trip was twenty-five to thirty miles and required me to drive through Huế.

On one particular day, I was accompanied by a master sergeant (E-8). We delivered the supplies and were driving through Huế on the way back when a guy on a scooter pulled in front of me, forcing me to slam on the brakes and downshift. As I stopped, concentrating on the scooter, another guy jumped on the running boards, grabbed my wristwatch, and ripped it from my wrist. He then ran into a crowd of people and disappeared. Chasing him would have had all kinds of negative consequences, from getting killed to getting mugged to having the truck stolen. These guys worked in packs in order to steal and were well-known as cowboys. Because I had a credible witness with me, I was eventually reimbursed for my watch. But, in typical military fashion, it took months and several visits to support my claim.

This trip was not over, however. We were on Highway One traveling south when the truck broke down in the middle of nowhere. We were surrounded by rice paddies, and no buildings were in sight. After a time, another vehicle drove by, and the sergeant was given a ride to the 85th to get help. This left me alone to stay with the deuce-and-a-half. A couple of hours passed as I watched the rice paddies, looking for any activity. These children came out of nowhere and began climbing on the truck. I allowed this, hoping it would deter any possible attack, knowing full well that it wouldn't matter.

Darkness was approaching, and the children eventually disappeared the same way that they appeared. I decided that I was not going to stay with the truck after darkness set in and located an area in the ditch on the side of the road that would provide a defensive position. I was going to move in after dark to avoid giving away my position. I had an M-16 and one bandolier of ammunition. As I was preparing to vacate the truck, headlights approached; it was my rescue truck. My truck was connected to a tow bar and towed safely back to the motor pool.

***

The hospital provided a PX (post exchange) run once a week. The PX was at the south end of the compound, a mile away. I sometimes drove the deuce-and-a-half, but most of the time, I rode in the back. The PX was like a general store, and it generally didn't have much. We could get some personal items and occasional luxury items like beer, liquor, wine and cigarettes. Everyone was issued a ration card that allowed six cartons of cigarettes, three bottles of wine, three bottles of liquor, and three cases of beer.

When I first arrived, a person had to be a sergeant E-6 to buy liquor or wine; it didn't make a difference how old you were. This was later changed to twenty years old. It was okay to carry an M-16 but not okay to buy a bottle of booze. This was another regulation that was not enforced. ID was not checked, and oftentimes the ration card was not stamped. I could buy a liter of Gordon's vodka for ninety cents and a case of tomato juice (twelve cans) for a dollar twenty. On occasion, we could get Mateus wine. There was never a guarantee that anything would be available. Beer was mostly Hamm's of Carling Black Label. Once in a while we could get Bud, but you had to be there at the right time because it sold out fast.

Ration cards were used to keep guys from selling items on the black market for a profit. Some of the guys would buy cigarettes for their *mama-san* so she could make some extra money. Cigarettes were six dollars a carton. Electronics would make their way that far north every so often, and they sold out fast. Word traveled fast when cameras or stereo equipment were available. I was able to get a nice Canon SLR from the PX.

We got a truck to go to the PX at Camp Eagle for electronics one day. There was a whorehouse just off camp, and while we were driving by, a Vietnamese male ran out of the building. He was followed not far behind by another Vietnamese male with a knife about eight inches long. He caught up to the first guy and stabbed him in the chest at least a half dozen times. This was a restricted area, and we did not stop.

There was a catalog from the PX with items that could be ordered from Japan and shipped home. Many items were available duty-free. I was able to buy twelve place settings of Noritake China and ship it home for forty-eight dollars. My 200-watt stereo was less than two hundred. I purchased several items from this catalog and sent them to Connie.

***

Bob Hope was always a big deal in Vietnam. He toured the country every year after monsoon season. The tour started in the south and went north from base to base. One of the shows was at Camp Eagle, and anyone not on duty that day was able to go. I was fortunate enough to attend. We took a deuce-and-a-half to Camp Eagle and back. Les Brown and his Band of Renown provided the music. The Golddiggers were there with Lola Falana and Johnny Bench. There were several acts performed with comedy between each act. At times, the acts would be stopped in the middle and restarted because it wasn't good enough for the cameras. One act was done three times.

After the show, Bob and the other entertainers came to the 85th Evac to visit with the wounded and ill soldiers. We were able to get back in time to meet and greet them as they arrived. They went from ward to ward talking to the patients and lifting spirits of everyone. I was able to meet Bob Hope and shake his hand.

***

When the rain stopped, warm weather activities started. We had a fast-pitch softball team and played about four other teams on-base. Warrant Officer Smith from the mess hall was the pitcher. I was the catcher. We won some and lost some but had a pretty good team. We had a slow-pitch league made up of teams from different departments. The OR/CMS team was one of the better teams; the docs, not so much. We counted on a win when we played them.

We got a little cocky, and there was a challenge game scheduled. We made a mistake by betting a case of beer. If we had bet twenty dollars, I'm certain we would have won, but a case of beer—we got our asses handed to us! And I still hear about it at our reunions. The softball diamond was like playing a links golf course with narrow fairways through condos; there were a lot of obstructions. Into the road in left field was a home run. If the ball hit the ammo bunker in center, it was a ground-rule double. Over the bunker was a home run. Hitting the side of the hooch in right meant the ball was in play. On the roof was a ground-rule double, and over the hooch was a home run. The infield had two areas where the sand eroded when it rained. There were a lot of bad hops when I played short stop.

The hospital chaplain, Captain Hunt, arranged for a Chinook to Eagle Beach every Sunday. Those who weren't scheduled to work could go to the beach for a day of sun and swimming in the South China Sea. There were floor shows and a bar at the beach. It was good to get away and forget about the events of the previous week, if only for a few hours.

I took my in-country R & R at Eagle Beach. We were allowed to go to an in-country destination for three days to relax. I stayed at the 85th Evac Aid Station. I helped out some in the clinic, but mostly vegetated.

I was sitting on the beach with about eight other guys passing a bowl (*took fin*) when I heard someone say in a monotone, under his breath, "Put it away." I looked up and saw an MP staring at me with an unhappy look on his face. I put the bowl in the sand next to me on the opposite side from the MP. Questions were asked, and the two MPs left without questioning what was in the bowl. I suspect if there had been fewer of us, there would have been consequences.

I went to a floor show one afternoon and was pretty well under the influence. The group was Australian and did a great job. They did a rendition of "Joy to the World" that is still in my mind. I remember that every time I hear the song. I also remember going to the snack shop that afternoon and buying a cheeseburger. The *mama-san* shorted me a dollar in change, and I essentially thought, *Oh well*, and did nothing about it.

Maybe I was too mellow, and a dollar wasn't enough to destroy the mood. The cheeseburger tasted good.

The beach was closed one day because a poisonous sea snake was caught and killed in the water.

***

I was promoted to Specialist E-5 on March 15, 1971. I was put in for promotion after fifteen months, the minimum time allowable with a maximum waiver. This was the second promotion that wasn't automatic or meritorious, and I had to go before a board of review and be approved. Several questions were asked to determine if the candidate was qualified for promotion, theoretically. Rarely was a candidate denied a promotion after being recommended by his commanding officer.

To me, the promotion was just another stripe and pay raise. To many others, it meant power. A guy could be a good friend one day until he got promoted. There was an overnight change, and he felt he was allowed to tell you what to do and how to do it the next day. It was disturbing to see these changes, and I never really understood this. A true friend is a friend always.

***

R & R was greatly anticipated by all. We were allowed a one-week leave and a one-week R & R. The R & R was guaranteed, but the leave was on a space-available basis. If the destination was filled by guys on R & R, the leave would be denied. I wanted to go to Sydney, Australia, but it was a popular destination and not available for a leave. Hawaii was a less popular destination, but I was meeting Connie there on R & R and didn't dare chance using my R & R for Sydney. As it turns out, I could have gone both places, but I don't regret my choice for a minute. I wouldn't have taken any chance that would have jeopardized my chance to spend a week with Connie.

Murchio served at the 85th. He was Hawaiian and lived in Honolulu. He contacted his girlfriend, and she greeted Connie at the airport a couple of days prior to my arrival. They saw the sights and went shopping together. This gave Connie ideas about places to go when I arrived.

My R & R started on a flight to Da Nang on a C-130. After a night there, I boarded a Pan Am jet headed for Hawaii. It was mid-April, and the only contact I'd had with Connie during the last several months, other than the MARS call, was by letter. Our reunion was greatly anticipated.

There was a stop in Guam, where I bought a bottle of champagne. Connie met me in the airport with a lei to place around my neck. Our hotel was a block off the beach because we couldn't afford the others. We rented a Honda 450cc motorcycle for transportation. It was not only less expensive but a great way to tour the countryside. I recommend seeing Hawaii on a motorcycle.

We went to a restaurant called the Lanai on the first night and sat on the lanai. During dinner, someone slid a table across the floor, making a noise that sounded too much like a 122 rocket. I was under the table without even thinking about what had happened. I felt foolish after realizing the truth, but it went relatively unnoticed.

I wanted to go to Pearl Harbor, but I couldn't bring myself to go onto a miliary base while on R & R. I still hope to go there. We visited the zoo, the international marketplace, and the beach. We toured the island on the Honda and just enjoyed riding and being together. While in the room, we watched a mockingbird that occupied our balcony as its residence. We opened the bottle of champagne the first night and agreed after one sip that it was the worst thing we had ever tasted. The rest of the bottle was discarded.

We went to see Don Ho one evening and enjoyed the dinner and show. A week goes by much too fast, and I was back in Vietnam so abruptly that it was like waking up from a fabulous dream. Upon returning, I quickly learned about the cook who got mad at his roommate and killed him with an M-16.

***

May 4, 1970, was a big day: I became a two-digit midget. This is the day you have less than a hundred days left in-country. I had my calendar and colored in the appropriate area of the corresponding day.

I was now entitled to yell "*Short*" when around a group of guys. That wasn't usually done until the last few weeks because someone would yell, "*Shorter!*" Then the competition began. The person yelling "*Short*" would have to give his DROS (Date returning from overseas). The other person would either be disappointed or gleefully announce a one-digit midget. This was too short-lived to exploit.

In the spring of 1971, the 18th Surgical Hospital in Quang Tri closed. This left the 85th Evac as the northernmost hospital in South Vietnam. The 18th continued to operate while it was closing. One of the functions that closed was the incinerator. This was the furnace where body parts were burned. As a result, we would get garbage cans full of body parts sent to us by chopper for incineration weekly.

Obviously, some of the parts were a week old and had been in 100-plus-degree temperatures. There were several arms, legs, and body parts that were unidentifiable. Surgical masks gave little relief from the odor. The incinerator would only hold a few extremities at a time, and this took an afternoon to complete. The garbage cans arrived for several weeks.

***

One summer evening, several of us decided to have a bonfire. A sand pit was dug and lined with firebrick obtained from somewhere. Marsh had worked as a mason and laid the bricks. A bright fire was lit, and cake and tea provided.

The cake was cooked by Freaky, who worked in the mess hall. He was also the supplier of took fin, and he didn't let us down that night. The cake had ample amounts of marijuana in it, and the tea was made from the stems and seeds. The colonel in charge of the hospital paid a visit and helped himself to the cake and tea. He left not long afterward, but I swear his feet never touched the ground as he did.

The big project at the officer's club that spring was building a patio and grill. As enlisted men, we were not supposed to fraternize with the officers, but working side by side every day had us on a first name basis. This drove the lifers nuts. They were always insisting we exercise proper military courtesy. It became a joke, and many pronouns were added to their names. Gus would be referred to as "Doctor Major Gus, sir." Anything else that came to mind would be added, and it became humorous. That is how we wound up helping out with the cement patio.

After the slab was poured, one of the surgeons, Joe, constructed a grill from firebricks. He had also worked as a mason while in college. With construction completed, a celebration was in order. Steaks being cooked on the grill for those who'd helped with the construction. A good time was being enjoyed when the word came through that there were casualties and help was needed in the OR.

I was not under the influence and reported to the OR. I was describing the party when one of the surgeons threw a bloody sponge at me, hitting me in the face. This was an attempt at humor, but I didn't find it funny. I was pissed in an instant, and it was all I could do to keep from jumping over the table and attacking him. If there hadn't been an injured GI on the table, I would have been court-martialed that night. I left the OR and retreated to my hiding place on the back steps of Sham Palace to cool down. The surgeon apologized later, but some things can't be taken back. You have to avoid doing them in the first place.

I turned twenty-one in June 1971. Everyone knows this is a birthday of celebration. I can't remember anything about that day—not because I was under the influence, but because it was just another day. There was no celebration. It was the most unimportant birthday I have ever had.

***

Joe was one of the OR techs. He was older than the rest of us and tended to spend time with others more his age. Before the army, he was twenty-five years old with a wife and two children. His wife and children were killed in a car accident, and he received his draft notice within three months, before he turned twenty-six. Now he was in the army trying to make sense of life.

Deeg was from Michigan, about two hours from Marshall. Dew was from California, and Tree was from Minnesota. Tree wasn't happy about being in the army. On his first day in the OR, he was asked what his name was. He responded, "What's in a name? You can call me anything—house, garage, tree, anything." Tree was the name that stuck. We were together for nearly the entire year.

Dew and Deeg were in the same class as I was at MFSS, and we arrived at about the same time. We did everything together. We ate together, worked together, laughed and cried together, slept in the same quarters, and confided in each other. We knew each other unconditionally. And we knew that the others would be respectful of our feelings. I could express feelings that I couldn't discuss with anyone else, not even my wife. I've never felt camaraderie like this before or after. We became brothers in Vietnam. This provided the stability necessary for me to come home as normally as possible. Although we only contact each other on occasion, they are with me every day.

There were five nurses in the OR at the 85th Evac at any time. Many came and went. Patti volunteered for Vietnam. She was from Washington state. She was there to help and make a difference. Patti was not a lifer and treated the enlisted men with respect. In turn, she was respected. If she needed something done. It was always reasonable and always done. She married a flyboy while in Vietnam. He was shot down about seven times during his tour, but he lived to go home.

Darlene was a career army nurse. She was by-the-book and often treated us as property. She was a good nurse, but I didn't care for working with her. Jennie, for the most part, was fun to work with, although she had her Regular Army moments. She tended to treat guys according to their level of competence. She was very complimentary of me when I left, comparing me to Mitch.

Lieutenant Lynch was a guy and gay. Gays weren't allowed in the army at that time. He was caught with a sergeant in a compromising situation one night and forced to resign his commission. The sergeant was given an undesirable discharge. The sergeant said he was so drunk he didn't recall anything. I'd known him for several months and believed him.

On nights when we were too intoxicated to know better, we would do what we called, "the turkey circus." There would be a group of us, and we would say "*owa, owa, owa, owa*" loudly, rapidly, and in a high pitch to make it sound like a turkey (kinda). We would then surround someone and whine in a high voice while picking at their skin. This would give most people the heebie-jeebies and send them off running, never to be the same. We did this to Lieutenant Lynch as he was returning from the shower one night, and he loved it so much he gave us a liter of whiskey. His eyes shone bright, and he had a huge smile that said *I'll take you, then you, then you*. We left him alone after that.

Helicopter pilots, aka flyboys, were notoriously crazy. They had to be to do what they did. We frequently got pilots in who had been shot down. The choppers almost always exploded and burned. That is where the term "crash and burn" came from. We would take them to the OR and, under anesthesia, use a brush and Phisohex to scrub and remove the burnt skin. The smell of burning flesh is unmistakable. Often, their ears and nose were burnt off; sometimes their eyes were burnt out. The pain associated with this, I don't even want to imagine. Most often, the severely burned became septic and died after a living hell. We stopped using Phisohex when it was discovered it would actually grow pseudomonas.

The 85th was blessed with some excellent trauma surgeons. We knew the wounded had the best chance possible when working with Gus, Roger, or Joe. Not only were they excellent surgeons, but they were excellent to work with. There was a chemistry between most of us that made the sum greater than the individual parts. The statistics speak for themselves: if they arrived at the 85th alive, there was an excellent chance they would survive.

We had general and orthopedic surgeons only. The general surgeons did vascular when needed. The Neurosurgical cases were transferred to the 95th in Da Nang, weather permitting. There was a time during the monsoon season when we could not transfer a patient with a head injury. It was do something, or the patient would die. I remember the circulating nurse turning the pages of the book as the surgeon read up on how to do burr holes. The patient survived and was eventually transferred.

Casey was the chief of anesthesia. He was a little general in the OR and held everyone to the highest standards. There was only one way to accomplish a task: his way. He was firm but fair and not abusive. If you varied from protocol, guaranteed you would remember not to do it again. He was responsible for getting medication not usually available in Vietnam. He was driven to provide the best care possible.

Sergeant Russell (E-6) was the NCOIC of the department. He was career army but didn't act the part. He was only interested in the end result, and he always worked side by side with everyone to achieve this. He was able to accomplish tasks in spite of the army red tape.

Mitch was from the Cleveland area and was a physics teacher. He was a pensive, soft-spoken guy and very professional. Mitch was the guy everyone wanted to be like. He always did a superb job, and he felt like he was just doing his job. He expected no accolades.

Bergy was our shit magnet. He was from Toledo and a huge Jimi Hendrix fan. He could go in on a case that was supposed to be a simple debridement of an extremity and wind up doing a thoracotomy for a fragment in the chest. It was always an adventure with Bergy.

Ron was from Wisconsin. He was a conscientious objector and avoided stepping on insects when walking on the sidewalk. He had a large wax sculpture made by lighting various colored drip candles and allowing the wax to flow and harden. This made a small mountain of wax with air spaces between the wax stalagmites. He became infuriated one day when he found his candle had become a cockroach hotel and destroyed the candle, killing the roaches.

Chuck was from Southern California and enjoyed a good argument. He could take the opposite side of any topic and make a good case for his position.

Dennis was a career soldier, but he was one of us. He had been kicked in the mouth by a horse when he was younger and had dentures. He was able to do acrobatics with his dentures that, when under the influence, were always funny.

At the 85th, we supported troops in the A Shau Valley, primarily the 101st Airborne Division. The A Shau was twenty-five miles long north to south, and a mile wide, surrounded by densely forested mountains. The valley was flat and covered by elephant grass. It was bordered just to the west by Laos and was a main entry point for the Ho Chi Minh trail. The NVA controlled the A Shau, and entering the valley meant fierce fighting.

Some of the biggest battles were fought in and around the valley, including Signal Hill, Ripcord, and Hill 937, aka Hamburger Hill.

The NVA was deeply entrenched in the hillsides and had tunnels running everywhere. In cases of extreme pressure, they could quickly retreat to Laos, where we couldn't follow them. There are records of NVA tanks being destroyed in the A Shau valley.

I often heard the comment that the war was winding down in 1970 and 1971. Tell that to the guys fighting in the A Shau. Signal Hill was fought in 1968. Hamburger Hill in 1969. Ripcord was fought in July 1970, three weeks before I arrived. Phu Bai was under enemy control in 1968 and again in 1973. The 85th Evac was busy on a daily basis, and we did not do elective surgery.

***

The days ran together, and I can't remember what I was doing on any specific day. Amputations were a daily occurrence, and often several times a day. Mines and booby traps destroyed legs beyond salvage, and they had to be removed. Oftentimes, there would be nothing left but a bloody stump with hamburger at the end. The leg would be removed to the nearest point of viable tissue, the bone would be trimmed, and a flap would be closed over the stump. Arm amputations were less common than legs but not uncommon.

All wounds were dirty and oftentimes were debrided and left open for several days. They would be debrided on a later day and then closed. This was called a DPC (delayed primary closure). It was done this way to reduce the risk of infection. The DPC was done with stainless-steel wire for strength. This would leave large scars but saved life and limb. Better to have a leg with a scar than to have no leg.

The chest, abdomen, and pelvis were certainly not spared, and we spent hours on individual cases performing bowel resections and vascular repairs. I scrubbed in on four cases where the vena cava was damaged behind the liver. This posed a problem because it is much more difficult to repair a vein than it is to repair an artery, and the location made it impossible to get to the site for repair. An attempt was made to pass a shunt (bypass) into the superior vena cava, toward the heart, then inferiorly, toward the feet, in order to maintain circulation while a repair was performed. Passing the plastic tube superiorly had to be done by feel because the unbelievable gush of blood made it impossible to see. There were only two, perhaps three chances to get this done before the patient exsanguinated. None of the four patients I scrubbed in on survived.

Although I can't remember specific days, I still remember specific cases, and for a long time, I could remember their names. I can only recall one name anymore, and I will never forget Richard. It was probably April or May 1971 when I scrubbed in to relieve Dennis for lunch. There was a case just underway on a guy who stepped on a mine and had damage to his legs and lower torso. Gus was trying to find the most distal point of viable tissue to determine where to remove the damaged tissue. The search proceeded up the legs to the pelvis. Ultimately, the legs and pelvis were removed. There was nothing below the umbilicus remaining. A colostomy and two ureterostomies were performed to allow the intestines and kidneys to drain. This is known as a *hemicorporectomy*. His right arm was amputated below the elbow as well.

Upon completion of the case, we learned that his commanding officer and a couple of buddies were waiting between the OR and the ICU to see Richard. We placed pillows under the sheets to make it look like there was a complete body underneath and moved him to the ICU. Richard died of sepsis three days later. I was horrified and in a deep depression for a week afterward, but I was supported by my brothers. I will never forget you, Richard. I think of you often, and when I do, I still cry.

***

Some of the more difficult memories from the 85th occurred in the ER. It was common to get mass casualties, and assessment and treatment were done at a furious pace. They were young men arriving injured and afraid for their lives. They all knew they were injured but did not understand the severity of their injuries. They were all under the influence of a full-blown adrenaline rush, making them anxious and hyperverbal. And they were all searching for hope and reassurance. There was a constant stream of screams and questions.

"Doc, am I going to live?"

"Doc, am I going to die?"

"Doc, did they get my leg?"

"You gotta help me, doc, I've never seen my kid!"

"Doc, did they get my dick?"

"Don't cut off my leg, doc. If you cut off my leg, just let me die!"

"Doc, you gotta tell my wife I was thinking about her until the end!"

"Doc, you gotta get this letter to my mother!"

True or false, the message we gave was always one of reassurance. "We're going to take good care of you. Just hang on. You're going to be all right." They were automatic responses to requests only half-heard. This wasn't out of disrespect, but the primary focus was on trying to accomplish a task in order to save a life. A distraction could mean the difference between living and dying.

Some of the injuries were minor and could wait. Others were more serious and needed immediate attention. If we were too overwhelmed, some of the wounded would be evacuated to the naval hospital ship in the gulf. Some of the wounded were so serious that they had little chance of survival. If they were treated first, others might die. The difficult decision of who to take care of first was made by the ER docs and the surgeons. I'm glad I never had to make that decision.

It was in the last couple of weeks of my tour that we received the body of a major. He was in command of the helicopter unit at Camp Eagle. He was scheduled to go home but volunteered to go on one last mission. It was, in fact, his last mission. He was shot down by a B-40 rocket and arrived for processing by Graves Registration. When the body bag was opened, he was found to still have agonal breathing, and the shit hit the fan. He was taken to the ER for IVs and fluids. There was a quick pass through X-ray and then into the OR.

Tree was the primary OR tech on the case, but I scrubbed in to work with him because the pace was so furious. The scrub was more of a quick rinse, as there was no time for a true scrub. We were still setting up when they brought him into the room. When the abdomen was opened, it was obvious that nothing could be done. The intestines were hamburger, and there were, essentially, no two ends of anything to be sewn together. A futile attempt was made to save him but he was called after a couple of hours.

***

Orders came down dated 13 June 1971 for my reassignment. I was to report to Fort Lewis, Washington, on 11 August 1971—home. It was still two months away, but it was becoming a reality. My calendar was filling in nicely, and anticipation was setting in.

Dew and I were awarded the Army Commendation Medal on June 29. This is an award for meritorious service. The OIC (officer in charge) of the OR, Rey, put us in for this award. It read:

> The Army Commendation Medal is presented to Specialist Five Michael D. Clark, US Army, who distinguished himself by meritorious service in support of military operations against communist aggression in the republic of Vietnam. During the period September 1970 to August 1971, he astutely performed under extremely adverse conditions to obtain consistently superior results as a technician in both the Operating Room and Central Materials Section of the 85th Evacuation Hospital (SMBL). His superior versatility in responding to the needs of both the patients and surgeons has been outstanding. His conscientious follow through, demonstrated in any endeavor he undertook is an example for those with lesser experience. His skill, knowledge, devotion to duty has achieved outstanding results and has been keeping with the highest traditions and standards of military service and reflect great credit upon himself, his unit and the United States Army.

I didn't know how much of this was a form letter, and I didn't appreciate it much when it was first received, but I do now. I was also given a plaque from the guys in my unit that simply states, "Just a token of thanks for a job well done." This was not previously a tradition. Dew was going to get one also but stated he wanted no part of it. He was given a scrub shirt with a large question mark on it, as his other nickname was "Question Man."

The first Monday of the month usually found us on the back steps of my hooch watching for the three rockets to slam into the ARVN camp. This was no ordinary Monday; it was the first Monday in August, and I was a one-digit midget. I was going home in a week, and I was taking no chances. I put on my flak jacket and steel pot and sat in the bunker until it was over. Dew and Deeg had just left for home, and I was next.

There was a big turnover in personnel during this time at the 85th, and there was a big party the night before I left. Somehow, someone got hold of a five-gallon container of ethyl alcohol. It came in an OD-green container with a serial number and everything; it was official army issue. I have no idea why the army needed a five-gallon container of ethyl alcohol, but we got one. The alcohol was not served, as it was too high of a proof. Instead, fruit cocktail was the dish of the night. The fruit cocktail was added to the bucket and then served in a dish with a spoon. This was dangerously deceiving, and people got dangerously drunk.

Rey, the OR OIC, ran up to me, jumped into my arms with his arms and legs wrapped around me, kissed me on the cheek, and yelled, "Clark, I love you!" One of the surgeons tried to jump from a bunker into a tank of water and missed, breaking his elbow. I was going home in a few hours, but he was evacuated that night and beat me home. I had a confirmed flight on a C-130 the next day and couldn't imagine making that flight hungover. I only had one dish of the fruit cocktail.

The trip to the Phu Bai airport was in the a.m. Tree and Chuck rode with me in the back of the deuce-and-a-half. I was happy beyond words to be going home alive, not getting a Purple Heart, and making a difference in someone else's life. Although I was happy to go home, I was also emotional about leaving guys I considered to be my brothers. I knew we had the kind of relationship that I would never experience again. Camaraderie developed in Vietnam isn't attainable at home. If you bare your innermost thoughts here, they won't be understood and will be used against you at some point.

***

Processing out consisted of some debriefing and turning in of equipment. It took a couple of days, and we stayed in transient barracks, much like basic and AIT, until we were placed on a flight manifest. We were given eight weeks of antimalarial tablets to be continued at home to ensure we would not get malaria. I was standing in formation after dark when a sergeant climbed some steps onto a platform and started calling the names of those scheduled to be on the next flight. It was starting to sound like another disappointing manifest when I finally heard my name called. It was reality at last.

We flew home on Flying Tiger Airlines, exchanging fish stories during the flight. For many guys, the stewardesses were the first round-eyes they had seen in months, and their conversations made this very obvious. I'm certain there was a stopover on the way home, but I don't remember where it was. After a sixteen-hour flight, the plane was set to touch down in Washington state. All I could think about was, "I survived a year in hell. Don't let anything happen now that I'm home." Cheers lit up the plane as it touched the ground. Getting off the plane, I dropped to my knees and kissed the asphalt tarmac and rejoiced at being on American soil.

Arriving at Fort Lewis, we were told we could take a couple of days to process out or complete everything in one long day. There was no decision to be made. I planned on being home with my wife by that time the next day.

There were several stations to be cleared. Some of them were run by civilian subcontractors. I went into a large building to complete a part of my processing. I can't even remember what it was. As I entered the building, my heart sank. There were antiwar protest posters covering the walls. I can't describe my disappointment at seeing this. I was on an army base, and there were protest posters on the wall. I was so happy to be home, but I was already being subjected to the negativity associated with the war. This was just wrong, and it hurt deeply.

I was still in the building when a full-bird colonel came into the room and ripped the inside apart. There were pieces of posters flying all around the room in the midst of screamed obscenities. There was no doubt in my mind that someone paid a high price for such inappropriate actions.

At one of the stations, we were required to review the information on our DD214s for accuracy. If there were errors, getting them corrected would delay processing by one full day. Otherwise, we could write to a station in Iowa to get them corrected. My DD214 had two minor errors, and I was determined not to allow this to delay my departure. Letters to Iowa were no help, and the errors remain. It was late at night when I finished processing.

It was August 11, the day after my third wedding anniversary. Five of us loaded into a cab headed for the airport. The driver was a retired first sergeant, and there was ample conversation during the ten-mile ride. We had to be in dress uniform in order to fly military standby, and I was apprehensive walking through the airport. No one yelled at me or spit on me in the airport. I am happy for this, but it seemed unfair to return from fighting a war for your country and worry about being mistreated by your countrymen for it.

Karen and Leo drove Connie to the airport in Detroit. They were waiting for me as I got off the plane. After hugs and handshakes, I took the bag of civilian clothing from Connie, as was prearranged, and went into the bathroom and changed clothes. I have never worn the uniform since. It still hangs in my closet, but it is tailored for a much smaller man than I am now. The first stop after arriving in Marshall was the A & W for a cheeseburger.

I am proud to have served at the 85th, but if given the opportunity to relive that part of my life again, I would avoid the army. Although I still silently struggle with my experience, I have been able to live through it and contribute to society. We were blessed at the 85th with a group of dedicated professionals focused on doing their best and giving the best care possible. It was the strength of the people, sometimes in spite of the army, that made the hospital a shining star of hope for those in daily combat.

The words that appeared on the shield of the 85th were *Miracularum Laborantes*, "miracle workers," and we were. I am forever grateful for many things that occurred during my tour. I am grateful I had a roof over my head. I am grateful I saw limited combat. I am grateful for a bunk every night. I am grateful for my one electrical outlet. I am grateful I had an electric blanket. I am grateful for flush toilets and indoor plumbing. I am grateful for dry socks. I am grateful for a shower with an inch of green moss on the floor. Most of all, I am grateful for the people I served with. We did our best. But sometimes our best was not good enough. And we have to live with reality every day.

There is some peace in knowing that we are human and, as such, subject to human limitations. There were some things beyond our control, and as much as we wished for different results, ultimately, there was nothing we could do. This was never due to a lack of effort. Although I am not in contact with many of the guys I served with, they are in my thoughts every day, and I owe them a debt of gratitude.

Excerpt from One Man's Story: Memoirs of a Vietnam Vet
by Michael Clark.
Published in 2014 by Michael Clark and Lulu Publishing Services.
Reprinted with permission from Michael Clark.

Duane Wall

My military history from getting my draft notice to arriving home.

The Letter & CO Status

I graduated in June 1969, finally in the real world. Independent life was about to begin! Four years of college had given me a solid foundation, and I was ready for the world.

During my senior year of college, I joined an insurance company to sell life insurance, which is not the easiest sixteen products to sell. When I graduated, I already had boots on the ground. I was good at selling life insurance and being rewarded with a reasonable income and accolades from the company. I rented an apartment in town; I was on my own. My apartment had bare necessities but no character. On routine trips to town, my parents stopped by to visit and bring food that my mother knew I loved.

In early October, I received a call from my mother. "Son, there is a letter from the government here that you better come home and see what it has to say." I drove the sixteen miles home and opened the official-looking envelope. "Greetings…." It was my draft notice. I was being drafted. My immediate gut feeling was I would be sent to Vietnam. But I had not heard of any other classmates being drafted so soon after graduation.

Colleges were packed during those years due to the baby boomer generation. Being enrolled in college was a way to avoid being drafted. A 2-S deferment for carrying a full load in college had kept me out of the service, but now that I had graduated, I was a target, and Vietnam was on the news every night. Body counts were the focus.

My Napa draft board had to fill a lot of slots. The draft board was pressured to draft the prescribed number of young men, and they earnestly went after whomever they could. A couple of years earlier, during my sophomore year, the draft board had tried to reach into the 2-S deferred students and pull me out. I had to defend my Conscientious Objector (CO) status and show I was taking the required number of college courses to remain a student and not be drafted. Now, my deferment had expired, and I was being drafted.

I broke my apartment agreement, packed my Volkswagen, and went to my older brother's place on the Keys of South Tahoe to think this issue over. I spent a week landscaping and toying with the idea of going to Canada. Some draftees had decided going to war was not an option and left for the sanctuary of Canada. That option was not palatable to me.

My brother, who is 22 years older, had been drafted during World War II, became a pilot, and was headed for Germany as a captain. This was just after the Desmond Doss experience, shown in the movie Hacksaw Ridge, which created the Conscientious Objector (CO) status. Having a Seventh-day Adventist upbringing and having no desire to bomb from on high, he chose to activate the CO status, which had become applicable. The military was not happy. They busted him from a captain to a buck private and sent him to a lab in Naples, Italy. Later in life, he said that was the best thing that could have happened to him. The doctor in charge of the lab became a mentor, which positively affected the rest of his life.

So, following the stay in South Tahoe, I turned the Volkswagen toward Mexico, crossed the border, and ended up in Ensenada. I found a quiet room on the beach and continued considering the Canada option. It still was not in my character to be a draft dodger. I went fishing off the coast of Ensenada, caught barracudas, and sat on the beach. Coming to the conclusion I was destined to go into the service, I headed north to the California-Mexico border.

Approaching the immigration checkpoint, I must have looked like the typical drug smuggler. The border guards pulled me out of the checkpoint and proceeded to dismantle my Volkswagen, looking for drugs. I guess a young male in a Volkswagen was the anticipated drug runner. I fit the profile. After they tore my car apart, it took a couple of hours to replace the door panels, the seats, the air intake to the carburetor, and all the items from the trunk to make the car functional again.

Back on the road, I was glad to have those border guards behind me. I thought my future in the military would be easier than coming home from Mexico. Returning home, I reluctantly packed a small suitcase. My parents took me to the bus headed for Oakland and the induction center.

Arriving in Oakland, I found the line of young men headed for the physical exam required for draftees. I asked myself, "Maybe I will be rejected for some medical issue." If those with flat feet were rejected, there must be other medical issues that the Army would find as cause for rejection. Maybe…maybe. I passed all the required stations, had no flat feet, turned my head to the side, and coughed, no issues. I was then sent to a room with others who passed their physical. My hard work and healthy upbringing had provided the Army with another healthy, qualified draftee.

Once all the young men who passed the physical had assembled in this room, an officer came in, ordered some form of lines, and proceeded to swear us in. "I, _____, do solemnly swear (or affirm) that I will support and defend the Constitution of the United States against all enemies, foreign and domestic…" We were now in the Army and soldiers whether we wanted to be or not.

What a motley crew of unwilling, apprehensive new soldiers. A real cross-section of young men from the Bay Area. One guy stood out. He was short, poorly dressed, had long red hair, and had a noxious vocabulary. He said he had been ordered to go into the service or go to jail. He was not sure he made the right choice, but now he was a soldier.

The sergeant stood on the platform and pointed to two green draftees. I was one of the two. What had I done? Why had I been singled out of around 300 men? I had been a soldier for only minutes, and now it appeared I was in trouble; how could that be? The sergeant escorted the two of us into a side room. He said, "You two are now in charge of this detail, which is headed to Travis Air Force Base, there to board a plane and go to McCord Air Force Base in Washington State." This was not said as a request. It was the first order made as a demand, not a request. Buses were outside, and the now "troops" loaded up. The little red-headed guy continued swearing and being obnoxious to everyone in his vicinity, a real pain… The other guy who had been ordered to be in charge and I just ignored this problem. After all, the only order we were given was to get this group to Washington.

It was a rainy, cold night when we arrived at McCord, where we boarded more buses and were taken to the processing complex. The two of us in charge were now relieved of our responsibility. What a relief. It turned out the two of us were the biggest in the group—not always a good evaluation of leadership. I guess the Army made quick decisions to assign authority by size, but that was all they had to go with at that moment.

The only thing between us troops and the weather was a corrugated roof, no sides. We were not protected from the elements, except the roof kept the rain off. The wind was still cold. We stood under that roof until around 4:00 A.M. when a sergeant ordered us into a building where we were ordered to take a test. I guess it was supposed to evaluate each draftee in some way the Army wanted evaluated. The little red-headed guy continued swearing and being obnoxious. He objected to taking the test but finally did take it. I have no idea what the outcome of his test results was, but I imagined some swear words were written on the answer sheets.

We went to some "Mess Hall" and had the first military food, not bad considering how many they had to feed. Then we were ordered to stand in line in front of a small building where troops entered and came out the other end with no hair. Swearing and being obnoxious, the little red-headed guy entered and came out the other side. He was almost unrecognizable. Only his clothes identified who had gone into that building. If we had not seen him go in and come out the other side with the same clothes, we would have thought he had disappeared.

From that moment on, he was docile, timid, and cooperative. What a difference. His hair had been his armor, and now it was gone. For the remainder of my time with that group, that little now bald guy started to become a soldier. I wonder what became of him. Did he go to Vietnam? Did he get wounded? Did he go Absent Without Leave—AWOL?

The next day found our group in a large room. This time, we had chairs to sit on, a real improvement. As we sat there, occasionally, the loudspeaker would come on announcing the name of a draftee who had to report to a numbered office on either side of the room. My name was called out and said to report to room ___. Again, I wondered what I had done. Why was I singled out again? This should not be happening. I wanted to "keep my head down" and go through this journey without issues.

I entered the room, and an officer told me to sit down. He looked at the paperwork and announced I had done very well on the test. He also saw on my paperwork that I had graduated college. He then informed me, "Because you scored so high on the test and you are a college graduate, we would like you to become an officer." Well, at least I was not being singled out because I had done something wrong. They wanted me to be an officer. That would be a reward. Wow! I was a little proud to be offered a better status than a grunt. But what about my CO status? The officer rifled through my paperwork and found the form that allowed me the CO status.

So I asked the officer, "Can I be an officer and keep my Conscientious Objector status?" He replied, "No, to be an officer, you will need to abandon the Conscientious Objector status and enlist for a three-year tour versus the two-year drafted term." My immediate reply was, "No, thank you." I then returned to the group - never to be an officer, but glad to have stuck with my convictions. Later, in Vietnam, it became apparent that new officers had a very high mortality rate due to various reasons. I was glad and relieved I was just a regular draftee with the CO status. The next day, we all were bald and introduced to our Drill Sergeant. He seemed mad and glad to have a new set of troops to beat up. He was good at everything except being cordial or pleasant. His uniform was immaculate. He was tall, had a loud voice, and considered all of us draftees as scum, or at least that was how he made us feel. His words were, "I will make soldiers out of you regardless of how stupid and dysfunctional you are."

It took some time to organize this motley crew into a military formation. The Drill Sergeant marched us around a little and told us how disgusted he was with all of us and that he would make soldiers out of us even if we could not do something so simple as march in a straight line or know which foot was our left foot.

The next day, we were standing in formation when the Drill Sergeant singled me out and called me to the front of the formation. What had I done this time? I followed instructions well, marched properly, and kept my head down. But here I was in front of the formation and the Drill Sergeant.

He said, "Wall, I see you are a Conscientious Objector!"

I replied, "Yes, sir."

He replied, "I am not an officer; do not call me sir. I am a Sergeant, and remember that."

I replied, "Yes, Sergeant."

The whole formation had just been informed of how to address this man in charge of us regardless of the words we had formed in our minds.

The Drill Sergeant said, "So you are a Conscientious Objector. No one under my authority is or will be a Conscientious Objector. I am going to make a soldier out of you if it is the last thing I do." He went on, "Conscientious Objectors are cowards and cannot be trusted on the front lines to defend the other soldiers."

He must not have seen combat on the front lines in Vietnam because Conscientious Objectors became medics, and medics were highly respected by the troops on the ground, as I found out much later.

I already knew orders would remove me from this base and send me to Fort Sam Houston, TX, where all Conscientious Objectors took basic training in Echo 4 Company, where there was no training with weapons. It took most of a week and a half before those orders came down, during which time that Drill Sergeant did his best to demean and downgrade me personally and my CO status in front of all the other troops. He was crestfallen when my orders arrived, and he no longer had his grip on this soldier to abuse. I still wonder if that Drill Sergeant ever went to the front and experienced what a medic did for the soldiers in his unit.

My orders gave me over ten days to go to Fort Sam Houston and a ticket to San Antonio, TX. I packed and was driven to the airport. At the United Airlines ticket counter, I told the staff I wanted to go to San Francisco, not San Antonio.

They looked at me, a bald-headed recruit saying he wanted to disobey his orders and go to San Francisco. They must have thought, "Another deserter."

My sales skills came to good use, and I later boarded a plane to San Francisco. My mother and sister picked me up at the airport, and we stopped at my mother's close friend's home in the San Francisco Sunset District.

The husband of my mother's close childhood friend was Bud. After some conversation, Bud assured me I would not go to Vietnam as he controlled the finances for the 7th Army and had considerable influence. "Do not worry. I will keep you from going to Vietnam."

With the assurance that I was not going to Vietnam, I noted immediate relief from that knot in my chest present since the day I read my draft notice, confident that I would be going to Vietnam.

At home during that brief interlude, I worked with my father for about a week, got in my car, and headed for Fort Sam Houston.

United Airlines benefited from my short trip to San Francisco as I was now driving to Texas. After traveling for a short time, I became extremely homesick and anxious. I was a mess; my mind was crazy with imagined consequences of being in the Army. I needed to talk to someone. I stopped east of Phoenix and called a Seventh-day Adventist preacher in Las Cruces, NM, along the way to San Antonio, TX. It took a few hours to get to Las Cruces, and the anxiety and panic continued. When I arrived at the church, the preacher met me and invited me into his study. It was apparent I was emotionally disturbed, and all he had to do was listen. Like many issues, talking it out solves most of the problems. I poured out my grief, and the preacher listened. He sent me on my way, and I headed into the night and the heart of Texas.

Driving south along the border and east to San Antonio, the road was desolate and lonely. It was a cold November night. No cars were going in either direction. I was very alone and cold. The anxiety and crazy thoughts were under control but not gone. The Volkswagen heater is not known for efficiency; the heater was on high, but I was still cold.

Then, in the distance, I saw a light. I drove for what seemed like an hour, and then the light went past me very fast. It was a train, not a car. I was still alone and cold, in the dark, and headed into the unknown future.

The next morning, I arrived at the Seventh-day Adventist Serviceman's Center in San Antonio, TX. There were a lot of troops housed there. It was an oasis away from the military base. The next day I found a soldier who would take care of my Volkswagen while I was in basic training. I blindly trusted this soldier. It was still there when I got out of basic training just before Christmas. I drove home to the ranch above Napa, helped my father do jobs around the farm, slept in my childhood bed, ate my mother's cooking, then returned to Fort Sam Houston in early January, where I went to Basic Training and then Advanced Individual Training (AIT) to become a medic. All medics went to Vietnam.

BUD

I had been drafted but with the assurance that I wasn't going to Vietnam. My mother's close childhood friend and her husband in San Francisco always came to our home for Thanksgiving and Christmas. They were our extended family. Her husband, Bud, had taken mortars in France during World War II, which resulted in the loss of his right leg well above the knee, his left leg pinned straight, but he still had use of that foot. Remarkably, Bud could climb stairs after many years of personal fortitude and work. He had a car modified to manipulate the gas pedal with his only foot, and the brakes were operated by hand.

Bud told me he oversaw the monies of the 7th Army function at the Presidio in San Franciso, which gave him significant influence in the Army. So, Bud informed me right after I received my draft notice that he would keep me from going to Vietnam, even though almost all draftees ended up in Vietnam. "You do not have to worry about Vietnam. I will arrange for you to stay on the West Coast. You will not go to Vietnam, and I can have you placed on the West Coast so you can still spend time at home and with us on Thanksgiving and Christmas."

Well, that promise provided no worries about being shipped off to the "front." I attended basic training at Fort Sam Houston in San Antonio, TX, where all Conscientious Objectors took basic training in Echo 4 Company. No worries, I was comfortable, and under Bud's authority, those other draftees must be tormented by the worries of going to Vietnam, but not me.

At that time, almost all Conscientious Objectors underwent Advanced Individual Training (AIT) to become medics. That medic training was very educational and completed with a good understanding of anatomy and how the general body functioned. Also, there was obligatory education on how to defend oneself in hand-to-hand combat. I was told I was now listed as an expert in hand-to-hand combat. No worries, I was comfortable. I would not have to use that hand-to-hand combat training; I wasn't headed to a combat zone.

By this time, I had successfully completed the AIT medic training and the Operating Room Technician (OR Tech) course at Fort Sam Houston.

After the OR Tech course, I was assigned on-the-job training (OJT) at Madigan General Hospital in Tacoma, WA. As in the OR Tech courses in San Antonio, I could live in the Seventh-day Adventist Serviceman's Center at Lake Steilacoom, WA. Being in such a comfortable environment with other soldiers was a blessing. This OJT training provided direct surgical experience following the classroom training. This continued until I had been in the service for eight months and had received an outstanding education to be a medic and OR Tech. No worries, I was comfortable.

I received orders to report to Travis Air Force Base in Fairfield, California, which was not far from home.

After OJT training, soldiers were usually allowed leave before going to their duty assignments. I took leave with no worries. I was comfortable. Bud had my back. I spent the time at home helping my father with jobs around the farm. I did not pay much attention to the orders to report to Travis AFB. Bud assured me they had to give me those orders, but other orders were forthcoming.

Day after day, I looked in the mailbox with no relief. The day was coming that required me to go to Travis. Where were my orders for the West Coast?? Bud said I should go to Travis Air Force Base, and there would be orders at Travis assigning me to a hospital on the West Coast. So, like a lamb headed to slaughter without worries and still comfortable, I made my way to Travis.

At Travis, I reported in, made sure the staff knew who I was and that I expected orders to arrive for reassignment. They accommodatingly smiled and showed me where I could wait. I waited for a couple of days. I looked at the manifests periodically to see if I recognized anyone on the lists. And then, to my horror, my name showed up on one of the manifests for boarding a plane within a few hours.

"They must be wrong, maybe uninformed, but I am not going to Vietnam," was my thought. They hadn't gotten the orders that I had been promised. I was not going to Vietnam. I knew it. I had no worries. I was comfortable.

I went to the line of dozens of phone booths to call Bud to get this straightened out. After all, Bud was an influential person. He controlled the money that made the army operate. I had his assurances. I dialed Bud's number and put in the required coins. It was like Bud was sitting right by the phone and picked it up on the first ring.

"Bud! My name is on a manifest for Vietnam! What is going on?"

Bud did not hesitate and answered my panicked question. "Well, it did not work."

"What? You cannot mean that!"

"Yes, my efforts failed."

I sat there in a daze. I had lived with no worries. I was comfortable. Knowing I was not going to Vietnam had comforted me for all those months of training. I hung up the phone without saying the responses in my mind. I sat there in that small, smoke-smelling phone booth for some time. All those promises had left me abandoned and exposed to the war machine. What can I do? What can I do?

After some time, I regained consciousness and realized I was going to Vietnam. All those months of no worries and comfort left me in the arms of the war…I was going to Vietnam!!! The only conclusion I could draw from this heart-sinking realization was, "This is going to be a life-changing experience…an adventure… I will make the most out of what comes my direction… The security of "No worries, I am comfortable" was gone. I felt exposed, naked to the war I had dismissed for all that time.

The flight left at night because protestors were around during the day. We lifted off in a packed stretch jet which held around 300 soldiers. Looking around, I wondered how many of these soldiers would not come back alive. Would I be one to survive or not?

We stopped in Anchorage, AK, and I enjoyed a walk around the terminal observing a giant stuffed Alaska brown bear. I was impressed. Then the flight followed the Aleutian Chain to the southwest. Stopped again in Yokota, Japan, for fuel. The soldiers on board were jovial and spirited throughout the flight. When the plane passed over the Vietnam beach, the plane went silent. The reality of Vietnam took away the jovial spirit.

A short time later, the pilot announced, "We are approaching the Ben Hua airport where they have been receiving action lately, so we will be making a steep descent into the airport."

It was steep, like a rock falling straight down, though the landing went well. I was about four seats back from the plane's door. They opened the door, and I felt the hot, humid August weather like a hot dish rag thrown across my face. I was worried and not comfortable.

Bud was home in San Francisco without worries and comfortable. Actually, I realized how lucky I had been to not worry about going to Vietnam during those months of training. I did not experience the fear of Vietnam, along with the baggage of anxiety for all that time. Bud had been a blessing, although I never gave him the satisfaction of knowing how I had reacted to all those months of feeling comfortable with no worries about Vietnam being a part of my future. My subsequent relationship with Bud was not so trusting.

AIT, OR Tech & OJT

Medic training was very educational. After basic training, most CO soldiers went to the Advanced Individual Training (AIT) at Fort Sam Houston. I learned anatomy, physiology, medications, and how to treat wounded in the field. It was much more interesting and inclusive than I expected. At the end of those couple months of schooling, I felt reasonably comfortable with my future duties.

NOTE: That education was useful when I was on patrol in the 101st Airborne Division. There were many minor issues—insect bites, scrapes, rashes, but blisters were the most common. Rumors spread around the group in medic training that we would be walking around with a big target on our back, the Red Cross on our field medic bag. As it turned out, the troops protected the medic and radio operator more than anyone else. They ensured the two of us in the unit were in the middle of the group. If we were going to get shot, the enemy would have to go through those troops to get to us. We were their lifeline. Unfortunately, the lieutenant would hang out with us. He knew that was the safest place. Our concern was that he was a prime target, and we could be collateral damage if the lieutenant were targeted.

As AIT medic training came to an end, we would either be sent to Vietnam or get orders for advanced schools. I received the American Spirit Honor Medal at the end of basic training. Why, I do not know, but I did not refuse it. It is a civilian medal issued to the occasional basic trainee who shows promise. The reverse side of the medal reads, "For High Example to Comrades in Arms." I remain unaware as to why I received that medal.

That medal resulted in being ordered to the office of the commander of Fort Sam Houston. I put on my dress uniform and went to the colonel's office. There were two other trainees there who were being honored with some other medals. Pictures with the colonel that were supposed to be published in our hometown newspaper were taken. I never heard of anyone seeing that picture.

During this ceremony, the colonel asked me if there was something he could do for me. What do you ask for after being in the service for less than two months? Do I ask not to be sent to Vietnam? That would be quite presumptuous. Maybe I could ask to accompany my picture back home.

Well, I knew that would not work, and I didn't want to be offensive, so I asked for another training course.

Previously at Fort Lewis, Washington, where I had been assigned before going to C.O. Basic at Fort Sam, I had the opportunity to go to the Seventh-day Adventist Serviceman's Center for my Sabbath. The cranky first sergeant there informed me I had to go to the base chapel for my Saturday Sabbath, sit in the balcony all day, and come back for dinner at 1800 hours at the mess hall. He neglected to tell me the entire process.

I obeyed and was sitting on the balcony when I heard the door open.

Someone said, "Is there anyone in the chapel?"

I faintly replied, "Yes, I am up in the balcony."

This person asked me to come down. He was a civilian chaplain with the authority to take me off the base to church and the Serviceman's Center.

I was very reluctant because not following orders could be a serious matter that included the term "brig."

The chaplain convinced me he had the authority, so I went with him. After church, I went to the Serviceman's Center to find some college classmates. Wow, what a deal, but I still hoped this activity would not put me in the brig. I was assured I was in good hands.

At the Serviceman's Center, I was glad to see John, who had graduated a year before me and had been in the service for about a year. Like me, he had been drafted right out of college. John sat me down, got out a set of orders, and educated me on how to read orders. A valuable education for my future. He also told me the best duty I could try for was "Operating Room Technician" (OR Tech).

Standing before the colonel at Fort Sam Houston weeks after John educated me, I asked the colonel if I could go to the Operating Room Technician course. He looked surprised, expecting something less impacting. After a minute, he replied, "I do not know about that, but I will look into it."

When my orders arrived at the end of AIT, I expected to see my destination would be Vietnam. Bud would be sure to keep me from going to Vietnam – right? To my surprise, the orders were to stand down for about ten days and join the next OR Tech school. Wow, what a relief. I was thrilled I had asked for that school when receiving that American Spirit Honor Medal. That colonel had come through and gotten me into that school.

The stand-down time was spent at the Seventh-day Adventist Serviceman's Center in San Antonio. I had my car and made the most of this free time, including on the beach outside Corpus Christi. At the designated time, I reported for the OR Tech school.

The first activity in the OR Tech school was to weed out those who could not deal with blood. We were marched into Brooks Army Hospital and into an amphitheater where we watched an operation in progress. Three soldiers excused themselves. They could not take the blood. Those three soldiers were reassigned to some other duty.

We learned how to scrub in, use and apply various surgical instruments, and set up and maintain a sterile field. Again, this course was very educational, and at the end, I knew how to set up a sterile field, set out an instrument tray for various surgical specialties, anticipate the surgeon's needs, and all the details of being a "scrub tech."

This OR Tech course required training in surgery. The On-The-Job-Training (OJT) course included an assignment to a military hospital somewhere stateside. My orders came for Madigan General Hospital at Fort Lewis, near Tacoma, WA. I traveled there with a few days stopover at my home in Napa, CA.

Reporting to Madigan General Hospital, I informed the sergeant overseeing my stay at Fort Lewis that I had accommodations off base at the Seventh-day Adventist Serviceman's Center. He checked and agreed I could stay there but needed to report to him every week. No problem, and very happy I was not sleeping in barracks.

By this time, John, my earlier educator, had left, and I got acquainted with the other military personnel in the Center. The chaplain and his wife were accommodating, positive, and generally, parents away from home.

At the beginning of OJT at Madigan General Hospital, I was assigned various surgeries. I did well enough to be transferred to the Ear, Nose, and Throat room, where surgery was primarily done on the inner ears. Often, the surgery was performed as the surgeon looked through a microscope with dual eye lenses. I had a separate lens to keep abreast of what was happening and anticipate what the surgeon would need.

Many operating rooms did not have specific designations for specific types of surgery but were used for any surgeries that arose. As I did not stay on the compound, I did not develop close relations with the OR staff but knew most of them casually.

One day, word got around the OR pavilion that a special procedure would happen in room #5 and that if anyone were finished with their procedures, word would be provided for when we could enter room #5. The surgeries I was involved with that day finished early, so I waited around with the other staff who were excited about this surgery that was uncommon to this surgery suite.

The announcement came that the patient was under anesthesia, and we could enter the room. It was packed. I stood at the foot of the table. The sheet covering the patient was pulled down. I was familiar with OR protocol and accepted it was normal for a patient to be naked during surgery.

The patient was a middle-aged woman. Most of our patients were men. Interestingly, the woman, maybe in her 40s, was undraped to the waist. Most of the patients were men—soldiers. She was the wife of an officer.

The surgeon entered the room and announced he was today performing a Mammoplasty, a breast augmentation. The room was quiet except for a few unwelcomed comments. The necessary incisions were made, and tissues opened for the implants.

The instrument table held six blobs of sterile silicone. There were two each of three different sizes. The differences in sizes were obvious. The surgery proceeded to prepare the breasts for the implants. At this point, the surgeon, who had a good sense of humor, held up the two small implants, then the mid-sized ones, followed by the large implants. He eyed each one with questioning comments.

Then, as someone who did not want to be responsible for the outcome, he asked the audience their opinion. Debate followed. The men chose the large implants. The women decided the medium one was appropriate. The mid-sized implants were finally chosen, and the procedure was completed. Those blobs had created bigger boobs. Unfortunately, I never knew if I ever saw that woman later at the base or in town. Probably for the best. I might have gotten caught looking at the wrong thing.

Toward the end of my OJT, orders were delivered. The orders were to report to Travis Air Force Base on August 6th for processing to Vietnam. Obviously, the military had not gotten the word that I would be assigned a location on the West Coast, not Vietnam. Bud had assured me I would be assigned stateside, and Vietnam was not in my future.

I called Bud, who reassured me the order for Vietnam was necessary, and other orders would follow, assigning me to one of the three major army hospitals on the West Coast—Madigan, Letterman. Like a lamb to the slaughter, I proceeded without question!

Mortars

One way the Viet Cong harassed the American compounds was the occasional mortar attack. There would be no warning, no preparation, just sudden explosions. Sometimes, it was just one mortar. Other times, it might be multiple.

To reduce danger for the Viet Cong responsible for the mortar, they set a timer to activate the mortar without being present. The tube would be aimed in the intended direction, then some delaying mechanism would be assembled, and the perpetrator would leave the area. Radar could pick up the mortar, and its point of origin could be calculated, and our artillery responding would destroy the point of origin. By then, the perpetrator was somewhere else, maybe even close to the target, to see his effectiveness.

Following the in-country training near Quang Tre, I was assigned to the 326th Medical Battalion of the 101st Airborne Division at Camp Eagle. After getting settled, I familiarized myself with the compound. Knowing the location of the bunker was important. It was not far from the hooches. I laid out a route in my mind so when needed, there wouldn't be much time to waste.

For entertainment, occasionally movies would be shown for our distraction. Soon after arrival at the 326th Medical Battalion, the evening movie was started in a hooch set up for movies and other gatherings. There must have been 25 to 30 guys in the hooch. I had arrived late with Mike. We ended up close to the one door. The movie had started, and all of us were enjoying the distraction from the monotonous day. All was well, and we relaxed with the entertainment.

A horrendous explosion was close. Mike and I were unsure if it was "outgoing" or "incoming." We looked at each other for an idea as to what to do. When we came to our senses, the hooch was empty, leaving Mike and me standing there looking at each other.

"That must be incoming," Mike said.

"I guess so. Everybody is gone. They must be in the bunker," I replied. "Let's go."

We got out of the hooch when another mortar hit, which forced us back behind the 5-foot-high sandbags designed to protect us during mortar attacks like this.

"Let's get to the bunker!" Mike yelled.

"If we get out there, we have no protection. Here we have some protection," I replied.

"Well, staying here leaves us exposed. Everyone else knew what to do. We need to get to the bunker," Mike demanded. Right about then, another mortar hit close by. Gravel, dirt, and dust poured down on us. It had hit along a driveway on the side of the hooch.

Mike and I continued our debate as to whether or not we should go to the bunker for what seemed a long time. The mortars ended, and Mike and I were still arguing. We had not been hit, but our understanding between "incoming" and "outgoing" was now well understood. We would not make the same mistake again.

Future mortar attacks were not often, but we respected the results of not moving quickly to a bunker. However, as time passed, I became jaded. The fear of being hit by a mortar gradually went away. I was not invincible, but the fear of dying decreased. I would make my way to the bunker but not go inside. I would join some of the other troops on the top of the bunker to see where the mortars were hitting. Most were somewhere else on the base. It appeared the perpetrators could not aim properly. The rounds would hit randomly.

Another good use of the top of the bunkers was sunbathing and watching the helicopters coming and going. It was above the dirt and some of the dust. A retreat location, not the protection as originally intended. A friend in the company and I ended up on the bunker where he taught me how to play chess. Fall was beginning, and the weather cooperated to make the top of the bunker a place of retreat and escape. Even the officers seemed to overlook those of us on top of the bunkers. Then I found my way to the 85th Evac Hospital, a better retreat with doctors, nurses, and educated people, not the "grunts" of the 101st. Mortars did not find their way to the hospital as much as other compounds, maybe because some of the "locals" who worked in the hospital might have positioned the mortars or knew the people who did.

Eagle Dust-Off

"You got a letter from home before you were assigned to this unit," a mail delivery soldier told me a few days after I had been assigned to the Headquarters and Support Company, 326th Medical Battalion, 101st Airborne Division. Those at mail call were amazed I got a letter right after I arrived. After all, I had just been assigned to the unit, and my first letter home probably had not even arrived home in "The World" announcing my address.

But, earlier that year, my second cousin had been drafted, trained as a medic, and assigned to Charlie Company, 326th Medical Battalion, the Dust-Off company—the helicopter company that picked up wounded in the field. My industrious mother had decided there must be only one medical battalion in Vietnam, so sending a letter to her son at that location was the right thing to do.

A Dust-Off was a Huey Helicopter, UH1H, that had the duty to pick up wounded soldiers in the field as soon as possible, aiming for the "Golden Hour" timeframe. That Golden Hour was defined as the time lapsed from being wounded to getting to a MASH unit. If it took less than an hour, the patient was more likely to survive and sustain less long-term damage. Charlie Company delivered that Golden Hour in I Corps with tremendous risk and valor.

I had not met that second cousin before arriving in Vietnam and was surprised to find a relative within the battalion. He had been there for around 9 months and would go home after his one-year requirement.

During the three months we overlapped, I spent as much time as I could flying with that outfit. The company seemed to adopt me as I was a cousin of one of their medics. So, when there was an opportunity to fly, I took it. I would sit in the "hell hole" with my back to the engine and my feet on the edge of the helicopter and behind the medic. Dust-off choppers flew without doors to accommodate getting a wounded soldier more quickly into the helicopter and out later at the hospital. If doors remained on the Dust-off, they were pulled back and not brought forward unless weather required enclosing the inside open area. Sometimes, the wounded would have bamboo poles through their fatigues, making a self-contained stretcher. The bamboo poles would hang outside their fatigues and occasionally outside the chopper. If there were many wounded, some wounded would sit on the floor of the helicopter with their legs dangling out the door.

During the three months I overlapped with the Dust-off unit, there were 37 pilots, copilots, crew chiefs, and medics. At the end of those three months, twelve of those guys had died. Each mission required one of each position. Of course, the pilots, the medic, and then the crew chief who manned the gun on the right side of the helicopter. The crew chief also operated the penetrator, if needed, which would be dropped through the jungle foliage where the penetrator would open into a couple of small metal seats that could accommodate one or two wounded soldiers. If necessary, the wounded soldier would be tied to the penetrator. The penetrator would be raised through the jungle and moved into the helicopter. All this time, the helicopter had to hover and be very stable. The medic would receive the wounded, take whatever actions were required, stabilize as best as possible, and monitor the wounded soldier during the trip to the 85th Evac.

One day, I was in the Dust-off operations room where the radio was broadcasting activity within I Corps. As I listened to the radio with around fifteen unit members, a call came in for a Dust-off to pick up a wounded soldier at such and such coordinates. Immediately, the next crew in the duty line-up jumped into a Dust-off. Take off was quick. The pilot could be heard over the radio. The Dust-Off took some time to arrive over the coordinates. The pilot said it was a pretty open area and that this pickup would be easy.

As the chopper started to move into position, the crew chief could be heard over the speaker yelling, "RPG!!!!"

The next sound was not pleasant. A squealing sound like an electrical short in a microphone. The chopper was down. It had been hit by the RPG. (RPG = Rocket-Propelled Grenade–a shoulder-fired missile)

Without a second passing and no orders given, the next crew was into the next Dust-off, in the air and on their way to those coordinates. No orders had been announced. Nobody had said anything. There was no hesitation. No thought of the risk of going to the same place the first chopper had gone down. Mental images of the downed Dust-off went through everyone's mind: exploding fuel tanks, rotors digging into the ground or into the crew, the crew dying or severely wounded. Soon after the second Dust-off was airborne, two Cobra Gunships were alongside, headed to the same coordinates. Dust-off crews are the most courageous people I have ever known. Some of them died that day. My respect for those crews, their courage, and their bravery is beyond description. They saved so many lives at their own peril.

In heavy jungles, sometimes the chopper would lower down into the foliage to get out of sight of the enemy who might be on hillsides ready to launch an RPG. The helicopter blades would chop off the tender growth. Sitting in the "hell hole," you could pick the leaves off the jungle. It was noisy, but I was blessed to be out in the Dust-offs as often as possible.

When flying high in those Dust-Offs, above where small arms fire was lethal, Vietnam was beautiful. In contrast to the humid summer heat close to the ground, high above the ground, it was cool and enjoyable. I could tag along with those guys traveling from the DMZ to the mountains above Da Nang, near the hills that formed the A Shau Valley, and out to the beautiful beaches along the South China Sea. We never got too close to the A Shau Valley, knowing it was a dangerous place to be.

One day at the 85th, word came over the radio that a small helicopter, called a "Loach," was being piloted by a crew chief. The pilot had been shot and was unconscious. They had flown too close to the A Shau Valley, and a 50 mm round hit the pilot. Fortunately, the helicopter was still flyable. The crew chief had enough experience to know the helicopter's general operations and fly it to our area. This crew chief was not very experienced. The helicopter swerved from side to side and up and down. We could hear the tower communications with the crew chief. The crew chief was directed to the main airport next to the 85th.

The crew chief would have nothing to do with that. "I am taking my pilot to the 85th Evac. Period. Do not try to change my mind!" he said over the radio.

That crew chief brought the Loach over the helipad at the 85th Evac. We watched from a distance as the erratic Loach tried to hover and land. Eventually, the tower told the crew chief to "turn it off." The crew chief did as ordered. The Loach slowly, then faster, dropped to the helipad. The crew chief got his pilot to the hospital. The Loach required some work after that hard landing.

We took the wounded pilot into surgery. They had ventured near the ridge of the A Shau Valley to peek in and see what they could see. Fortunately, the pilot survived. The actions of that crew chief radically decreased the time it took to get that pilot into surgery. The large bullet had passed through his arm and his chest and lodged close to his carotid artery. Much more time, and that pilot would have been dead. His crew chief was a hero that day. The next day, a Chinook helicopter came and lifted the Loach from our helipad and took it to a maintenance facility. Like so many brave members of the Dust-off unit, this crew chief deserved a Medal of Honor.

Command Sergeant Major

"No one gets out of the 101st Airborne Division," stated the Command Sergeant Major when I asked how I could get out of the 101st. The Sergeant Major's comment was accurate and practiced throughout the history of the 101st Airborne Division. After all, most soldiers wanted out of the 101st. It was in the most active area in Vietnam.

After landing at Ben Hua Airbase near Saigon in August 1970, I was herded with the masses to a holding area without seating or accommodations for those just arriving in Vietnam. We were tired, nervous, hungry, and apprehensive of everything, and now we were in a holding area that was less than inviting to the new troops coming into Vietnam.

It took days of processing for us to get assigned to a company and transported to an "in-country training" location. During the days, we slept on the cement floor, got meager food, and it was hot and humid. In general, we were not happy to be there. Some got very upset and yelled obscenities at those in charge. Those comments were not received well. Those receiving those comments were seasoned soldiers. It did not make any difference. The attitude of those soldiers was, "If I am obnoxious, what are you going to do? Send me to Vietnam? I am already in Vietnam."

A few times a day, I checked the manifest lists for my name, which told me where I would be assigned. The lists were long, but all I had was time. So I continued to look and finally found my name on a manifest and assignment to the 101st Airborne Division. Over a dozen divisions in Vietnam were shown on a map next to the manifest board. Vietnam was broken into four regions: I Corps, II Corps, III Corps, and IV Corps.

I looked at the map, starting at the bottom, the delta area and IV Corps. The 101st was not in that region. There were several divisions in the III Corps. Some of them I didn't recognize. Nope, not there either. Then I looked high on the map. The 101st Airborne Division was at the top. Wow, not far from the DMZ and North Vietnam. It took some time for me to settle down and realize I was headed to the top of the map, close to danger and North Vietnam. I boarded the C 130, and the flight north never seemed to end.

Finally, the C 130 landed, and everyone got off the plane with wide eyes and anxiety. We were ordered to place our duffle bags in the middle of a long trailer and stand around the plywood sides. In front and behind this "cattle truck" were two jeeps with large automatic guns mounted on standards, locked and loaded for action in the hands of soldiers, ready for anything that became a threat. The truck started, and away we went, north some more. Going north never seemed to end, the C 130 by air and ground transport by land. This trip gave us our first sight of the natives farming their rice paddies, riding their water buffaloes, and row crops that turned out to be their profit crops—marijuana or opium poppies.

After what seemed forever, the truck and jeeps came to rest at the in-country training area. We were taught about the local people, their customs, and what to do or not do when in the field. Whenever with a group of new soldiers, one buddies up with someone. Having a buddy makes life a little more tolerable when you are apprehensive among strangers. So I got acquainted with two guys, a Chinook pilot and a Command Sergeant Major. How those acquaintances happened, I don't know, but the Command Sergeant Magor would be instrumental in my future.

The in-country training included marching into the unknown. Everyone but me, a Conscientious Objector, carried their weapon and were on guard. I had the medic's bag of supplies essential to helping a wounded soldier stay alive. The medic was always in the middle of the group, any group, with the radio operator. Both of us were their lifeline, so they protected us. One day, we went out to a location with bleachers. Bleachers out here? What? We sat on the bleachers and were given instructions for that particular part of the training.

Something that got my attention was the Cobra Gunship that drilled a circle in a tree stump with its minigun. For the next demonstration, the ordnance officer called in three rounds from the artillery at the base. The first landed about ten feet from a steel barrel. The officer talked to the artillery officer at the base, and the next two rounds lifted the barrel out of the ground. Wow, they are accurate. Glad to know they are that accurate.

During this training, I became friends with the pilot and Command Sergeant Major. The Command Sergeant Major was the NCO in charge of the 101st personnel department. That information was filed in the back of my mind for future recall.

On the first night of in-country training, we were assigned to barracks-like buildings with bunk beds. We were instructed that if we received incoming mortars, drop to the floor and put that thin mattress over you for protection.

About the time I started to fall asleep, there was an explosion. I jumped out of the bed and put the mattress over me.

A few seasoned soldiers laughed. "That is outgoing, not incoming," they said.

How was I to know? I learned.

After in-country training, I was taken to Camp Eagle where I reported to the Headquarters and Support Company, 326th Medical Battalion, 101st Airborne Division. The quarters were uncomfortable. Dust and the smell of burning diesel mixed with feces polluted the air. Human waste was mixed with diesel and burned. There was no sewer system, only 50-gallon drums cut in half and placed in outhouses. I had arrived at what was to be my base for the next 365 days. Not impressed. Those 50-gallon drums were probably Agent Orange drums.

My job was occasionally to go out with a unit on a mission when someone was on leave or sick. Each unit had a medic. Fortunately, I was never in a firefight. I treated insect bites, rashes, blisters, and any ailment a soldier got in the field. Those missions were uneventful. I was glad to return to my company at Camp Eagle each time. I had become the company clerk because I could type and the company carpenter because I knew which end of a nail to hit with a hammer.

At the Headquarters and Support Company, there were a couple of rarely-seen doctors, a bunch of OR Techs, and corpsmen. No surgery was performed there unless a crisis happened close by. All the wounded flew overhead to the 85th Evac Hospital in Phu Bai. The most common activity was to give massive amounts of penicillin in each "cheek" of those returning from R&R who suspected they might be carrying a "disease" back with them after involvement with someone of the opposite sex.

One guy in the unit decided he needed to be circumcised. A self-confident OR Tech chose to perform this surgery.

"After all, how hard is a circumcision?"

The operation was probably the messiest and bloodiest surgery I witnessed until assignment at the 85th. Poor guy. I wonder about the result of that procedure. Malpractice comes to mind.

After being a multipurpose corpsman in the 326th Med., I had to get out of there. Either I would go to Charlie Company, the Dust-off company, as a medic with a short life expectancy or get out of the 101st. I went to that Command Sergeant Major, who was at the personnel headquarters of the 101st in Camp Eagle. He was surprised to see me. We visited a bit. Then I told him I needed to get out of the 101st and go somewhere the army could use my training.

He told me, "No one gets out of the 101st Airborne Division!"

I was crestfallen. I knew getting out was not easy, and I persisted.

The Sergeant Major finally, after much persuasion, said, "If you can find an open slot for your MOS, I will see what I can do."

At least he had not driven home the "No one gets out of the 101st Airborne Division." There was hope.

The 85th Evac Hospital was a few miles down Highway 1 from Camp Eagle. I went down there and asked for the officer in charge of the operating room. I was directed to one of the wards and told the major was under quarantine with hepatitis, but I could speak to her over the isolation curtain. I introduced myself and told her my plight. She eagerly said they had slots open and would welcome another scrub tech to the hospital.

I returned to the Command Sergeant Major with the news that the 85th had open slots.

He reminded me, "No one gets out of the 101st Airborne Division," but he would look into it.

A week later, I received orders for reassignment to the 85th Evacuation Hospital in Phu Bai.

Unless one experienced the things I did at the 101st, one cannot understand what exhilaration is. With little explanation to the officers at the 326th, I packed and thumbed a ride to the 85th Evac. The only times I returned to the 101st were to go to Charlie Company and fly with the Dust-off unit.

That Command Sergeant Major probably saved my life.

Drugs

"Drugs? What do you mean? I am in a combat zone, 8,000 miles from home in a strange place, people are shooting at me, and I can't sleep!" is the reply to the question confronting a soldier in Vietnam in 1971 about his drug use. That soldier has been drafted and sent to Vietnam against his common sense.

The availability of any drug is immediate, maybe a few hours away or less. The "contact" can provide anything you want, is close by, and probably already has what you want available. That "contact" is probably in your company and may live in a hooch nearby. If you are on patrol, availability is not immediate, but it will be when you return to base. It was common knowledge that drugs were carried into the field.

There were two groups of people in our area. "Lifers" who made the military their career and had decent liquor available at a reasonable price at the PX, usually a short distance away. The second group consisted of those using drugs. Most soldiers in Vietnam were in one of those two groups.

Those using drugs could be broken down into many categories: experimenters, occasional users, and regular users. Each of those categories could be broken down by type: marijuana, acid, mescaline, heroin, opium, etc. It was common for a person to stay with one drug, though some progressed to more powerful drugs, including hallucinogenic ones. Mixing drugs could be fatal.

There was a guy at the 85th who was a typical heroin user. One day, he was in horrible condition and taken to the emergency room, where he was revived. A few weeks later, he took a larger amount of heroin and didn't survive. The name he went by is not found on "The Wall" in Washington, D.C. His correct name is unknown.

A guy at the hospital compound could provide what you wanted. One day we played baseball not far from the compound gate. This guy walked out the gate, got on a scooter with a local kid, and went into Phu Long. About an hour later, he returned and walked by the baseball game with a clear plastic bag full of "Nickel" and "Dime" caps. That represents the cost of the vial of heroin, some five dollars and some ten dollars. No one said anything.

During 1970-71, while I was at the 85th, if someone got into an argument or got mad at another, it was not uncommon for that person not to see the next morning's sunrise. "Fragging" was too common. A person with a gripe would shoot or booby-trap that person to eliminate their disagreement.

If the drug "contact" was challenged, that challenger might not see the sunrise. The risk was too frequent. One night, a soldier who had been "fragged" was brought to the 85th Evac.

The sergeant was a dog trainer who trained dogs to sniff out the enemy. Those dogs were a tremendous help in the jungle. That sergeant was hard on those under him. Someone put a claymore mine under his bed that night, so it exploded when he laid his head on his pillow. The top quarter of his body and part of his hooch were gone. He did not suffer. He should have been taken to Graves Registration, not the hospital.

Another method of eliminating opposition took place in the field. The officer who oversaw a company was to follow orders from the command at base camp. If those orders were to take a location, sometimes previously taken with heavy casualties, that officer ordered his company to take that location again. The senior enlisted soldier, usually a sergeant, was given the order by the officer. The sergeant's job was to order his men to take that location. That sergeant knew the casualties would be bad and might refuse the order. By refusing, the sergeant could be court-martialed. Somewhere along the way, that officer might be shot, often in the back. One casualty was better than many. "Friendly fire." If that officer were smart, he would take the advice of the experienced sergeant or consider other options. Retaking a specific location, often a hill, would cost more lives. Too often, a hill taken by our soldiers would be abandoned, then retaken by the enemy, which set it up for another assault by our soldiers.

Back to drugs. One guy in our unit took mescaline. He ended up frying his brains and never being normal again. When he ate in the mess hall, he would take the same novel out of his pocket and reread the first chapter. I never knew his name, but he was a walking casualty of war.

From my vantage point, it appeared around a quarter of the casualties in 1970-71 were drug overdose casualties. Another quarter were from "friendly fire," and the remainder were from "they shot us."

It is a sad commentary to talk about the casualties from drugs and "friendly fire," but that was part of our life, primarily at the 101st.

And the guy who said, "Drugs? What do you mean? I am in a combat zone, 8,000 miles from home in a strange place, people are shooting at me, and I cannot sleep," was the husband, son, father, brother of those back in "The World" who thought the only casualties were from "they shot us."

War is a messy business, even when the enemy is obvious. With drugs rampant, a population back home that does not support the soldier, and field orders that are just wrong, the consequences will be destructive to the overall society and the soldier. And then there are the "Rules of Engagement."

X-Ray

"I know my fiancée will quit me...for sure," the GI on the X-ray table said with painful emotion. For the first time since he had stepped on a booby trap in the Vietnam jungle, he was alone. When wounded, he was with his buddies, then in the Dust-off and the 85th Evac emergency room. The X-ray table was plastic and cold. X-Ray was one of two areas with air conditioners, the other being the operating rooms.

After witnessing wounded soldiers lying on this cold table, alone for the first time since incurring unimaginable trauma, I assigned myself to that room to place my hand behind the neck of the soldier on that uncomfortably rigid table and let him know someone was there, that he was not alone with his wandering bitter emotions of fear, anger, anxiety, and anything else his mind would imagine during the time the technician developed the negatives before the soldier would be put back on the gurney for the short trip to surgery. As soon as he was in the operating room, he would be given sedatives and anesthesia.

The most common cause of the soldier's injury was the booby trap that exploded when stepped on. The soldier would be thrown some distance with both legs seriously damaged. One leg would usually be gone below or above the knee, and the other leg would have compound fractures and mangled to the point it would remain connected but dangling. Both legs would be impregnated with debris—dirt, grass, twigs. The booby trap had done its work. This soldier was no longer in action.

Wounded soldiers were attended to by a field medic who could do nothing more than apply a tourniquet. It is incredible that major arteries, like the femoral artery, would automatically close themselves off during the intense trauma these young soldiers experienced. A tourniquet was usually not applied, but bleeding was controlled.

His buddies were doing and saying whatever they could to keep him as calm as possible. Now, he was alone for the first time in the X-ray room.

The "magic first-hour" Dust-off action brought the wounded soldier to the 85th Evac Hospital. He was put on a gurney and wheeled into the Emergency Room. Doctors, nurses, and corpsmen swarmed over the soldier. The first job was to cut off the remaining clothes so he could be inspected for hidden wounds. The primary wounds were apparent, but often, other wounds would be discovered that could be as deadly as the primary wound.

Intravenous bottles and blood would be hung and run into his veins. If necessary, cutdowns would be made to get bigger needles into the veins to get more fluids into the depleted body. Sometimes, blood pressure cuffs would be placed around plastic bags to force blood and IVs to infuse at a faster rate to keep the soldier alive.

After the heroics performed in the emergency room, the wounded soldier was wheeled into the X-ray room. The X-rays would show how far the debris penetrated the legs and other body parts, allowing the surgeon to debride as much as possible.

When a soldier stepped on a booby trap, the legs were not the only body parts affected. Often, the face, genitals, hands, and arms were damaged. The soldier would look down but not see the trap set for his demise, so the face often was involved.

This soldier now finds himself alone in the X-ray room with his own tormenting thoughts. Most comments were about spouses, fiancées, girlfriends, family, and sometimes sports. Their lives had just taken a massive turn, and they imagined the worst. Comments about how their spouse, fiancée, or girlfriend would abandon them were foremost. Their imagination, probably correctly, was that their relationships would be broken or radically changed because they no longer had a completely normal body.

And then came the questions about what would happen. "Am I going to lose my leg? Is my leg gone?" "What damage is there to my genitals? Can I still have kids?" "What about my buddies? Did they get wounded also?"

At the 85th Evac, we did the emergency surgeries to stabilize the patient, and then they would be transported to a hospital out of the country. That could be days to weeks, depending on the severity of the wounds and how the patient responded.

There was an occasional response that was hard for me to swallow. "This means I cannot go back and shoot more Gooks!" Although this response was not often heard, it penetrated my soul that one could be so callous, bitter, angry, and want to go back just to shoot another person. The core reason for war is to kill the other guy and make him die for his beliefs and his country. I was glad to be a Conscientious Objector.

I did not carry a weapon, nor could I be placed in a situation where I would have to shoot another person.

It has been said that the soldier wants war to end more than any other person. The soldier experiences the tragedy of war along with the ensuing mental and physical disabilities. A society that lives where war does not exist and/or does not see the casualties of war, is blind to the consequences. As a result of not experiencing the consequences of war, we are inclined to be victims of war. Ignorance blindly walks into the arms of war.

America has sacrificed for the liberty and freedom of other societies and to sustain our own. The wars America fought brought liberty and freedom to many around the world. America continues to sacrifice so that others can experience freedom from oppression and tyranny. Some do not understand that and foolishly think life on Earth is Pollyannish.

I have often asked, "What are you willing to die for?" That is a hard question for the young soldier who goes off to war. Now, in the later years of this life, it is easier to say I am willing to give my life for the liberty and freedom of others. The young soldier, however, feels invincible, and war is a distant theory that will not affect them. Listening to those on the X-ray table with their legs blown off and their future compromised brings the reality of the cost of liberty and freedom. Some of us are also foolish and do not take history into account. The cost of liberty and freedom is high. Just ask a soldier who has paid that price!

Question Man

Some people like to be educators. Some people like to be dictators. Some want to do their job and not be bothered. As a draftee with a two-year commitment, I was anxious to learn as much as possible. After all, this would be an adventure, and if I could learn something, so much the better.

The operating room was usually a stress-filled arena where everyone worked for one goal: save the wounded guy's life! The amount of blood loss resulting from massive trauma was incredible. I added up those I worked on who lost a limb—leg, arm, both legs. You get the idea. There were twenty-eight soldiers in total. I was one of several OR Techs at the 85th Evac. We were one MASH unit, but there were many similar units in Vietnam. Do the math.

A special amputation tray was organized for such work. That tray included hammers, saws, osteotomes, and many clamps for the bleeding. The work had similarities to carpentry, but carpentry was not part of our training. A carpenter works on lumber, the surgeon in a MASH unit works on a living being whose life is in that surgeon's hands, and the outcome is life-changing.

Most surgeons in those conditions are uncertain and apprehensive. Working with the doctors would sometimes be stressful for the scrub technician (OR Tech). These trauma surgeries did not have a textbook guide on accomplishing the desired goal for the surgeon or the tech. Because of the uncertainty and apprehension, some doctors were quiet, some talkative, some joking, some pensive, and then there was the occasional doctor who was comfortable enough to answer questions, and I had a lot.

"What is that?"

"Why are you doing that?"

"What does that do?"

As the inquirer, I did a lot of questioning and received various responses. Most docs were helpful but not really educators. I finally connected with Gus, who was comfortable doing what he did and enjoyed educating. Gus was a vascular surgeon who could stitch the most beautiful resection but did whatever surgery was next. Splicing a saphenous vein section into an artery that was blown apart was tricky business. When Gus sutured the inside and outside of those connections, it looked like a machine had done it. The spliced sections did not leak and accomplished the goal of blood flow to the needed tissue.

Because of Gus's educator temperament, I tried to work with him whenever possible. He was obliging. My questions were voluminous. We got along great. I tried my best to do my job as a scrub technician as well as possible. Each surgeon had their share of amputations. Whoever was on duty got what arrived on the Dust-off. During mass casualties, there were occasions of chaos, but things usually turned out well. It has been said that the 85th Evac had the highest survival rate, even though we received around 50% of all the casualties in all of Vietnam combined. I (Eye) Corps was where the action was.

The operating room team—doctors, nurses, and OR Techs—was a remarkable cohesive group that all worked in unison for one goal: save the guy's life on the table. Most of the time, the team performed well together. It was a pleasure to work with a team in the Army that did not "pull rank" or get in conflict with others. I believe that is why we had such a high success rate. It is also why we still have reunions every couple of years, trying to vary the reunion place from one coast to the other. It is a privilege to have worked with such a team - a good group of people. No one was better than another; each had a duty to perform, and the combined efforts proved successful.

During the surgeries, Gus answered many of my questions, and I was blessed to have that education. When I came home, I helped a dentist friend do oral surgery, and he was impressed with my ability. All those questions paid off! That dentist offered to put me through medical school, all paid. By then, I knew my temperament well enough that being a surgeon would be too confining and require too much focused time. A surgeon knows where and what he will be doing two weeks from now. I made the right choice and was privileged to start a revolutionary cooperage (specialty wine barrels) that provided worldwide travel, friends throughout the wine industry, and an enjoyable lifestyle through hard work.

As a result of all those questions that Gus answered, he chose a moniker for me, "Question Man," which has survived the years.

At the first reunion, I was late getting to the event in San Diego due to work and airline delays. When I entered the packed restaurant, I heard, "Question Man!" I knew I was in the right place.

Gus even had a scrub shirt embroidered with a huge question mark on the front. I wore it with pride. Wish it still fit today. I wore that scrub shirt during my last few weeks in Phu Bai.

My experience at the 85th Evac Hospital enriched my life and gave me a concrete understanding of how a team should work. We were blessed, and our reunions continue to exemplify that blessing.

Cremation

It was said that there were several Viet Cong or their sympathizers working within the 85th Evac Hospital. I do not know who they were, but I was suspicious of a few. They were good workers, and the hospital needed those people for some tasks. We were lucky to have most of them. They generally showed a sense of humor and were there when required.

However, one issue revealed its ugly head. When we did amputations, the parts were discarded without much security. Some of those body parts had been found, packaged, and sent to families in the states with the message that this was part of your son. That was horrifying. It was ordered that all parts be cremated at the earliest convenience.

The earliest convenience was sometimes much later. That required a storage system. Where is the best place to store those parts? In a hot and humid climate, the best location was the refrigerated room for the mess hall. That worked. (Do not let your imagination go wild about the body parts in the Mess Hall refrigerator.)

Later, when another evacuation hospital in our area was dismantled, a chopper from that unit flew their two garbage cans full of amputated body parts to the 85th. The OR officer got the scrub technicians together and asked who would do the unpleasant job of cremating the body parts. No one volunteered. No one wanted to touch, let alone cremate, parts from somewhere else. Doing our own was difficult enough.

The officer knew his people well, including their backgrounds. He knew Mike had a hunting background and "volunteered" him for the job. It takes two people to do a job like this, so another person was "volunteered." Who else but me? The officer knew I had been raised on a farm and unpleasant jobs were commonplace. Mike and I cremated the two garbage cans full of parts. It took time as the brick structure built for cremation could only accommodate small amounts. You can visualize the rest. Finally, the job was completed, and life returned to normal. Being a farm boy that day did not work out well, but I am glad I did not grow up in the city. Had I been raised in the city, I could have stood around like those others and escaped the gruesome job, but I would not have been blessed with the farm country life.

Then there was the day a remains-filled body bag arrived at our little shed. Why it came to the 85th Evac vs. Graves Registration never got answered. One of the doctors ordered me to help with identifying the remains.

We went to the shed next to the helipad where the Dust-offs delivered wounded. We gloved and opened the zippered bag. The body had ballooned to the point we couldn't determine race, sex, or anything about him. He had been sitting in the "hell hole"—the rear seat of the helicopter with his back to the engine and right next to the fuel tank.

An RPG (rocket-propelled grenade) hit the fuel tank, which exploded on impact. The soldier died quickly. He was heavily burned but not incinerated by the fuel. The force of the explosion broke most of the bones in his body. |The fuel flash over burned his clothes off and charred his body. The dog tags were missing. We couldn't give a reasonable report identifying his body, so he probably went out as an "unknown." That bothered me.

When Graves Registration properly processed the remains, hopefully, the list of those on board the helicopter helped identify that soldier. If there was even a manifest listing those on board?

Side note: I was NOT documented when I rode with Charlie Company, 326th Medical Battalion, 101st Airborne Division, the Dust-off unit. Having friends in the unit allowed me to ride along, but there were no lists of me being on board. My name wouldn't have appeared if I had been aboard when a Dust-off went down. I could have ended up like that body we tried to identify. Being a medic, I contributed some value to the mission. The experience was worth the risk to me. My place in the Dust-off was sitting on that narrow seat with my back to the fuel tank.

X-Mas

"Bob Hope is coming!" We were excited to see him and all the entertainers with him. We watched Bob Hope on TV back home. The shows he presented to soldiers throughout the world for many decades. That man should have a colossal memorial and a holiday named in his honor!

As the day approached, word came down that the Bob Hope USO show had been canceled due to heavy action in our area. The risk of endangerment to Bob Hope and his entertainers was too great. That was accepted as the only excuse for cancellation we could handle. Bob Hope is a national treasure. He cannot be harmed.

A bit discouraged, we plugged along with our duties, but in the back of our minds, we wanted to see that show. Could we get on a plane and go somewhere where Bob Hope was performing, where danger was not so great? Not feasible, so we buckled down and kept going.

Early one morning, word spread that Bob Hope was coming. We had to get as many stable wounded soldiers as possible onto deuce and a half trucks (2 ½ ton cargo weight trucks) to travel to Camp Eagle. We scurried around getting those wounded soldiers onto the trucks, and we, of course, had to attend to them. We all got on the trucks and headed to Camp Eagle. The guards directed us to a spot near the front of the amphitheater where we unloaded and hauled the wounded, some ambulatory and some on stretchers, to the left front of the stage. And, yes, we had to stay with the wounded.

The amphitheater was packed with soldiers dressed in their field fatigues, showing the grunge from the jungle. No one cared. We were here, and Bob Hope was close by.

There must have been over 10,000 soldiers. It was impressive to see so many soldiers in one place. What if there was a mortar attack? A well-placed mortar could take out a lot of soldiers at one time. This was dangerous. We knew V.C. worked in the various compounds and could have gotten the word out about the show. We kept that thought in the back of our minds while getting our wounded settled in, then looked toward the stage with great anticipation.

Without fear, Bob Hope walked out onto the wide stage and leaned against his golf club. This was the real deal. That was Bob Hope in person, not on a TV. It was him. The show continued with Johnny Bench, Les Brown and his Band of Renown, Miss World, a few male groups but mostly scantily dressed female singing groups. The troops went wild! It was unreal but very real. We had the area right in front of the stage. We saw everything up close. What a time we had!

At the show's end, all the performers stood on the stage. Bob Hope was in the middle, still with his golf club. With that cue, Les Brown and his Band of Renown played the song "Silent Night, Holy Night..."

As the band faded away, all the singers, now acapella, the 10,000 soldiers chimed in, and a chorus like none ever heard before or since sang "Silent Night, Holy Night..." Looking over my shoulder at the 10,000 soldiers, I could not find a dry eye anywhere. That song brought home to each soldier the memories of times past. Memories of family and friends at home, opening presents, having Christmas dinner. Only Bob Hope and that song could bring those tears that those troops will not forget. Whenever I hear "Silent Night, Holy Night," I cannot sing for the emotion it carries. That memory of those 10,000 troops in chorus. The tears always come. Though we can never again experience Bob Hope and the spirit he brought to us in Vietnam, the memories still come to life every Christmas season.

We were the first to leave the amphitheater with our wounded and soon arrived back at the 85th Evac. Memories of the show were still emblazoned in our minds. What a blessing. We got to see Bob Hope up close.

Then, a helicopter approached our helipad. Not a Dust-off. Out came Bob Hope, Miss World, and many of the girls from the bands. Wow! The head honchos greeted Bob Hope, then directed him into the hospital. He moved with no hesitation and looked casual and at ease. I figured he would go to the Recovery/ICU unit, and I went inside, where I could see how things developed.

We had several seriously wounded soldiers in the Recovery/ICU who had come in the day before from a friendly fire artillery attack. Most of the soldiers had been near a hill where artillery had been called in incorrectly. The ordnance officer had called in the strike on the wrong hill. These soldiers took severe casualties. (Nine KIA, nine wounded, with two subsequently dying.) Friendly fire.

Bob Hope casually approached each bed of those soldiers. Most of them had received severe wounds, including loss of legs. Bob Hope sat on each bed and talked with each one face-to-face. I do not know what Bob Hope said, but you could see the pleased look that Bob Hope had taken the time to sit on their bed and talk to them. Their despair, pain, and joy at seeing Mr. Hope. A full range of emotions was on display. Bob Hope did just like he had over the decades in previous wars. I cannot say much more about that event, but I respect and honor that man.

Miss World and the other girls accompanying Bob Hope brought staring and smiles to each of us. The girls were warm and accepting. They were wonderful. Instantly, I fell in love with one performer. She was kind enough to spend about a minute talking with me. The hospital staff had a big infusion of good. Home was not far away that day. Bob Hope left, but he infused our hospital with an unforgettable spirit.

Christmas had come without family, a tree, or presents. We had Christmas when Bob Hope and his performers visited us at Camp Eagle, I Corps, Vietnam, and the 85th Evac. Hospital. Wow!

Blood and Guts

"How could you deal with all the blood and guts?" The question asked back in "The World" about the surgeries we did in the war zone. We were busy with wounded. Half of the casualties during my time in Vietnam came through I Corps, and our evacuation hospital was the first in line.

When a Dust-off arrived at the 85th, usually there was more than one wounded soldier. Landmines inflicted the most common wounds. One leg would be mostly gone, the other barely attached, badly damaged with compound fractures, but hopefully with the blood flow maintained. The soldier would most likely have additional wounds on the face, hands, and arms. Shrapnel, dirt, rocks, grass, twigs, etc., would be blown into the ragged stump and the remains of the other leg. There was a lot of blood.

During surgery, the doctors, nurses, and OR Techs would often end up covered with blood from their waists down, including their boots. Yes, we wore combat boots in the operating room, along with fatigue pants and a scrub shirt.

A garden hose on the side of each operating room hung long enough to stretch across the room. After surgery, we OR Technicians had the job of cleaning up. Depending on the mess left after surgery, the hose might be the best way to eliminate the bulk of blood and miscellaneous tissue pieces. A large, grated drain was in the middle of the floor and underneath the operating table. On bad surgeries, the hose would push the debris to the drain. Sometimes, the grating would plug, necessitating debris removal by hand.

As many sponges were used during these surgeries, the cloth blood-soaked sponges would be around the room on the floor. Minimal attention was paid to how much blood had been absorbed by the sponges. It is expected in elective surgeries to note the estimated volume of blood absorbed by the sponges or even weigh them for proper fluid loss to be calculated. Those sponges would eventually plug the drain. They had to be picked up and discarded.

Throughout these surgeries, blood covered everything: the floor, the table, the personnel. We hoped it would not get onto the cabinets that held instruments. Wherever it ended up, it had to be cleaned up. A mixture of water and iodine would be broomed on the floor to sanitize it as much as possible before the next patient was wheeled in.

The blood and guts were not the focus. Saving the wounded soldier's life was the focus. All the blood and guts were part of saving the soldier's life. The OR team, surgeon, nurses, and techs focused on that one objective. The rest was incidental.

One day, a soldier came in with multiple wounds. He had been hit by mortars that landed close. Wounds were from head to foot. As the surgery progressed, several surgeons worked on this guy simultaneously. There were so many wounds it took a long time, and the patient started to decline. Eventually, the soldier died. The surgeons and nurses instructed Mike and me to close the wounds before the body was taken to Graves Registration.

That was one time I truly saw the blood, the guts, the wounds, the torn tissues. Mike and I worked on that soldier for hours. I was relieved when we finished. That time, the blood and guts affected me. The soldier was dead. There was no life to save that could hide the dirty part of the job.

Hong Kong

Everyone was allowed a week of Rest and Relaxation (R&R) at various destinations of our choice. I chose Hong Kong. Arriving at the Hong Kong airport, I took a cab to a hotel on the west side of the Kowloon peninsula. My room looked out on the bay inlet and across to the airport.

Once settled, I explored the commercial district, a short walk away. Humphrey Street was the area I focused on with electronics, tailors, meat markets, and other commercial stores.

I happened on "Petones," a tailor shop with an excellent display in the front window. Entering, I introduced myself to the two proprietors, Peter and Tony, whose names combined to form "Petones." They were welcoming and eager to show me their products. As I was not a standard issue size, we agreed something could be made specifically for me. Not one to make quick decisions, I held off for another day. Upon my return, we discussed various jackets.

Wanting a versatile jacket, they proposed making a reversible jacket. What an idea. I went for it, understanding it would be available for fitting within a couple of days. It was. They marked the jacket for resizing, and a day later, I had a reversible jacket. What a unique item. One side had a light pattern, and the reverse a darker different pattern. One side could be appropriate for daytime activities and the other for evening attire. Cool, I could swap sides depending on where I was going. That jacket was functional for many years until it appeared to "shrink" after I returned to "The World."

The Petones invited me to their home for an authentic Indian dinner. After arriving, I observed their native custom. Women ate in a separate room, such as the kitchen. We sat, and I was introduced to a curry dish that is common in India and delicious. It took a few days, however, to regrow my stomach lining. That curry was hot, hot, hot!

During one of my "fitting" days, the Petones invited me for lunch. We walked a couple of blocks away from their store, climbed a stairway on the side of a building, across a roof, up another stairway, and across another roof. They opened the door. I could barely see across the dining room for the steam. We were in an authentic Chinese restaurant. We sat. There was no menu.

Soon, a waiter came to our table with at least a dozen baskets hanging from a shoulder support. One basket was opened.

My hosts said, "Oh, you must try this."

I did. Another set of baskets came, but this time they refused, and another arrived, they agreed, and again we ate from the steamed baskets. We had four or five baskets of various vegetables and meats. With curiosity, I asked about the meats.

Peter and Tony smiled and said, "Maybe we should ask you how much you liked them."

I said, "They were very tasty and spicy."

They replied, "We are glad you liked them."

To this day, I have no idea what I ate.

Many years later, a similar event hosted by friends at Ago Bay, Japan, resulted in no specific answers regarding the multiple small dishes presented to me. My host stated most were from the ocean. One dish was said to be an everyday food. I asked what it was. They said they did not know, but it was a typical dish consumed by most of the people of Japan.

For variety, one day, I decided to take the ferry across to Victoria Island. I found an English-speaking cab driver and asked him, "Please show me the sites of Victoria Island."

First, we went to Aberdeen, the fishing village on the east side. What an interesting ocean of vessels, mostly small with living quarters. The taxi driver informed me that it is said some people are born, live, and die on those vessels without ever coming to land.

Later, the taxi driver took me up the mountain with a marvelous view of Hong Kong. I took the tram back down on the north side, delivering me to the high-rise business district. I walked back to the ferry and returned to the mainland. An exciting trip which cost me little. Years later, I took a taxi in various West Coast Canadian towns with excellent results. Often, these outings would not last long and always be inexpensive. These excursions would give one the big picture of the area and the culture.

I looked across the ocean bay from my hotel room at the Hong Kong Airport. I saw many planes coming and going. I found it entertaining. But one day, I watched a plane take off. It seemed to hang in the sky and travel slowly. I did not understand this phenomenon and wondered if some new form of aerodynamics had been invented. Later, I came to understand that plane was the Boeing 747. With its huge size, the proportions of size to speed changes your visual perception, and it's not the same as smaller aircraft. So, it did not use a new form of aerodynamics, but it was a massive aircraft.

In an electronics store, I saw a calculator incorporating a printer and a screen showing the calculation with electric numbers. What a machine! I had never seen one with the electric numbers before and decided to get one. I bought it and sent it home for future use. After the war, I used that bulky calculator. Not long after, the electronic industry had handheld, credit card-sized, cheap calculators for everyday use. I was proud of my calculator investment, even for a few years.

Following my stay in Hong Kong, I returned to Vietnam a little more educated and understanding the oriental culture and aircraft. Also, I learned a lot about Indian and Chinese cuisine…be careful!

Eight Dead Soldiers

Usually, when a helicopter approached the 85th Evac, information regarding the number of stretchers and walking wounded was communicated via the radio from the Med-Evac to the communications office in the ER area. This day, the entire ER crew was already working on a mass casualty event which required everyone available to do triage and get the wounded stabilized enough to either go to X-ray or directly to the operating room.

I was an extra pair of hands in the emergency room that day to assist where most needed. All personnel were dealing with the many wounded. The radio did not announce a chopper coming in, but I could hear it. I took a gurney and headed to the helipad. The chopper was not a Dust-off. It was not normal, but the doors were open. I could see wounded soldiers. As the chopper landed, I moved forward with the gurney.

As I approached, I saw several soldiers soaked with blood. I went to the first, who was leaning toward the pilot and grabbed him to move him to the gurney. He did not respond. What was going on? Typically, a wounded soldier responded. This one did not. I looked him over and determined he was already dead. His fatigues were covered in blood and debris. There was nothing I could do for him.

I grabbed the next one. He did not respond, also dead. They were stacked in there, one on top of another. Some lying, some sitting against the chopper or another body. The smell of blood was powerful. I grabbed the next, then the next, the next, and the next. I got into the helicopter, stepping on a couple of dead soldiers, trying to find someone alive whom I could help save. All of them were dead.

"No, no," I thought to myself. We could always find someone to help, someone alive. I kept pulling, moving a dead soldier off another. The wounds were grotesque. A couple did not show wounds from my angle, but they were dead. From one to the next, I went grabbing for someone to help, to save. All were dead.

Some had bamboo stalks run through their clothing to make stretchers. No one was alive. This was not right. We always had someone to "save," but there was no one to save. That chopper should not have come to the 85th. It should have gone straight to Graves Registration. I informed the pilot all these soldiers were dead. The pilot talked on his radio and then took off, I assume to Graves.

That was one of the hardest events in my experience in Vietnam. We were trained to save lives, and there was no one to save. I retreated from the helipad and had a visceral, emotional reaction. After I got control of myself, I went back to the emergency room and helped where I could to help save someone's life, then went into surgery. I am glad I was the only one who went out to the helipad that day, so no one else suffered such an intense experience. That event still bothers me today. The image of all those dead soldiers does not go away.

In defense of those young, inexperienced pilots, they were probably new to the area and perhaps did not receive instructions to Graves Registration but knew the location of the 85th Evac. They took those casualties to where someone might help. Maybe they thought some were still alive. Perhaps some of those soldiers were alive when they picked them up but were gone by the time they reached the 85th.

Our whole mission was to save lives. We trained, worked, and even lived through the occasional patient dying while trying to save them. Digging through those eight bodies for one to help was extremely difficult. With great effort, we, the team, saved so many people with severe wounds. We are blessed to have those memories and are proud of our accomplishments. That heartbreaking event is soothed by the many lives we saved, but it does not go away.

Aspiration

The left foot had a gunshot wound. He was right-handed. At first, this wounded soldier took everyone's attention as he was worked through the emergency room, then X-ray, and wheeled into the operating room. The X-ray showed the bones involved, and the procedure was started, not unlike other foot wounds. But this wound was isolated, different from the others, which mostly came from booby traps. Some booby traps caused puncture wounds, some from small rounds triggered by stepping on a mechanism. This one was different. The bullet entered the top of the boot and then through the foot.

The soldier said it was from "Cleaning my weapon."

A soldier with significant wounds would be taken out of the Vietnam theater and either discharged or assigned a position stateside. This process was acknowledged throughout the troops. It was also known as the way to get out of Vietnam. Here was another one trying to get out of Vietnam by seriously injuring himself.

Knowing he was headed to a hospital, the soldier found a big beef steak. He ate big chunks of that meat. Shortly after that great meal, he was wounded and rushed to the 85th Evac Hospital.

The operation was routine. His left foot was in the process of being debrided as anesthesia was gradually reduced. It is not uncommon for a person coming out of anesthesia to have gagging reactions. This soldier gagged and upchucked big pieces of the meat he had eaten. During the gagging reflex, a person can aspirate. Some of the stomach ingredients are quite acidic. This soldier aspirated, and a big piece of meat lodged in his airway. He was losing air and retching, the normal bodily reaction. The staff got a long-handled clamp and attempted to remove the chunk of meat. Finally, they succeeded, and the airway cleared. But during the gagging, he had aspirated some acidic bile from his stomach into his lungs. He was breathing but not getting oxygen. The stomach acid caused his lungs to excrete copious amounts of fluid to protect the lining. Bubbles started to appear in his mouth. He was drowning in his own fluids. Suction tubes were placed down his throat to get the fluid out. It was ugly for some time. Then, it became apparent this soldier was dead. Oxygen could not get through the fluid bubbles.

This soldier's name appears on "The Wall" in Washington, D.C., as a soldier who died in action. Sometimes, it is best not to know the details.

When a soldier trying to get out of their duty shoots themselves in the foot, it is usually to the opposite side of their dominant hand.

Most soldiers want to escape the war and do anything to make that happen. Taking extreme measures is usually not wise and can result in unintended consequences. This soldier died because his desire to escape the war thoroughly diminished any rational thinking. Those of us who lived through the war have some memories that bring us rewarding thoughts, some not so good, but we remain to tell the stories. Trying to get out of Vietnam, this soldier died - not worth it.

Alone

It had been months since I was with her, and now our lives had changed for the better or worse.

I returned to "The World" on August 8, 1971, landed at McCord Air Force Base in Tacoma, WA, knelt, and kissed the earth. I was on my way to being a real person again, not a soldier who was ordered, controlled, and confined.

The plane with around 300 troops left Cam Ranh Bay, Vietnam, earlier that day and passed the time zone, landing thirteen hours later, but on the same day we departed. We had seen the first land of the Americas along the west coast of Canada. A transformation started taking place. This soldier, who felt like he had finally escaped, began feeling relief but was a much more experienced person going forward.

That flight was probably a few of the same boisterous soldiers on the flight 365 days earlier until we saw the coast of Vietnam when the airplane became quiet and sober. Returning to "The World," this plane was as quiet as when we first saw Vietnam, knowing we were headed into a war zone. A year had passed. Most of our lives were different now. Some would never come home. But, for varied reasons for those of us coming home, some came back wiser, some dependent on drugs, but every one of us was different than a year before. Every aspect of our lives was now different.

But this silence was disparate, contemplative. The war was behind us. As we traveled further from that war zone, the reality of living life as a citizen, a human again, was on our minds. We didn't know how we would be received. We had heard of soldiers returning home being spat on at airports by those opposed to the war, our neighbors, our fellow Americans. What would I face? How would my family and friends receive me?

I had left a nurse, Barbara, with whom I tentatively planned to join and possibly marry once she returned home. She became very close to me through shared experiences, similar faith foundations, similar values, the war, and the bitterness of death. Sharing that time together had brought us close together. We bonded, and that was wonderful in that crazy, abnormal world. That bonding brought me some peace and comfort in a world that was not "The World."

I was closer to her than any other woman in my life. I was not alone. Now, how was this relationship going to endure and grow? Would we have the same bond when we reunited? How different would she or I be? I saw myself changing from what I was in Vietnam. I was different.

When I arrived at the discharge quarters in Fort Lewis, WA., I knew I could go home. I was discharged and given a ticket for San Francisco. Recalling the bitter homecoming many soldiers had experienced, I stayed in the Tacoma area for a few days. The Seventh-day Adventist Serviceman's Center was nearby, where I lived during my on-the-job training at Madigan General Hospital.

I arrived to open arms and stayed for three days. I changed my flight to three days later. During that time, I called home and family with my arrival details—sister, brother, aunts, uncles, friends, and anyone who would be glad I had survived the war. I dug out the civilian clothes I had purchased on R&R in Hong Kong three months earlier. I wanted to arrive at the San Francisco Airport in civilian attire, not a military uniform. I could not disguise my duffle bag, but those were common, so no problem.

The flight from Seattle/Tacoma airport was relaxed. I was anxious to see my friends and family. They would greet me at the gate. The war was behind me. I was no longer a soldier. I was home. An American with a lot of trauma behind me, but that trauma and those experiences will live with me for the rest of my life. How good it would be to be welcomed back by family and friends.

Looking out the window, I identified places where I had worked in Oregon and Northern California. The August weather was typical for San Francisco, cool with some fog burning off. Finally, I was home. I let most of the passengers leave before I went to the door and exited into the terminal. I looked around. My parents were there.

"Where were the others, my family and friends?" I said to myself. "They must be waiting somewhere. They for sure are here." Just my parents. God bless them.

My parents hugged me. "So glad you are home, son."

They turned and started walking down the airport way. They argued about who was going to drive home. My year in Vietnam was gone, not to be talked about or wanting to be understood. No one was there but my dear parents, no one!!!! (Some things can never be cried away; they live on.) All that was left were the experiences and bonds made with those close to me in Vietnam.

I retrieved my duffle bag at baggage claim and got in the car. Mother drove home. I thought about the friends who had seen me off at the Phu Bai Airport and how my sendoff was more heartfelt than my reception at home. Barbara was there at Phu Bai. So was Mike, Donn, "Tree," Gus, Patti, and a few other friends. Now, home. That year had disappeared into an unknown, unwelcomed oblivion. The sacrifice for liberty and freedom was not acknowledged.

The anticipated family and friends never showed up. In the years to follow, I was an enigma to them. My experience only talked about superficially. We reacquainted, and a few insignificant stories were told. Life was renewing. I had to readjust. Would the mortars, the pain of the wounded soldiers on the X-ray table, the bonds of the "BROTHERS FOREVER," the helicopter missions, the missions with the 101st, the dead soldiers on that chopper, ever go away?

The civilian clothes worked. No one at the airport paid attention to me. My uniform was buried in my duffle bag. My haircut had grown and was not an indicator of where I had come from. No one paid attention to me. Not even my family. My parents received me probably the only way they knew how. Part of my greater family and soul was still in Vietnam—Barbara, Mike, Donn, "Tree," Gus, Patti, Roger, Joe, Sergeant Russell… They were part of my family. Some remain "BROTHERS FOREVER." That does and will not ever change.

The next day, my father told me to get in the truck. We went to town. I needed to get a driver's license again. That was accomplished then Dad took me to the County Recorder, where I had my DD-214 recorded. That had been a very wise action. Whenever I needed my DD-214, it was, and remains, available.

Back on the farm, my energy was focused on the projects my dad needed done. Correspondence continued with Barbara. As the days went by, my Vietnam and my Vietnam family members gradually started to fade. They might fade, but never, never forgotten. My life is impregnated with those people and experiences.

A planned meeting was scheduled with Barbara for a rendezvous in Kaanapali, Hawaii, which coincided with her R&R. For some unrecalled reason, that didn't happen. Later that year, she returned to "The World." I would meet up with her on her journey back east where her family resided and she grew up.

That day arrived, but by that time, four months later, I had met another lady with whom I fell in love—Roberta. I took a job as a Hospital Administrator. The organization told me they needed someone with medical experience. After Vietnam, I certainly had that. It was logical I would be the right person for the job. However, I did not correlate being an OR Tech in Vietnam with running a hospital as having the right experience. I didn't care. I wanted a job. That lasted a year and ended because I could not make patients, family, owners, or employees happy. It was not for me. Meeting Roberta there had changed something inside me.

When Barbara arrived in San Francisco on the expected date, she called and told me where we would meet. I got in my car and headed the sixty miles into the city, parked, and went into the hotel. My stomach was in a knot when I took the elevator to the prescribed floor. I found the door. What was I going to do? How did I feel after all these months without Barbara and having met someone filling that emptiness? There was no answer to that question. I knocked on the hotel door.

Barbara opened the door, and I went in. We hugged. We talked about her trip, friends still in Vietnam, and nothing. It was the same Barbara I had left in Vietnam. She had not changed. I had changed. What I knew had to be said. I lost the Barbara I knew in Vietnam, but I still carried her in my heart. We visited for some time, then I told her. My life with her in Vietnam was gone. The intense feelings for her had faded. I met a lady I considered spending the rest of my life with. It was awkward. I was not comfortable. I had never seen enough old movies to help me with this awkward conversation. I did not know how to say what I needed to say. How do I tell someone I feel so strongly that I cannot continue with the commitment we made in Vietnam and that we both need to move on? I said the words that came from somewhere, not my conscious self. After the awkwardness became unbearable, I excused myself and left Barbara alone. Tears followed in the elevator and car. I wish I would have had the right words. But it was done.

Right or wrong, I headed back to Stockton, thinking about what happened. That has bothered me for the rest of my life. Perhaps someday I'll have the opportunity to meet Barbara again and apologize for not knowing the right words, but what was said had to be said. It was a learning and growing experience. Maybe Puccini could tell the story better.

Barbara was alone. I had another relationship to cover my wounds. She did not. I sincerely pray she found peace after that whole experience and is not alone.

Epilogue

As a draftee and a Conscientious Objector, I had a two-year commitment. During DEROSing (Date Eligible for Return from Overseas) at Fort Lewis, WA, the processor said, "You have less than four months left in service. It is not worth sending you to another station where it takes a few months to get oriented so you can go home."

Without hesitation, I said, "Thank you."

The previous twenty months and six days had given me an education I had not expected: foreign travel, friends (BROTHERS FOREVER), a better appreciation of life, an unexpected relationship with a nurse, and the realization that every day is truly a gift. Enjoy and appreciate every day because far too many soldiers have died for us to have choice, freedom, and liberty. Those who have not "served" have little understanding of what that means and will not know how precious those blessings are to all of us.

My twenty months and six days gave me a better understanding of who I am. It was only twenty months and six days out of these 76 years, but how else could I have gotten that much education and appreciation for the life we have without that experience?

In an interview by Colonel Franklin for the Witness to War, which now is part of the Library of Congress, he asked me what my service meant to me. I answered, "I did my service willingly to help support the freedom and liberty we are accorded in this country." The sacrifice I made is insignificant to the sacrifice so many have and will continue to make.

Those who take for granted or do not recognize or appreciate the blessings provided by our liberty and freedom are driving our world into another war that will very likely alter our life of liberty and freedom. They do not understand or appreciate the sacrifice others have made for them.

I am one of the most blessed people on the earth. My Vietnam experience educated me on what we have and the price paid.

God bless America!

Definitions

BROTHERS FOREVER: Mike Clark, Dave "Tree" Anderson, and Donn Gates. "Tree" is gone now. Mike and Donn have had cancer attributed to Agent Orange.

Conscientious Objector: A person convinced not to kill others but will serve their country in time of war.

Conscientious Abstainer: A person convinced not to kill or support the military. Often, they do three years of alternate duty.

DEROS: Date Eligible for Return from Overseas.

AIT: Advanced Individual Training.

OJT: On-the-job training is the practical application of the training.

DD-214: Discharge paperwork required for Veteran Affairs.

Seventh-day Adventist Serviceman's Center: Homes for on-duty servicemen in various cities where Adventist servicemen were assigned. A chaplain oversaw the center. The chaplain had military recognition and was authorized to take soldiers off base.

DUST-OFF: A helicopter, usually a Bell UH-1H, assigned to pick up wounded troops in the field. Often, the doors were removed to allow easier access to board and exit the wounded.

Camp Eagle: Base camp for the 101st Airborne Division near Phu Long, Vietnam.

85th Evacuation Hospital: A Semi-mobile hospital that could move if required. From 1965 to 1969, it was based at Qui Non, South Vietnam. From 1969 to 1972, it resided near Phu Bai, South Vietnam.

OR: Operating Room.

OR Tech: Technician of sterile fields, surgical procedures, and surgical hardware.

Agent Orange: A mixture of herbicides that U.S. military forces sprayed in Vietnam from 1962 to 1971 during the Vietnam War for the dual purpose of defoliating forest areas that might conceal Viet Cong and North Vietnamese forces and destroying crops that might feed the enemy. The defoliant, sprayed from low-flying aircraft, consisted of approximately equal amounts of the unpurified butyl esters of 2,4-dichlorophenoxyacetic acid (2,4-D) and 2,4,5-trichlorophenoxyacetic acid (2,4,5-T). Agent Orange also contained small, variable proportions of 2,3,7,8-tetrachlorodibenzo-p-dioxin—commonly called "dioxin"—which is a by-product of the manufacture of 2,4,5-T and is toxic even in minute quantities. About 50 million liters (13 million gallons) of Agent Orange—containing about 170 kg (375 pounds) of dioxin—were dropped on Vietnam.

ANTHOLOGY:
85th Evacuation Hospital, Phu Bai Vietnam 1970-71

By
Patti Hendrix

Early Journey

In seventh grade, an assignment to read the newspaper daily and another to write an essay on career choices resulted in reading an article in the Cleveland Plain Dealer about Army Nurse Anesthetists. I was intrigued. Already aware I would choose a career in the health field, I did some more research about army nurses. Back then (1960s), girls had only a few career choices to aspire to: secretarial, teaching, or nursing. I would be the first in my family to opt for education after high school, and I knew I would need additional funds to further my education. That made the military an attractive option for me. Uncle Sam would be footing the bill!

The more I researched about Certified Registered Nurse Anesthetists (CRNAs), the more I realized that it would be a career field I would enjoy. CRNAs are responsible for providing anesthesia to patients and maintaining their safety and well-being during surgical procedures. How difficult could that be? So naïve!

In the Army, they work in various hospital settings ranging from large university teaching hospitals to small outposts in some of the most remote places in the world. I was sold. I knew in the seventh grade I would pursue a career as an Army Nurse Anesthetist. Now, I just had to figure out how to accomplish that mission.

In nursing school, a three-year diploma was the generally accepted program. I was accepted into the St. Luke's Hospital Nursing program in Cleveland. I spent my first year at Kent State University taking basic college classes before moving to St. Luke's for nursing classes. I chose that program because of the university credits, hoping to complete a degree later. I joined the Army nursing program while at St. Luke's. They paid for my last year of school and paid me a stipend! I was paid as a PFC (Private First Class), an E-3 on the pay chart for that year. This enabled me to purchase my first car. A brand-new Mercury Cougar XR-7 with a manual transmission since my dad taught me to drive a stick utilizing our family VW Bug.

I graduated in 1969 and drove from Euclid, Ohio, to Ft. Sam Houston at San Antonio, TX, for basic officer's training. We had no military commitments while in school, so I knew nothing about the military until arriving in Texas. That several days' drive was my introduction to being completely and utterly on my own.

In-processing meant never-ending paperwork in triplicate, multiple shots simultaneously, which brought very sore arms and mild fevers with it. The all-day classes consisted of military history, protocols, traditions, rank structure for all the military branches, how/when to salute, and the ubiquitous marching. We marched everywhere as a medical "company" from class to class and listened to the rest of the troops on base ridicule our efforts. Medical Officer troops were not adept at marching. We were a prime example of that perception.

Toward the end of our indoctrination into Army life (late Oct '69), we were asked for preferences for our next assignment. I needed to spend eighteen months on active duty before applying to the Nurse Anesthetist course. It was a lengthy, prestigious school, and the Army wanted to ensure you were suited to military life. In nursing school, I spent several weeks in the Operating Room (OR) learning about circulating and scrubbing for surgical cases, and I loved it. I asked about the OR Nursing Course. I was told one slot was left at a "remote" base. I said sure. I didn't mind where it was located. They laughed at me and asked if I would like to attend school in Hawaii. "Let me think on that for a moment." What an opportunity! Hawaii on Uncle Sam's dime!

While at school at Tripler Army Medical Center in Oahu, Hawaii in Nov '69, I already knew I'd be requesting Vietnam as my next assignment, and then after that year, I could apply to CRNA school. I would go in at night to the OR and ask to help out on the late-night emergency cases to have as much experience as possible before heading to 'Nam. The surgeons got used to me being there. I became more of a first assistant instead of a scrub on many surgeries. Sometimes, I was scrub and first assist, but most of the time, someone else scrubbed in, too. I tried to make sure the scrub person didn't take offense at my unusual participation.

I spent as much off-duty time as possible at the beach. I asked the OR techs which were the better beaches and was generally included with the enlisted group heading to the beach most days. They taught me some surfing basics, which went well until I hit myself in the head with the board one day. I decided to settle for the body surfing beaches and spent most days at Makapuu Beach hanging with the guys and perfecting surfing without a board.

One day, I was called to the Chief Nurses' Office after someone reported me hanging out in the CMS (supply) area talking to the enlisted techs. We were setting up logistics of when/where to meet for the next beach excursion. Long before cell phones and texting were invented. The CN was stern and noted I shouldn't be fraternizing with the enlisted folks, especially while in uniform. As I left her office, she smiled and said she remembered what it was like to be young once, to be more discreet and not be in uniform when interacting with the techs. I don't recall any official statements put into my file for that "infraction." I continued to hang out with the OR techs and live the good life on the beach most days.

When the orders came out for our graduating class of eight students (spring '70), everyone except me received orders for 'Nam or Korea. I received orders to remain in Hawaii. I was confused. Everyone else had asked to stay in Hawaii or return to CONUS (mainland USA). I was the only one to request Vietnam and didn't get that assignment.

My instructor said it was because several staff OR nurses were being sent to Vietnam, and I was the one the OR supervisors decided was most prepared to take calls right away. All my hard work didn't pay off as I had expected. I said OK (not that my opinion counted), but I would apply for 'Nam again after the next class finished. I did, but then I was told again I'd be staying in Hawaii. Any other time, I would have been overjoyed to remain. I decided to make the most of my continued time in paradise. I agreed to rent an apartment in Honolulu with another nurse, enrolled in the University of Hawaii, and, of course, received my orders to 'Nam the following week for a mid-August '70 deployment. I quickly backtracked to get out of all the above agreements.

Shortly after arriving in Hawaii (Nov '69), I learned through letters that my younger brother Gary (age 13) was letting his grades slip. He normally was an A-B student. I knew that didn't go over well with our parents and told him that if he brought them back up to As and Bs, I'd bring him to Hawaii for the summer if I was still here. Great incentive because he did get his grades up, and I was duty-bound to bring him over.

I graduated from the OR course and was now on staff. My parents let him fly to Hawaii by himself once school was out for the summer. He had to change planes in Los Angeles, and the agents in LA bumped him from the flight. Thankfully, he had the gumption to speak with the gate agents and questioned his removal from the flight. He didn't think they could do that as he was a minor traveling alone to Hawaii. They quickly got him listed back on the flight! This was well before cell phones. I wouldn't have known he wasn't on the flight until he was a no-show at the terminal. I am glad I didn't have to call home and tell my parents that their only son, the youngest of the four kids, was alone on the West Coast!

Gary stayed with me in the BOQ on base. I never inquired if that was permitted. I didn't have the money for us to stay elsewhere. He quickly adapted to island life. However, he was a teenager, and keeping him amply fed was no easy feat. We made sure to hit the Officers' Club Buffet as often as possible, and he did his part to ensure they didn't profit from him.

Most of my paycheck, $375/month as a Second Lieutenant, went back home to pay for my '69 XR-7. My dad was trying to sell it for me and not having much luck because it was a manual transmission. Everyone wanted a second car for the "wife," but it had to be an automatic. When I was first sent to Hawaii, it was temporary school duty. I wasn't authorized to send my car over. I did manage to pick up an older Austin Healey Sprite in Hawaii to get around on the island. Loved that car even though it had issues. Not the least of which was that I needed to park on a hill or at least an incline to "pop the clutch" to get it moving. The top didn't go up easily, so I would often continue to drive with the top down through the frequent daily but thankfully short rain showers. Gary enjoyed that car, too.

The other nurses in the BOQ quickly became accustomed to Gary. No one questioned his presence. They often asked if they could take him along on their excursions while I was working or on-call and restricted on how far away I could go. He was having the time of his life and spent many days at the beach with my friends while I toiled away in the OR. They even took him to concerts in Honolulu while I never even made it to one.

When my orders came through assigning me to 'Nam, Gary was not a happy camper. He even asked if he could stay with the other nurses instead of returning to Ohio. I could imagine our parents' reaction to that. He knew that at some point, he would need to return to the reality of home and school in Ohio, promising to keep his grades up after having had a fantastic summer-long vacation in paradise.

My departure date to Vietnam soon approached, as did my anxiety level, not knowing what to expect. Just prior to leaving for 'Nam, one of the surgeons who had been to 'Nam was doing a late-night appendectomy and asked me to assist when I showed up at the OR. I was more than a first assist that night. He talked me through the whole procedure, from skin incision to closure. It took longer than the normal Appy. No one challenged his decision to instruct me on performing the procedure. He stated, "In 'Nam, I would never know what would be coming through the OR doors, and I needed to be prepared, even knowing how to do procedures and suture wounds." I'm sure my former instructor found out about the case, but she never said a word.

Arrival in Vietnam

After receiving my orders, I wrote a letter to the Chief Nurse of Vietnam and requested to be stationed at the 85th Evacuation Hospital, as one of the OR nurses from my class, Darlene, was there. I didn't know if the letter had even been received when heading to the airport for the flight to 'Nam. The flight left in the middle of the night. We were allowed to bring one suitcase.

I recognized a young enlisted man in civilian clothes. Most of my friends at Tripler were enlisted. He was there to see all of our group off. I asked him why. He said he made it his duty to send off every flight possible as most troops were not from Hawaii and, therefore, had no family members there to say "goodbye" and let them know someone cared. This took me aback, and I never forgot his kind gesture. I wish I could remember his name.

The flight was long. Most of us settled in to sleep. We stopped en route to refuel, but I don't recall which airport as we never left the terminal. They herded us back onto the plane to continue our journey. I distinctly remember the extreme heat and humidity when the doors opened at Tan Son Nhat Airport and how the wonderful floral aroma of Hawaii was missing.

We were transported to the in-processing center via bus with wire mesh over the windows. This was done to discourage anyone from lobbing a grenade into the bus. Welcome to Vietnam! In-processing took several days, with us needing to acquire, among other things, fatigues and tropical combat boots. The boots only came in men's sizes. I wore a women's size 9 AA. I had long, narrow feet. Nothing was comparable in men's sizes.

The supply officer handed me a pair of boots, saying, "That was the best he could do." Of course, they didn't fit. I found Dr. Scholl types of inserts at the little base PX and doctored up the boots as much as possible. Blisters formed within days of constantly wearing the boots to "break them in." Quite the painful start to my tour of duty. I recall thinking how inconsequential my pain was compared to what the wounded GIs were experiencing.

The nurses in my in-processing group were all taken to meet the Chief Nurse of Vietnam. As we were standing there sweating profusely, waiting to be introduced, she remembered my name and letter requesting the 85th Evacuation Hospital. She chuckled, saying the only thing she knew about Phu Bai was the slogan "Phu Bai is All Right." She wasn't quite sure what those words meant. I wasn't sure how to take that or what I was getting myself into.

When the day arrived to head north to Phu Bai, we waited with our gear on the tarmac for the C-130 to load up and head to Da Nang. The heat and humidity were oppressive! Finally loading, I was stopped at the door and asked if I wanted to sit up front in the cockpit. The cockpit door was open, and I saw all the windows and the pilots doing their pre-flight checks. I looked back into the main body of the aircraft—no windows. That was all it took. I have significant motion sickness problems and always need to be by a window when riding in a car, usually with the window cracked open, no matter the weather outside. I wasn't sure how my gut would react in the windowless cargo compartment. A closed window was better than none, and hoping for a fresh air vent.

The ride up to Da Nang was uneventful and intriguing. They let me mostly hang out by the front window to the left of the pilots. They gave me running commentary about the countryside and answered all my questions. During take-off and landing, I sat in one of the "jump seats." If you looked beyond all the bomb craters…and plenty were visible during our flight…Vietnam was a beautiful tropical country even back then.

After arrival in Da Nang, there weren't any scheduled aircraft to Phu Bai. I would have to wait until a seat was available, which might take a while as there was a lot of "activity" in the area. I returned to the tarmac and sat with my one suitcase and duffle bag full of combat gear, waiting…for what, I wasn't sure.

After a few hours, I started to think that nothing was going out that day and I'd better plan on an overnight stay when a pilot asked if I was the nurse headed to Phu Bai. He was headed that way and could drop me off. He was a Huey pilot. I rode in the co-pilot seat for most of the trip while the actual co-pilot sat in the passenger compartment. An uneventful and beautiful flight from Da Nang to Phu Bai over the Hai Van Pass through the mountains.

My first view of the 85th was approaching the landing pad by the ER. Just over the concertina wire surrounding the 85th was an airfield with a long runway where most incoming personnel probably arrived. I felt lucky to have made the trip by helicopter to see the surrounding areas up close. The pilot only had time to drop me and my luggage off as more flights were inbound.

Upon entering the ER, I noted that everyone was busy caring for injured patients. A tech at the desk asked me who I was then handed me a clipboard to interview the next patient lying on a litter on the floor by the door. Turns out he was a lieutenant (LT) with a traumatic leg amputation. My first introduction to war wounds. The returning Vietnam patients at Tripler were all recovering from already medically treated wounds, and we did their follow-up surgery.

The lieutenant was awake and alert despite what remained of his leg resembling hamburger meat. I was surprised at the lack of blood present without a tourniquet in place. Having worked in surgery for several months now, I was well aware of how blood would free flow from incisional wounds until vessels were clamped or cauterized. His wound was certainly bloody, but not to the extent I had expected.

He answered my questions. I copied his dog tag info onto our paperwork for processing. In short order, his litter was placed on stanchions, allowing 360-degree access to him for initial treatment at standard bed height. The ER crew went to work on him. He was soon off to the X-ray and then the OR for initial surgery.

Toward the end of my tour in 'Nam, I wrote a letter to this LT as I had kept his home address, asking him how he was doing. If he was able to adapt and cope with his new reality. He wrote back that he was doing fine. He spent a long time in rehab, learned to ski with one ski, and adapted "outrigger poles." He met his girlfriend during rehab and generally had a positive outlook on life. Considering all the negative press the Vietnam War generated and the abuse heaped upon returning veterans, I was hopeful many of the returning disabled vets would be able to rise above it all.

After all the incoming patients were tended to that day, I was introduced to the crew and told I would spend my first ten days in the ER learning how to care for incoming trauma patients and the administrative paperwork that went along with it. Then, I would spend the next ten days in the Recovery/ICU area, taking care of patients and learning the process and paperwork for that area. Only then would I be assigned to the OR, working scheduled twelve-hour shifts and taking my share of on-call duty.

I hadn't yet encountered Darlene, my fellow Tripler OR nursing student. She was on leave and due to return soon. I did, however, meet another nurse, Carol, from my nursing school back in Cleveland, Ohio. I didn't realize she was even stationed at the 85th Evac. After graduation from nursing school and basic training, everyone went their separate ways. Once all the controlled chaos of the day ended and the ER was put back together, I spotted Carol sitting on a counter in the ER, chatting with the rest of the crew. It was great to see her and realize that I was starting my tour with more than one familiar face to share it with.

Meeting The One

In the ER, just a few short days later, I was hard at work along with the rest of the crew working on multiple GIs with the usual horrific wounds. A pilot came into the ER from the helipad looking for one of his friends who had been shot down. I asked him to wait off to the side somewhere else while we tended to the GIs.

Much later, I noticed him still waiting. Since there was a break in the hectic pace, I asked him for his friend's name. I checked our patient roster, but his friend wasn't listed. I suggested he try the hospital in Quang Tri (QT), just north of us, closer to the DMZ, or perhaps inquire in the Admin/Comms office, and maybe they could locate him. He said he would then left the ER.

Several days later, I went to the Officers Club after some prodding by the other nurses. I didn't drink and wasn't interested in the smoky atmosphere, so I didn't spend much time there.

A few years earlier, I swore off alcohol after a horrible night at a frat party at Case Western in Cleveland. Not realizing how much vodka was in the fruity punch, I spent hours upchucking in the bathroom. Someone told me later this frat house was known for spiking the punch with way too much vodka. I was an alcohol neophyte and quickly realized I didn't like relinquishing control, vowing never again to be in that position. Subsequently, I became the "designated driver" for our nursing class "outings."

I wasn't at the O' Club very long before noticing the same pilot I had spoken with in the ER. I approached him and asked if he had located his friend. He said *yes*, and his friend Brian had been taken to QT (Quang Tri). We started talking and exchanged names and phone contact info. His name was John, and he was a Loach pilot. The Loach (LOH: Light Observation Helicopter) is a Hughes OH-6A Cayuse Scout, single-engine helicopter, aka the "Little Bird." His "job" was to fly at tree-top level, get the enemy troops to shoot at him, and mark the location with smoke grenades. Then the Cobra gunships would roll in and take out the gun emplacement. In other words, "play chicken with Charlie."

John and I talked on the phone and occasionally met at the Officers Club. He was kind and considerate, a true gentleman. John was funny and intelligent and made me laugh. He told wonderful stories of his family and his crazy military life. One night, he invited me to take a ride in his helicopter. I said *sure*. I enjoyed all the helicopter traveling I had done so far. I was aware of the "no nurses joyriding in helicopters" edict, as there had been a few crashes and injuries. But what could happen? Right?

Flying in the little bubble helicopter was quite different from a Huey. There was not much to see that night as it was dark with no moon. Then came the green streaks of light. Not realizing what they were even though I had observed some night shooting at Camp Bullis during basic training, I asked John, "What's with the green lights?"

"They were tracers," he said.

Then I remembered the red ones from training.

"The green ones are from NVA/VC (North Vietnamese/Viet Cong) weapons, and we had better head back," John said.

I mentioned if we were to be shot down and I didn't die, my CO would probably kill me anyway.

John turned off the lights to make us less of a target. That night, I found out what a really crazy pilot he was as his evasive maneuvers brought on some motion sickness issues, but at least I didn't upchuck, managing to somehow keep my guts in place. Obviously, we made it back safely. I didn't mention encountering enemy weapons fire to anyone on base as I figured the consequences for flying in the helicopter would probably be severe enough. I don't know if any rounds hit the helicopter or not, but the tracers came pretty close.

A few days after arrival, I had my first introduction to mortar attacks. The siren for waking the entire compound was attached to the outside of my hooch. No wonder it was available when I arrived! I moved out as soon as something else was available. I had been instructed about where the nurses' bunker was located and to shelter there during the attacks. Needed to wear the steel helmet, flak jacket, and combat boots (not flip-flops) as there generally was several inches of stagnant water on the floor. Lights would be out all over the compound, so I had to make it to the bunker in the dark. Most of the nurses brought flashlights, and it would turn into a party. Someone always managed to bring food to share. On one occasion, I grabbed the bacon I had been cooking for late-night breakfast on my hot plate stove on the way out the door. It disappeared quickly.

The attacks were fairly frequent at first—every couple of nights. However, after the all-clear, they would start bringing patients to the ER. Lack of sleep became an issue, and fewer nurses made it to the bunker. Knowing that not everyone was on duty during the attacks, I found out a lot of nurses were rolling off their bunks and sheltering underneath, trying to sleep through it. I eventually did the same. We learned when a mortar attack was possible because the mama-sans wouldn't show up for work at the gate that day. We could hire local women to clean our hooches, wash our clothes, and polish our boots. I did that right away. I'm not one for domestic chores! My mama-san was very polite, friendly, and always tried to teach me how to speak and write Vietnamese. I appreciated her skills in getting the blood off my fatigues and boots.

From the sounds of the incoming rounds during the mortar attacks, it seemed like they tried to avoid the hospital area. However, the 85th was hit by a mortar attack on 12 March 1971. North Vietnamese Army 122mm rockets landed inside our compound. That night, the nurses went to the wards, not the bunkers, to protect the patients. I was not on the compound during the attack as John and I were in Hong Kong for R&R. We heard all about the attack after returning a few days later. To my knowledge, no deaths or significant injuries occurred, and nothing important was destroyed. The closest impact I saw was when they hit the transportation compound directly across QL-1 (the main N-S road in Vietnam) from us. I heard the tremendous explosion and watched the immense fireball from the entrance of the bunker. I think they hit the fuel tanks.

We were given weekly doses of anti-malaria meds in the mess hall and had to sign for them, probably so Uncle Sam could prove we were given the meds should we end up with malaria. Well, it wasn't long before I realized those pills were interfering with my ability to work – I would have to spend extended periods in the latrine after taking the pills. I always ran back to the nurse's latrine as we had the only flush toilets on base that I knew of. I quickly realized it was best to sign for the pills but never ingest them, figuring since they flushed directly through my GI tract, they didn't give me much protection against malaria.

The Orphanage and Other Adventures

There was an orphanage down the road from the 85th toward Huế. Not long after arriving in Phu Bai, I was asked if I wanted to tag along with some C-130 and reconnaissance pilots while they dropped off a generator for the nuns. Of course, I wanted to go. This was my first opportunity to interact with the Vietnamese people. The nuns were thankful and welcoming, and the kids were great. Had a fun time playing with them despite not understanding or speaking Vietnamese.

I spent a fair amount of my "off time" at the orphanage during the next few months. I didn't ask permission to travel to the orphanage. We were allowed to venture off post to the little PX, dental office, and a few other places without signing out, so I surmised it was OK if I occasionally went to the orphanage.

The first time I walked off the compound out the front gate, I was hesitant, unsure how to get to the orphanage on my own. I did it the American way. I hitchhiked. Stuck out my thumb and hoped someone would come along and pick me up. The orphanage was right off the main highway. Thankfully, no Vietnamese vehicles stopped, but the GIs did.

If the sun was shining, a ride would stop for me quickly. If it was raining and I had my rain gear hood up, it would take a while for someone to stop. They were always startled when I took off my boonie hat or pushed back my hood, and they realized I was a female officer, aka a "round-eye" officer. I was always driven directly to the field in front of the orphanage. From there, I would walk across the field and knock on the door. Not until much later did I realize the probable stupidity of my adventures. The field could have been mined, and it was also possible that local VC/NVA might have watched my unorthodox travels. There was never any routine to my visits, so no pattern to follow. Since I was there to help the nuns and the kids, perhaps that was enough for them not to take an interest in my actions.

The nuns were astonished but happy to see me the first time I showed up. One nun knew some English. She and the kids taught me Vietnamese while I helped them with the English language. As time progressed, I would stop at the mess hall before heading out the gate to see if the mess hall officer would spare a few food items, especially milk, to take to the orphanage. Then I would hitchhike carrying a large black plastic garbage bag filled with whatever he gave me.

The gate guards got used to my travels. I don't know if it was because I was an officer, but no one ever asked me what I was doing or where I was going. During any prolonged lull in the fighting, I would spend as much time as possible at the orphanage. The nuns always invited me to share whatever food they prepared and convinced me to try Nuoc Mam once. I'm not a fan of spicy foods, although I did enjoy several of their traditional dishes. When it was time to leave, I hitchhiked back to my unit, or occasionally one of the nuns would drive me. I was always back before dark.

I started visiting John's unit occasionally and traveled in the same manner. On one trip to Camp Eagle, the jeep that stopped for me was the head of a convoy on QL-1(the main N-S Highway in Vietnam). The enlisted driver asked me where I wanted to go and drove me to the Bravo 2/17th Cav. We chatted the entire time. John's area was off the beaten path of the 101st compound at Camp Eagle.

When the driver let me out, I turned to thank him. Then I realized the 8-10 vehicles behind him were part of his convoy headed to Huế, not Camp Eagle. I hope they didn't get into trouble being late to their destination. At least they had a good story about their detour, and the driver had witnesses to the truth. I imagine some of the other guys who stopped for me were probably told they were crazy, making up a story about a hitchhiking "round-eye" officer in the middle of Vietnam.

The Red Alert system was set up so you would know when you could and could not leave the 85th compound—the gate was "closed." A sign was always posted in the women's shower facility announcing that Red Alert status was active. I always made sure to check the status before venturing off post. I don't recall if I left base that particular day by helicopter or hitchhiking to visit John before the Alert status was supposedly posted. When I returned, Lieutenant Colonel Areola (sp), our chief nurse, was livid that I had been off base when Red Alert was in place. She threatened to court-martial me for being AWOL. It took a lot of finagling and apologizing from John to calm her down. That was my first and hoped last almost court-martial incident.

Angel 7

When I ventured to John's unit, his CO, Major Goff, always ensured I was cared for if John was out flying. He allowed me to sit and listen on the Comms to the ongoing missions. One of those days, a pretty fierce battle was going on. The pilots said the Dust-offs were headed to the 85th with several wounded, giving the number of litters and walking wounded.

Major Goff turned to me, and I said, "I need to head back to the 85th."

John was headed back to base. Major Goff allowed John to fly me back to the 85th.

John told me what to say over the mic as we approached the landing pad.

I asked permission to land using "Angel 7" as my call sign. The 2/17 Cav guys gave me that moniker. There was a bit of hesitation before a response came back. But he laughed about it and said it made his day.

We landed at the 85th. Thankfully, no one saw me get out of the Loach. I went directly into the ER and told them about the inbound casualties. No one believed me. The Comms guy said they didn't have any info on inbound Dust-offs. Just then, the call came in with precisely the same numbers I gave them. Everyone wanted to know how I had that information, but I was already headed to the OR area to get ready. It was going to be a long night in the OR.

On another of my adventures to Bravo Troop, 2/17 Cav, John was on a mission when I arrived. The gunners (in charge of the M60 Machine guns on board the "Little Bird") and other Loach pilots were in the middle of a squirt gun fight, running amok throughout the hooches, shooting each other.

Someone handed me a spare squirt gun, and I joined the fun. I soon discovered it was Kool-Aid, not water in the guns, and very sticky when you got shot. Someone chased me into John's hooch. I slammed the door in his face, but he reached up, shot into the room through the open transom above the door, and squirted Kool-Aid all over the photos tacked to John's locker. He was not happy when he saw them later.

That beautiful, playful summer day turned into a miserable, wet, stormy night. I was back at my hooch when John called about a missing Huey helicopter from Charlie Troop 2/17 that had picked up a patient on a long line in the field. C-Troop was located in Phu Bai across the runway from the 85th. He wanted to know if they were inbound and if anyone had heard from them. A long-line patient would be on a litter tethered underneath the helicopter if the pilots couldn't land due to terrain or dense jungle issues. I headed to the ER from my hooch. We were on "alert status" due to the enemy activity. The lights were off all over the compound.

I stumbled around in the pouring rain, trying to get to the ER. It was pitch black. I could not see anything until it was right in front of my face. Not a good night to be out in a helicopter. I went into the ER to see what they might know. They were aware of an inbound chopper with a long-line patient. Comms had lost contact with the chopper a few minutes prior. They thought the chopper went down close to the airfield perimeter. That was not good.

When I called John, he said one of their B Troop Hueys went out to find out what happened to the first one from C-Troop. He said some of the guys from the earlier squirt gunfight were on the second chopper.

Contact was lost with the second chopper. Anxiety levels increased exponentially. We waited in the ER for a long while. Ground searches were conducted to locate the choppers since contact was lost close to the 85th. Sometime later, a ground ambulance arrived and brought in several body bags to the ER. Both choppers had gone down.

Later, a report stated the first chopper couldn't see the wires/cables strung up around the airfield in the miserable weather. The litter got caught. The crew couldn't rectify the problem and release the litter in time. The chopper crashed. The second one flew too low and probably went down for the same reason. To this day, I'm not sure why the body bags were brought into the ER. It usually wasn't done that way. I was there when they opened them. There was hardly anything recognizable. The impact must have been quite severe.

I remember feeling gutted, realizing that some of the guys I had been having fun with a few hours earlier were now lying dead in the body bags. I went back to my hooch and cried for a long time. Many years later, I received an inquiry from someone connected to the incident. They were doing research for the family of the patient on the long-line litter and wanted details as to the sequence of events. I replied with what I knew.

Friendly Fire

At Christmas in 1970, John took some leave and went home to Yakima for ten days. There was a cease-fire for the holiday, and the 85th troops planned a pig roast for Christmas Eve. As I recall, the pig (from the orphanage) was being prepared Hawaiian luau style (Kālua puaʻa aka kālua pig), which is buried to cook in an underground oven called an imu. I wasn't part of the cooking team, but I was sure looking forward to an amazing meal. However, that was not to be.

We had multiple casualties arrive during the late afternoon and evening. It was a long night in the OR. Turns out it was a "Friendly Fire" incident. A second lieutenant had supposedly called in incorrect coordinates, bringing our own armament down on top of his troops.

We saw first-hand the horrific devastation wrought by our weapons. It was tense in the ER as the walking wounded were extremely irritated with the LT. I remember hoping he wasn't in the area as I feared tempers might erupt in the ER. We worked all night and were too exhausted to celebrate. I did eat some delicious food later, but it was a somber holiday.

Decades later, I received an inquiry from someone connected to the tragic incident. He said his group researched the incident from multiple angles. They found several missteps that could have contributed to the Christmas Eve Friendly Fire tragedy. There was a good chance that it wasn't the fault of the lieutenant, but no one could locate or even knew his correct name. He explained that the old information logs pointed to issues with the long-range guns utilized that night. It was noted in the logs that there were previous calibration problems for one of the weapons, and the rounds landed short. They weren't certain, but it was possible the error was not with the coordinates called in by the LT. It's sad that the young officer probably blamed himself for the entire debacle when it may not have been his fault. It was assumed he made the wrong call because he had been in-country only a few weeks.

We were lucky enough to have Bob Hope and his crew of celebrities perform at Camp Eagle over the Christmas—New Year holidays. Don't recall the actual date of the USO Show in 1970, but it was a great day. The weather cooperated, and the show was enjoyed by all. The nurses were invited to attend the show with the military "big-wigs" and watch it from the VIP area. I would have preferred to ride in the Deuce-and-a-half trucks and sit with the patients. It was an awesome all-star production with tight security. Considering the thousands of GIs and the VIP entertainers, security was a significant presence. Since I was at the mercy of the officers in charge for returning to the 85th, I missed seeing Bob Hope and his "troops" when they stopped to visit the 85th after the show. I caught a few USO shows as they came throughout the year, providing great entertainment in our O' Club for officers and enlisted personnel. Seeing Bob Hope on TV afterward always brought up memories of that Camp Eagle show.

John returned from leave after the holidays, came to the 85th before heading to B 2/17 Cav, and surprised me by proposing. I was working in the OR that night. He came to the OR area and asked to speak with me. One of the other nurses relieved me for a few minutes. We stood outside the OR. It was controlled chaos everywhere. He asked, and I said "Yes," hugged him, and hurried back to work. With all the noise, he wasn't sure of my answer until I finished work and returned to my quarters. Darlene, my roommate, and a few other nurses made some Chef Boyardee box pizzas sent to us in "care packages" from our families back in the "world." We celebrated until it was apparent how exhausted we all were. John returned to his unit, and the rest of us headed to bed.

Care packages from home were always coveted. My family was great in sending much appreciated, unable to secure items from the PX and extremely delicious home-baked goods. My sisters, Bonnie and Sally, would bake all sorts of cookies and individually wrap each one for shipment. Very few cookies in my packages were ever broken en route, and the techs were grateful when I opened my packages in the OR area. Not a whole lot made it back to my hooch.

People have complained about the chow hall food, but I thought "midnight chow" was pretty good. Perhaps it was good because I was too tired to care when we worked the late shift, but that was my favorite mealtime. I recall that our supply sergeant was adept at procuring great food by trading. I'm not sure what he used in exchange, but occasionally, we had steak and lobster on the barbeque. Nice boost for morale!

Hostage

One day, I was hanging out in the ER to see if they were sending anything to the OR. A Huey landed off to the side of the helipad in the dirt close to the perimeter wire. I looked out. Since it wasn't on the pad, I figured it was administrative-related and went about my duties. When I glanced out again, the pilot stood rigidly beside the chopper. That was unusual. Pilots never stood at attention if they could help it. There didn't appear to be anyone else in the area. I asked one of the ER crew to look and see what they thought. Definitely unusual, but they didn't think there was anything wrong. I went to see if he needed help.

As I approached the pilot, I saw another shorter person completely hidden behind the pilot. Then I noticed the gun pointed directly at the pilot's back and realized this was a bad situation. I spoke with the pilot. The young man behind him didn't say a word. The pilot said the GI requested to speak with one of our docs. I believe it was Dr Grossman.

The young man knew that we had an outreach group at the 85th. He said he needed to go home now. He was done with this war and wanted out. He appeared to be a young, scared GI. I said I wasn't sure if Dr. Grossman was on the compound right now, but I would check and be right back. To please not do anything rash in the meantime.

I hurried back to the ER and explained the situation to the crew. That set many things in motion, and I was denied permission to return to the chopper. The head ER nurse, Captain Hopkins, I believe, returned to speak with the pilot and GI. The ER notified the MPs. The CO tried to locate Dr. Grossman. All inbound 85th air traffic was re-routed until this crisis abated.

Word spread fast throughout the compound about the hostage situation. Multiple MPs and many weapons appeared quickly behind every sandbag in the area. I felt for the young man. This situation was not going to end well for him. As I saw it, he was a disillusioned young GI fed up with the war. If he made it out of here at all, he was going to spend a long time in prison, probably Ft. Leavenworth, Kansas. The pilot remained calm throughout my interaction with them. I wondered if he was acquainted with the young GI before this encounter.

John's helicopter took some hits one day. He unfortunately had a piece of shrapnel lodged in his temple, which bled a fair amount. He flew or was brought to the 85th and looked at, given a few stitches, and told to take the day off.

I was sitting outside my hooch when he wandered over from the ER. One of the ER nurses called to let me know he was on the way and not to worry because it was a small, superficial wound. However, John was pretty shaken up about the whole incident. He was fine physically, but I'm certain getting shot at and wounded amped up his emotional responses into the red zone. Took some time for him to settle down. I can only imagine all the what-ifs that went through his mind that day.

The Wedding(s)

John and I decided to go ahead and get married in Vietnam—he was from Washington State, and I was from Ohio. Neither family could afford to travel out of state to attend a wedding, so we thought it best to have it there amongst friends.

Getting married in a foreign country brought its own headaches. We had to have a marriage certificate from the local government in Huế to prove that we were not married in any other Vietnamese province. That meant bribing the Huế officials with Military Payment Certificates, "funny money," instead of piasters (Vietnamese currency), so they would expedite the process and sign the papers. We convinced the Vietnamese official in Huế that we were not married elsewhere, and he signed the papers. Next, we had to take those papers to Da Nang to the American Consulate. Our 85th Chaplain (Ray Hunt) encouraged us to have a "diplomatic wedding" before going on R&R in Hong Kong. The Consulate presided over a diplomatic marriage and gave us the official marriage certificate in March '71. We also decided to have a traditional marriage ceremony at the 85th.

On the way over the pass to Da Nang via helicopter to take care of the diplomatic paperwork and head to Hong Kong for a week of R&R, Steve Pullen, our pilot and John's Best Man for our wedding, noticed that there was a "skirmish" happening on the railroad. We were high enough that there was little chance of getting hit…unless they had an RPG (Rocket Propelled Grenade). Steve flew around the area, noted what was happening, and called it back to Phu Bai. We cautioned him not to do anything rash after he dropped us off in Da Nang. As with most pilots, he couldn't leave it alone. He returned to the area, ended up getting shot down, and injured his leg. When we returned from R&R, he was a patient at the 85th and a bit sheepish about the whole episode. Needless to say, that was the end of his flying for a while.

The Friday before our Sunday (11 April) wedding, I was in the ER/OR area when I heard several choppers coming in for a fast landing. I went outside to the helipad and noted Loaches all landing off to the side of the helipad. I recognized them from Bravo 2/17 Troop. I didn't see John's chopper among them. One of the guys came to me and said it wasn't John, but the CO. Major Grof's Huey was shot down, and he was severely injured. His newbie copilot managed to fly it back to a safe area. Another of their Hueys picked him up and was bringing him in. That chopper quickly landed, and I ran over to see what could be done. I got there before the litter. Major Grof was lying prone on the chopper floor with a fair amount of blood around his torso/neck area. I helped the techs turn him over onto the litter and then noted the gushing stream of blood pouring from his neck. He still had a pulse.

I immediately put my hand into his neck to compress the vessel and try to stem the flow of blood as we ran with him into the ER. When the ER crew saw what I was doing, the docs said to go straight to the OR where he was splashed with betadine while being intubated. Then, I let go as the surgeons took over. They were able to clamp and repair the damage with good vascularity returning. Next, they turned to the chest and abdominal wounds. Once he was opened, they tried in vain to stop all the hemorrhaging from multiple shrapnel wounds and tissue damage. It soon became evident there was no way to control all the bleeding or repair the extensive damage to multiple organs. Major Grof died on the OR table.

This man always made sure that I was welcomed over at B/2/17 and was much loved by all his troops. He was a good pilot and a respected leader. This was his second Vietnam tour. His death hit me especially hard as he was a friend. I left the OR, walked outside, slid down the wall, and just sat there and cried for a long time. One of the OR nurses came out to find me later and hugged me, knowing what a difficult situation it was for me.

Later, I found out that back in "the world," Major Grof was a musician—classical mostly I think, as was his wife. He was a business major in college at MSU in East Lansing, MI, played trombone and string bass, and sang with university groups. Not what one would think of as prerequisites for helicopter pilots and commanders.

In 2014, I was honored to be invited to MSU to attend the premier of a piece of American Music, "When Day is Done," composed by Joe Spaniola, adapted from a poem by Edgar Guest in memory of Major Grof by the Gamma Epsilon chapter. It was a very moving performance and a touching tribute to a truly amazing man.

John was understandably upset about Major Grof's death. He felt it should have been him instead, but Major Grof didn't fly the same types of missions as John, and everyone tried to explain that to him. Major Grof was actually on a reconnaissance mission to Laos that day. Later, I saw photos of the Huey with his entire side of the cockpit destroyed. It was amazing that the co-pilot was able to fly it back.

We discussed delaying the marriage ceremony as Major Grof was to walk me down the aisle. He had even come to the rehearsal earlier that week. In the end, we decided to go through with it as planned and try to remember all the good times with Major Grof. Colonel Sugiyama (sp?), our 85th CO, walked me down the aisle. Darlene was my maid of honor, and Jeannie sang and played the guitar. Colonel Arola even attended the ceremony wearing a nice dress. I had only ever seen her in fatigues before that. "Bridge Over Troubled Waters" was one of our songs. My short, white dress was made in Hong Kong for $50, and I wore it multiple times afterward. We bought our rings in Hong Kong. I had a friend ship over some special sola wood flowers from Hawaii for my "bouquet."

The nurses at the 85th took care of everything for our wedding, from having someone fix my frizzy hair to getting the mess hall ready to make a cake. It was a memorable day with B/2/17 guys and 85th troops helping to make it a success. Multiple photos of the day show a number of the 85th crew pouring cement for the barbeque pit. It was a multi-event day. We went on our honeymoon to Hawaii sometime later.

There was another 85th nurse married to a Huey pilot. They came to us already married. Her husband was shot down and killed. The guys who went to the crash site couldn't figure out if he was killed from injuries incurred during the crash or afterward by direct enemy confrontation. It was a difficult time for all of us as we were all friends working together, and this shouldn't be happening. She was whisked out of there very quickly afterward. I remember thinking how this could be John at any moment.

Neurosurgery at the 85th

During the summer of '71, football was an important pastime and stress reliever. The 85th team was quite talented. Our primary quarterback, Dr. Leo Flynn (Orthopedic Surgeon), played college ball with Auburn University and was on the '57 National Championship Team. Our center, Dr. Robert Agostinelli (Internal Medicine), was a big man—not much got past him. The techs rounded out the team and were also equally great players. Matches were set up with the surrounding units, and the 85th won most of the games. A match was then set up to play against a team in Da Nang. Our team and those off-duty were allowed to travel there for the game—which we won!

During the warmer months, a Chinook helicopter would set down on our helipad, and if you were off for the day, you could hop on and spend a few hours at China Beach (the real China Beach from the famed TV Series) in Da Nang. The chopper would do a reverse trip, dropping everyone off before sunset. I made the trip a few times and noted how nice the military compound and 95th Evacuation Hospital in Da Nang were compared to the 85th. The *Sanctuary*, a naval hospital ship, was stationed off the coast in Da Nang, and I met some of the nurses stationed on it. Offered to have them come to the 85th to check out how we lived and worked. None of the navy nurses wanted anything to do with our little mudhole/dustbowl in the middle of nowhere.

The 85th and 95th and others are considered "Semi-Mobile" Army Surgical Hospitals as opposed to MASH: Mobile Army Surgical Hospitals. MASH units are U.S. Army Field Hospitals that operated from the Korean War until the Gulf War and phased out in 2006. Our facility (85th) was basically wooden construction on stilts to handle the monsoon rains. We refer to the 85th as a "SMASH" Hospital. The movie MASH came out in 1970 and was shown in our O' Club to officers and enlisted troops together. It was a hoot. We could easily pick out corresponding 85th members to their counterparts in the movie. That was a great movie night!

Our hospital did not have neurosurgical capabilities. The I (Eye) Corps neurosurgeons were stationed in Da Nang at the 95th Evac. Any head trauma patient, no matter their other wounds, usually went directly to Da Nang after initial immediate treatment in the field. One very stormy night, two choppers tried to make it over the pass with their head trauma patients but turned back to Phu Bai due to severe weather. I happened to be the OR nurse on duty that night.

One patient had a closed head trauma with acute intracranial swelling, and the other had an open head trauma. I don't recall the surgeons involved that night and how they decided who would take which patient. I believe two general surgeons were the primary surgeons, but it was all hands on deck that night. This was one of the many times I had to send word to the enlisted hooches asking for any OR techs available to come to the OR to help out on cases. I am very grateful and appreciative of their dedication to duty. I always had the extra helping hands I needed.

We managed to find equipment for burr holes for the one patient. It was a manual drill, definitely low-tech, even at that time. We used a general surgery set with maybe some ENT and vascular types of instruments for the open head wound. It was debrided as best as possible under the circumstances. I remember standing in the doorway leading to both ORs with the medical-surgical textbook open, helping the techs and surgeons, and answering questions. Noting which instruments were recommended and trying to figure out which instruments we had that could be used as substitutes. I believe that this was the first burr hole procedure the surgeon had performed on his own, and it had been years since assisting on one during surgical residency. The open head trauma surgeons had never been responsible for debriding brain matter previously. We had the neurosurgeons in Da Nang on the phone for assistance. Miraculously, both patients survived the night and were transported as soon as possible to Da Nang.

I have to note that our surgeons were very innovative and made do with what we had on hand to do whatever surgery was presented to our facility. When the surgeons first arrived, they would request this or that particular instrument for cracking the chest or clamping a vessel but had to use whatever the scrub tech handed them. We had limited inventory concerning instruments. By the time surgeons DEROS'd (headed back to the states), they had become very efficient at getting in, performing the necessary procedures, and getting out as expeditiously as possible, with excellent outcomes, using whatever was handed to them by the techs. We were up north in I Corps and last in the supply line. Frequently, we had shortages of essential supplies, including anesthesia medications, which hampered the anesthesia providers. They, too, learned how to make do with the drugs available. But they made sure the CO knew we needed the drugs and medications ASAP if the GIs were to be adequately cared for. Lack of pentothal made intubations and general anesthesia induction more intense for the patient and provider alike.

We had at least two patients in separate events come in with live ammo embedded in their wounds during my tour. Those were intense moments when the rounds were discovered during in-processing in the ER. The surgeons decided who would operate on the patient—all volunteers and no females were allowed in the operating room during the procedures. A female CRNA may have been in on one of the cases, but I can't remember. We did, however, continue to assist from outside the surgery room. Patients were surrounded by sandbags on the OR table, and everyone in the area wore flak jackets and steel pots. Quiet, tense moments in the OR as the live munitions were removed. After the removal, the tension lifted, and normal OR banter resumed. Everyone was relieved to have survived the ordeal.

You learned to be prepared for anything that came through the ER doors. A soldier came in with multiple wounds, including a chest wound caused by his own leg that had been blown off and embedded itself boot first, with his foot still inside, into his lateral chest. White Phosphorous (WP) burns were horrible. The substance sticks to skin and clothing. The affected areas continue to burn, even smoke, and must be copiously irrigated with cold water/saline for extended periods. Re-ignition of the burn process can occur later unless all WP is meticulously removed. It was always amazing how awake and alert most of our trauma patients were when first brought to us, even the multiple amputation patients. Most of the time our horrifically physically traumatized patients were more concerned about their buddies than themselves. We were to "take care of them first. Please!"

One day, a pilot managed to roughly land his chopper on our helipad, only to die right then from his chest wound. A bullet caught him in his lateral chest, right where his "Chicken Plates" (hard ballistic vest) fastened, offering no protection. It was a Loach, and he was the only one on board.

Surgeries were obviously very bloody events for the most part. OR staff wore an OR cloth hat, scrub shirt, fatigue pants, and combat boots, which made for messy laundry and bloody boots for our mama-sans. If you were scrubbed in for the surgery, you wore a cloth "sterile" gown over your scrub shirt and fatigues and had sterile gloves. When the patient was wheeled out to the recovery room/ICU, then the unenviable task of cleaning up the OR for the next casualty commenced. In the middle of the OR floor (cement), there was a drain into which all manner of debris was flushed with a green garden hose that hung on the side wall of each OR.

Larger pieces of tissue were bagged and disposed of as no one wanted those drains to clog up. Each OR was also equipped with a Fly Swatter. It was the circulator's duty to try to keep the flies off the scrub's back table and other "sterile" areas as much as possible. Antibiotics were liberally provided to each patient! Not quite the normal surgical routine of a medical center back in "the world."

As incomprehensible as it is, we did not wear gloves when tending to patients unless we were utilizing a "sterile field" or scrubbed in. The circulator on the case did not wear gloves. Consequently, a lot of time was spent at the scrub sink cleaning up and scrubbing hands to clean the blood, guts, and gore off after finishing surgeries. The only gloves we had were the ones in packages for use in sterile procedures. Boxes of non-sterile gloves came out much later for routine medical care.

Blood was replaced as soon as possible during surgeries. We used a lot of whole blood during surgeries versus plasma, platelets, or RBCs (Red Blood Cells). When the blood bank ran short, the call would go out across the hospital compound for donors. Our soldiers would willingly line up and give blood. A lot of very fresh blood was pumped into our wounded GIs, which was beneficial for them. It was gratifying to witness the outpouring of support for the wounded troops. The donors were monitored to ensure their donations did not exceed the normal timeframe. If someone had a rare type, they were asked to donate when needed and not on a routine basis.

Not sure exactly when, but we had a GI who went crazy and set off tear gas canisters all over the compound. Took a while for someone to apprehend him. He set off a canister by the helipad, and I was in the area at the time. I was caught amid the heavy spray and, unfortunately, wearing contacts. By the time I made it into the ER, tears streaming down my face, both corneas were scratched even though I tried not to rub my eyes. I recall making several trips to our PX Optical shop for prescription glasses as I couldn't wear contacts comfortably for several months.

Tour Extension

John had extended his tour in Vietnam before we met. After we married, I extended my tour to remain in-country with him. We were given thirty days of leave before starting the extension. We elected to head to Washington State, where I would meet his family, and then to Euclid, Ohio, to meet mine. It was great to finally get to know his family and explore the Yakima area together. John showed me his favorite places growing up. My family was very excited to meet John. The neighbors all up and down the street had American flags out. My dad and neighbors erected a huge billboard-type sign saying "Welcome Home Pat and John" in our front yard. My family planned a big family reunion/wedding reception and held it at our house. Thankfully, the weather cooperated. John met all the cousins, aunts, uncles, and neighbors I grew up with. The only distraction was that John, unfortunately, drank his way through the celebration and was thoroughly inebriated by the end. Not a great introduction to my family, most of whom drank very little alcohol. I understood he didn't want to talk about 'Nam, and that was his coping mechanism. We had some long chats about what the need for alcohol to blunt the horror of Vietnam was doing to him and us.

Thirty days flew by, and we returned to Vietnam to finish our extra six months. It was September 1971, and nine days into our extension, John was once again shot down and wounded. The chopper blade broke through the fuselage and hit John in the leg with the flat side of the blade, breaking it just above the ankle. Unfortunately, that was the same leg that incurred the worst of the bullet wounds from his first 'Nam tour in 1968 with the 82nd Airborne in Chu Lai, spending time at the 312th Evac Hospital. He was about three months into that tour as a Scout pilot flying Loaches when he was shot down. John spent the better part of a year in and out of surgery and physical therapy for those wounds. Eventually, he was restored to flight status and requested to return to Vietnam, which was when we met.

September was the beginning of monsoon season, and the weather was quite rainy at the time. The docs were going to try to let him remain in-country but eventually decided to med-evac him home as they were worried about the circulation to that foot. We tried to see if they would let me accompany him home, but my CO, Lt. Colonel Garlick (sp?), decided that would not be necessary. John was sent on his way by mid-September, and I stayed in 'Nam to finish my extension.

The days and weeks passed after John was med-evac'd home. I received letters from my family and John's mom, assuring me he was doing just fine. There was NO mail from John whatsoever. I asked him why he wasn't writing with each letter I sent him. It was his leg that was injured, not his dominant left arm. Still no reply. The mail clerk became well acquainted with me as I showed up daily to see what he might have for me. He would see me coming and say without being asked that there was nothing from John.

Finally, toward the end of November or early December 1971, I wrote John a "Dear John" letter. I told him that he obviously didn't care about our marriage, and it was over as far as I was concerned. He should start the divorce process since he was in the states, but I would also initiate contacting the JAG (Legal) office here in 'Nam. Shortly thereafter, I received a MARS (Military Auxiliary Radio System) phone call from John. He had received my final letter.

We hashed out my anger over the MARS call doing the "Over" requirement so that the civilian shortwave operators could change the setup each time…not an easy way to argue. It was also much longer than the allotted five minutes per call. I'm sure that was a conversation the MARS operators and the rest of the 85th personnel waiting in line to use the system would remember for some time! John informed me he had been working on getting me home via political connections. That angered me even more as utilizing political influence did not set well with the military brass and imploded any chance of a military career, at least in the Army.

We sort of patched things over and agreed to keep trying to make things work. I knew it was going to be a rough road as alcohol had become his coping mechanism at home, per his family. In hindsight, I probably should have stood my ground and been more forceful in that context, but I was aware of the horrific situations he had endured in 'Nam and hoped that love, time, and working through this together would be enough. I had really thought at the time that I had married my soulmate.

Some of the other nurses were aware of the situation with John and knew that I was just not interested in socializing with anyone. However, one day before my phone call with John, a couple of them told me they were invited to Charlie Troop 2/17 for a get-together and wanted me to come along. I kept refusing, but they wouldn't take no for an answer. I eventually tagged along, and we went by jeep to their compound on the other side of the airfield behind the 85th.

It was just a small group gathering with a couple of the guys playing guitars and everyone joining in with the songs. No one paid much attention to the time, and when the party was breaking up, someone pointed out that the 85th gate would be closed as it was "after hours." I'd never been out after gate closing before, so this was news to me. It was decided that one of the pilots would fly us back. One of the nurses noted we would need to be careful that the MSC (Medical Service Corps) officer didn't see us, or we would still be in trouble. Again, I wasn't aware of that issue. Obviously, these nurses had encountered this situation before.

Of course, the by-the-book MSC guy was on that night. He heard the chopper and came over to investigate. The other two nurses waited until they thought he had left after we landed but ended up being confronted by him. I hung back in the chopper a while longer. The pilot just kept it running and waited it out.

I finally saw an escape moment, jumped out, and headed to the nurses' quarters by another route. I thought I was home free—not quite. Lt. Colonel Garlick confronted the other two nurses, but they never gave me up as the third nurse on the chopper. He was livid, and scuttlebutt had it that he was considering administrative penalties. After a few days, I requested an appointment with him and confessed that I was the third nurse on the chopper. He was stunned and said that of all the nurses, I was the last one he would have thought would be on that chopper. He didn't write any of us up as far as I know. He was, however, very emphatic about how any further unauthorized flying would result in severe punishment.

AWOL–Really?

I continued to leave the compound to spend time at the orphanage. The nuns and children were always welcoming, and I enjoyed spending as much time as possible with them, knowing my tour would be up soon. The kids were always asking to visit where I worked. I always put them off and explained I couldn't set it up. I wasn't quite sure how to explain that request to the CO.

One day in mid-December, I was working in the OR when a call came in requesting my presence in the CO's office. I had no idea what it was going to be about this time. When I entered, Lt. Colonel Garlick was quite enraged. He wanted to know what I knew about a truckload of kids and nuns at the front gate asking for me by name…

I had to come clean about my comings and goings off base for the past year plus. He insisted I submit a detailed written report about every time I was off base. He was livid when I explained how much paperwork that would entail and that I did not have a record of each time as I was off base frequently. He said he was considering a court-martial as I was AWOL. In my defense, I pointed out that there wasn't any system for signing in or out when leaving the base. He confined me to the post for the remainder of my tour. I wasn't allowed to leave unless I had permission directly from him, and he made certain I realized I wouldn't get that permission! I was grateful that I only had two months left on my six-month extension tour.

The enemy activity in our area was slowing down, at least for the GIs. I don't know how intense it was for the ARVN soldiers in the area, but there was an ARVN hospital in Huế, just up the road where their casualties were taken. I had been there a few times with our Med-Cap team to show the Vietnamese surgeons how we did certain surgeries.

The 85th was getting everything ready to transfer our supplies and equipment to other facilities and close up the "shop" sometime at the end of December or January. There was not much in the way of combat trauma wounds to deal with anymore, which was good for us and our GIs, but the boredom that ensued and the anger from the troops at just having to be there made for more frequent fragging incidents. If the GIs got frustrated with their superiors for coming up with busy work to occupy their time. They took it to the next level and set lethal traps in retaliation. Generally, a grenade under the bunk.

It was also sad to see all the overdoses coming in as the drugs the GIs encountered were much purer in form than what was available in the states. The DOA overdoses coming in were just heartbreaking. Another waste of young lives.

My orders to return to CONUS came through via Senator Jackson's (WA) letters to the Army command with a DEROS date of just before Christmas. I was happy to be finally leaving, but the politics involved would be a high price to pay. My total time in-country was sixteen months. I wouldn't be relocated elsewhere like the rest of the 85th crew. Lt. Colonel Garlick was probably thrilled to see me leave. I recall a monsoon storm about two days before heading out that took the roof off my hooch and cut my electricity too. I took all my mini-fridge food and other packaged food in the pouring rain and wind to the OR supply room and shared it with everyone before it all went bad.

I left the 85th and headed for Saigon to out-process and turn in the rest of my combat gear. I gave my well-worn but serviceable rain gear to John's unit ARVN liaison commander for his wife. I met the commander a few times at Camp Eagle during my visits. He spoke English very well and appeared to be highly educated. I often wondered how he and his family fared after our withdrawal from Vietnam. I later heard and read that the NVA pretty much eradicated the ARVN military and educated populace in retaliation for cooperation with the US military.

My out-processing was uneventful, and I headed home on the U.S. "Freedom Bird" like everyone else in my group, very happy to be landing in the states but anxious about the reception awaiting in the USA, considering the anti-war sentiment and the blame placed on the returning troops. We were advised to change into civilian clothes as soon as possible to avoid unnecessary confrontations in the airport.

If I'm being honest, had I been a senior officer and had a junior officer who did the things I did in Vietnam, I'm sure I would have been less accommodating than my superiors were! Vietnam was a much different cultural and political environment than the Middle East or Afghanistan. I would not have even considered off-base excursions alone in either of those areas.

After the Fact

Several nurses during my time at the 85th were awarded the Bronze Star for their service in-country. I, however, not surprisingly, wasn't. I also never received the Army Commendation medal (ARCOM) that I was awarded and didn't know about until years later while stationed at Ft Leonard Wood, MO. I did, however, receive a medal from the government of Vietnam—the Vietnam Technical Service Medal. The award was written in Vietnamese, so I had no idea what it said or why I received it. The paperwork was mailed to me to figure it out. There is a picture of the medal on the citation, so I figured out that it was approved to wear in my row of ribbons.

I was assigned to Madigan AMC after 'Nam as that was where John was sent upon leaving Vietnam after his last crash and wounding. He was doing quite well physically, considering his injury, but emotionally, he was having a difficult time coping with civilian life. Unfortunately, alcohol was his drug of choice, and more often than not, he was intensely inebriated. The Army included him in the "rift" of pilots that occurred after the war. He planned on making the army a career, which added to his stress level.

I settled in and worked as an OR nurse at Madigan. I sent my application for the Army School for Nurse Anesthetists as soon as possible. I had hoped the negative events in Vietnam wouldn't plague my application. I should have known better.

One day, while I was working in the OR, a call came from the personnel office asking me to sign some papers. I went as soon as I could. The tech handed me some paperwork to sign and set some other papers on his desk, angled in such a manner that I could read them should I look that way. The tech then excused himself for a few minutes. I signed the papers. While waiting for his return, I glanced at the documents. Two typed pages from the Chief Nurse of Madigan on why I should not be accepted into the Army Nurse Corps (ANC) Anesthesia program. She emphasized my utilization of political connections. My heart sank. I would never get into the program. When the tech came back, I thanked him profusely for his assistance.

I knew my only chance was to speak with the chief of the nurse anesthesia program at Madigan, Lt. Colonel Maziarski, CRNA. He had already approved my application. The didactic portion of the program was a six-month assignment at William Beaumont Army Medical Center (AMC) in El Paso, TX, with the clinical portion following at one of several

AMCs, Madigan being one of them. After explaining what I had just read in the administration office, Lt. Colonel Maziarski assured me he would take care of it. He did; he went over the Madigan Chief Nurse, straight to the program board, and pleaded my case…I was accepted into the program.

I am eternally grateful for his assistance in getting accepted into the program I had dreamed about for years! I started anesthesia school in the fall of 1972, about ten months after returning from Vietnam.

In 1975, after graduating and then while stationed at Fort Leonard Wood, MO, the chief nurse anesthetist, Colonel Gosling, CRNA, asked me why I didn't have any award ribbons for Vietnam service. I never had any, or so I thought, and told her that, in all probability, I was lucky not to have received my "immediate" discharge papers after 'Nam. The Chief Nurse at Madigan never forwarded the incoming award paperwork, and I was never presented with the ARCOM that was awarded. Colonel Gosling made the late presentation and presented me with my second ARCOM for my time at Leonard Wood. I was grateful that she took the time to research why there was no record of my first award in my file.

After Leonard Wood, I submitted a request for an assignment in Europe. I was locked into four more years in the Army for payback for my anesthesia training, and John was flying civilian helicopters worldwide. I received orders in March of 1976 to the 2nd General Hospital in Landstuhl, Germany, where I again met Fred Brockschmidt, CRNA, or perhaps at Fitzsimons in Denver 1973-74, where we reconnected. I remember he was part of the anesthesia department in one of my assignments.

Fred was very patient with me when we were in Nam as I would spend a lot of time at the head of the table watching closely what the anesthesia providers were doing and how they handled all the intricacies of anesthesia in a combat situation. I asked many questions, and Fred always calmly explained what he was doing and why. Not everyone had the patience to deal with my questions. However, I learned a lot from all those providing anesthesia at the 85th by observing their techniques whenever I could get away from the other duties of being the OR nurse.

John was still flying and keeping it all together at this point. He flew all over the Middle East and Africa for a company out of The Hague. He would be gone for two months then home for two weeks which is probably why our marriage survived. We'd meet up sometimes in other countries. I managed to travel to Iran for two weeks when he was there flying, and the Shah was still in power. We met for a vacation in Greece. Unfortunately, alcohol was still his drug of choice for dealing with life. Multiple people who cared deeply for him tried to help him see what was happening and how destructive his choices were. Whenever I gave him an ultimatum, he could stop for a few months. I was still hoping he could move beyond his need for emotionally and physically blocking the past. He needed to deal with the reality of life.

Exiting the Army

Upon completing my assignment in Germany, I opted to resign my commission. I hoped that by removing John from the military lifestyle, i.e., the Officers Club and its alcohol atmosphere, maybe we could settle into a "normal" life—whatever that was. The Army wanted to send me to Ft. Rucker, AL, but I had wanted to return to the West Coast. So we parted ways. I started my career as a student in '68 and was now resigning in '79. A lot of time to give up, but I thought it was for the best for our marriage to have any chance to succeed.

We resettled in the Tacoma/Seattle area, and all seemed to be going well. I was working as a civilian CRNA at Madigan and taking classes at Pacific Lutheran University to complete my degree in Biology with a lot of chemistry thrown in. John was still flying around the world and seemed to have more control over his alcohol needs. It was now 1981, and I thought we could consider raising a family. We talked, and John was enthusiastic and said he did not need the alcohol and all would be fine. The day we confirmed I was pregnant, he went out and got rip-roaring drunk. I knew then that it would not be an easy road into the future.

Eventually, we had three daughters—'82, '84, and '86, all of whom were brought up to be strong independent women. We were blessed that they were all healthy and very intelligent. I decided to look into reserve military duty as I wasn't willing to give up my tenure and enjoyed working in the military. We could also use the extra pay it provided. At that time, I worked as a GS-9 at Madigan for about $13 an hour while attending PLU full-time on the GI bill. I secured a position in 1981 as a CRNA at McChord Air Force Base, Tacoma, with a Medical Evacuation group.

This was my switch in military affiliation, hoping my negative Army exploits would not follow me. Apparently, all was well as I served fifteen years in the reserves and retired as a Lt. Colonel in the Air Force with about twenty-six years total time. I spent time in Korea and Japan and was called up for Desert Storm, serving three months on active duty. David Grant Hospital at Travis AFB, CA, was my duty station. Close enough to explore Napa and visit beautiful central California. The girls even came down by train to visit along with their nanny. The helicopter company John worked for provided us with a nanny since I had been called up to active duty, and he was away flying mostly in Canada.

When I notified the Army that I was switching to the Air Force, the admin officer said he wouldn't sign off my final resignation until I had secured the Air Force appointment to maintain continuity of service—no breaks in service meant that I could retire and receive credit for all years in service for pay purposes. I am very grateful for that as I now receive a monthly military retirement paycheck.

After graduating from PLU in December 1983, cum laude with a BA in "Biology with Chemistry Emphasis," just a physics class short of a Chemistry minor. We already had an eighteen-month-old daughter, and I needed to be working more to help financially support our growing family, so I opted for early graduation since I had enough credits. A few years later, I accepted an anesthesia position in Everett, WA. We bought a place in Granite Falls, WA, in 1986 and settled in. The girls grew up, became involved in horse 4-H, and all did well in school. John finally (1995) wrote his book about our time in Nam after telling me for years about the book he was working on. Turns out he is a talented writer. He let me edit his book initially. However, he embellished almost everything he wrote about the 85th. I made corrections as to how I recalled the 85th events since I was actually there.

He wasn't happy with my editing and refused to let me read anything more. I didn't have the opportunity to read the final product until it was published. Needless to say, I was not happy with how he portrayed events as they related to the 85th. I wasn't a fan of his book. He embellished and fictionalized events he wasn't even a part of. Whenever anyone asked me about specific events, I explained the reality of my recollections of the situation and always that they should read the book with "a grain of salt" in mind. In his defense, he was seriously wounded in '68. Bilateral gunshot wounds to both feet and ankles through the floorboard of his chopper. He never spoke about that time, but I imagine his experiences were reflected in his 85th memories as he wrote them.

John's book was written so that older elementary kids could read it as he left out any "colorful" language he was prone to using. Our girls read it, and one of their teachers, Mrs. Howell, read it and asked if her whole multi-age class (4th, 5th, & 6th graders) could read it, which they did. It became a very significant project for her class with two of our daughters in that class.

Belated Welcome Home

The students decided to try to locate one of John's pilot friends, Bob Donnelly, whom he had written about. They succeeded in finding him and some others written about in the book. They wrote to Weird Bob, as he was referred to in the book, and conversed via computer, asking questions about his escapades in 'Nam.

It became quite the undertaking for the class as they petitioned the city of Granite Falls, WA, to organize a Welcome Home Parade for Veterans Day in 1997. A year or so earlier, this same teacher, Mrs. Howell, asked me to arrange a speaker to come to school and talk about Veterans Day and Vietnam. I contacted VVA 423 in Snohomish, and they came and did a full presentation in the auditorium with the Color Guard and a speaker for the whole school.

These wonderful Vietnam vets and their wives (Dan and Linda, Roger and Pam, Ron, and Minda, Rob and Deb, LaDene, Mike, and Steve, to recall just a few) agreed to help with the Granite Falls parade organization. It turned into a massive project with an Air Force Fly-by during a huge parade with marching bands and veteran groups from all over the state participating.

A luncheon was held honoring all vets, which was quite an elaborate event. Kevin Benedict wrote and performed a song, "Angel 7," honoring all the nurses who served in 'Nam. Mardi Newman, an RN co-worker in Seattle and "chef," catered a memorable dinner at our farm for the multiple participants and film crew the night before the big day.

Our parade even made the national news broadcast that night. KOMO News from Seattle with Doug Tolmie did a whole program about our hometown parade over several days. You can still read about that magical "Welcome Home" day in 1997 on northwestvets.com. A YouTube video from 1997 is still available online: "A Vietnam Vet's Belated Homecoming Parade."

The children of the Multi-Age class did an outstanding job of welcoming home so many vets who felt lost and unappreciated after serving their country.

Coming to Grips with Reality

Life returned to "normal" after all the excitement with the Veteran's Day activities. As time passed, John tried but failed to take control of his life. He still insisted he didn't need any help in dealing with his demons. He went through the AA program, but he only did it for me, not for himself. He refused to see anyone or talk to a therapist...after all, "he didn't have a problem." Unfortunately, his alcoholism took a toll on our daughters. Having to deal with a father who poured himself sixteen ounces of rum with a dash of coke for color as his breakfast drink wasn't easy for them. His only saving grace was that he was a "congenial" drunk and not violent.

As time passed, I came closer to the divorce option for the sake of the girls. As I was researching options back then, I came across a court case in Seattle concerning a divorce involving an alcoholic husband/father and the main breadwinner wife/mother. He was given primary parental custody, and she had weekends and holiday time along with paying child support and alimony.

The article was very upfront about his alcoholic issues, but he was still given primary custody. I knew that could be a possibility for us as well. I wasn't ready to relinquish my parental rights to an alcoholic husband/father, so I put up with his continued alcohol use and tried very hard to help him see how that was destroying our family. I knew better than most wives what he endured in 'Nam, but no one could convince him to seek help. It was something he would need to acknowledge before he could "recover" from Vietnam, but sadly, he never was able to admit he needed help.

Years later, after thirty-three years of marriage, we separated. I thought it would be a good time to move on with my life. I accepted a position in November 2004 in Anchorage, Alaska. Far enough away, he couldn't just drive to my front door and plead for forgiveness again, as was his habit. The girls had all graduated high school, moved out of the house, and on with their lives—or so I thought. After telling them my plan, they all returned home for various reasons. I decided to bring them to Anchorage for one week each while I was there doing a "working interview" at the hospital. It was how the anesthesia group ensured you knew what you were getting into by agreeing to move to Alaska. The girls could check it out and see what they thought.

Heather, our oldest, was too involved in school and studying to take the time off and opted to remain in school in WA. Heidi and Hollyann came up individually for a week each. Heidi decided to make the move up too. When Hollyann stepped out into the many inches of snow in six-inch spike heels, I figured Alaska wouldn't be her preference. She was also confident she would be the one to help her father overcome his demons. She chose to remain in WA. Reluctantly, I left Heather and Hollyann back in Granite Falls. I had wanted John to have to make it or not on his own, not to have anyone he could rely on to take care of him. I had hoped it would wake him up to reality.

Unfortunately, my mother had a major stroke back in Ohio before my move to Alaska and died in August of 2005. I was back and forth to Ohio several times during this timeframe. Heather and Hollyann both lived at home in Granite while continuing their education. Hollyann, who tried her best to convince her father he needed help, instead started having health issues—increasingly frequent seizures. She had her first seizure the night after surgery for a broken leg (horse accident) in 2002. That seemed an isolated incident with no further occurrences, or so I thought. In 2005, the seizures started to come again. I was making plans with her to have her move to Alaska at the end of her school semester. She agreed to come but felt she had everything under control.

Earlier, I had come down and spent three days at Children's Hospital in Seattle with her for a neurology workup, staying in her room. They ruled out epilepsy. She was advised to continue with the anti-seizure medications, which she didn't like as they made her sleepy. She also said she would wake up with pain in her arms and legs after a seizure.

Back in Alaska, shortly thereafter, I couldn't reach her or John by phone and became more frantic as the hours passed. I spoke with her frequently and panicked when I couldn't get through. John finally called from the ER and calmly told me Hollyann had died. She was not able to be resuscitated after a seizure. The ER doctor told me she had traces of methadone along with her prescription meds in her system. The amount was fairly minimal, but she was new to the drug as it hadn't shown up on her previous tests. It was enough to end her life. Methadone was one of her father's prescriptions. This was Oct 2005.

My life fell apart. I was done.

My father, not wanting to be without Mom, died in March 2006.

We finalized our divorce in July 2006. I remained in Alaska. Heather was unfortunately left with the care of the farm and watching over her father as he slipped further into alcoholic decline. Something a child should never have to do. He was admitted for care several times but always signed himself out as soon as he sobered up, declining any mental health care. I had hoped he would wake up, deal with the reality of life, and reach out for the help he so desperately needed. Sadly, John passed away a few months later in November 2006, of an "accidental overdose" of alcohol, prescription and street drugs, never overcoming his demons.

I broke my wrist slipping on the ice in my driveway in Eagle River, AK, in December 2006. My fault for not wearing my "ice-walkers." I was unable to work, so I spent a few weeks in WA with Heather, taking care of John's personal effects. We went through many boxes of his worldwide flight and war memorabilia. We recalled many of the good times that so easily get lost in the daily trauma of living with an alcoholic. In the end, I'm glad Heather was there for her father, even though I had wanted him to finally hit rock bottom. She was a full-time UW student living at home, trying to watch over her father—not the usual carefree college life. I deeply appreciate all that she did for John in his last years of battling his demons.

Heidi was with me in Alaska, continuing her education and working as a nanny for a family she still is very close to. I am truly grateful for her support throughout those emotionally distraught months. She was there with me every step of the way with all the family health issues and funerals. Heidi was instrumental in taking care of Hollyann's funeral and later with spreading her ashes in Hawaii. We found the perfect rock formation on the coast that looked like a girl sitting with her arms around her bent knees, looking out over the ocean that she would forever be a part of. Heidi is an Everett Providence Medical Center RN and now a Recovery Room (PACU) nurse. She spent several years as a substance abuse nurse working in the Rehabilitation Unit. Unfortunately, she is well acquainted with addiction patients.

Epilogue

Our Vietnam journey was very different than most. I wish it had a happier ending. To move forward, I had to forgive John (and myself) for all the mental pain and anguish we went through as a family. I know now that I should have exited the marriage much earlier for the sake of our children's mental health. Hopefully, our girls understand that their father suffered intense emotional pain as well as physical pain from his Vietnam experiences and tried, though unsuccessful, to overcome his emotional wounds. I am eternally thankful for my daughters and now my grandchildren, whom I get to shamelessly spoil. "What Happens at Grandma's Stays at Grandma's"…is the motto on my door.

John led an interesting life, and had he taken the time to write about various events, he would probably have succeeded as a writer. He grew up in Seattle and Yakima. As a teen, he befriended a lost Tibetan boy on the streets of Seattle. The two families became fast friends. John convinced people to finance a trip for him to India in the mid-60s to assist with the Tibetan refugees. He was sixteen. He went as a young diplomat.

John has photos of himself meeting the Dali Lama. He brought back a large rug for Vice President Hubert Humphery, who had helped him secure the necessary paperwork, visas, and passports for his journey. Mr. Humphery sent us a letter congratulating us on our marriage. John was also a "guest" on the TV program "To Tell the Truth" concerning his exploits in India.

His descent into alcoholism and drug-induced escape from reality put an end to any of his talented story-telling abilities. He never left Vietnam…

Many Vietnam vet lives have been lost since the war ended. There are so many more than the currently 58,267 names listed on The Wall whose deaths are the direct result of their Vietnam experience.

Such a waste of humanity.

My 85th Evac family has helped me through the last many years with our reunion gatherings. My experiences at the 85th in 1970-71 set me on a path I had not expected—dealing with PTSD and Addiction. I accumulated a lot of "heartache" but also lots of love—my children, grandchildren, and the Gingell Clan over the years since '70-71. I'm very thankful for all the camaraderie and memories shared by our 85th family, which remind me of the outpouring of love and kindness to one another during our year in "Hell" and after. I'm glad to have reconnected with the people who shared that tumultuous time with me—the nurses, techs, and docs who understand the very nature of the beating heart that was the 85th back in 70-71. Looking forward, I know that our future reunions will become smaller and smaller gatherings, but the memories we shared will forever be a part of who we are… The 85th Evacuation Hospital Family, Phu Bai, Vietnam. Phu Bai truly is Alright!

Photographs

Contributed by Robert Jackson, MD

90th Replacement Battalion – Long Binh.

Enlisted Billets in background, 85th Evacuation Hospital.

Officers Billets at the 85th Evacuation Hospital, Phu Bai, Vietnam.

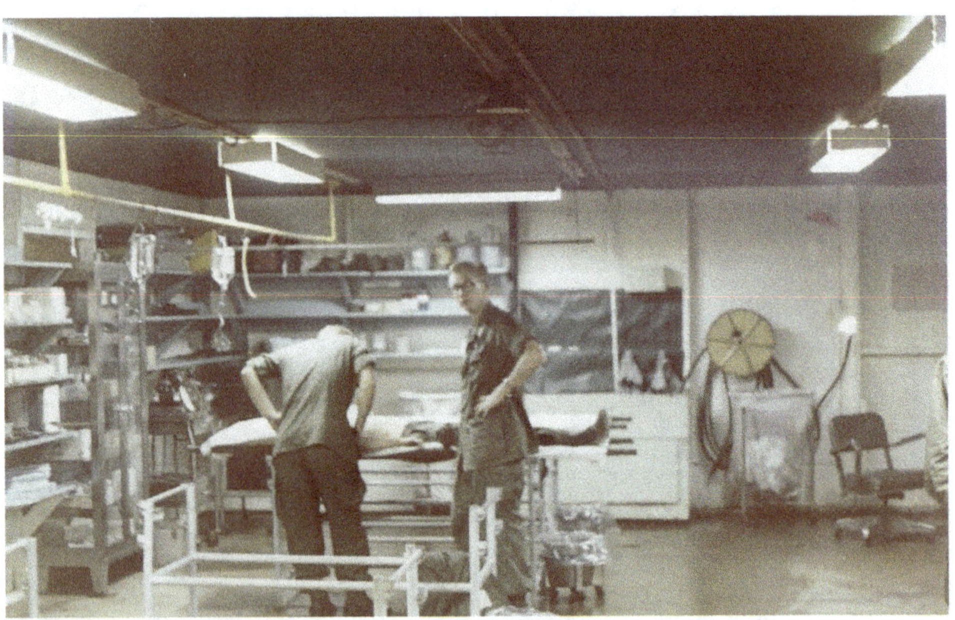

Emergency Room at the 85th Evacuation Hospital.

Left front Dr. Bill Harmon, Dr. Cary Conyers, Dr. Barry Powell in the middle and Dr. Robert Jackson on the far right.

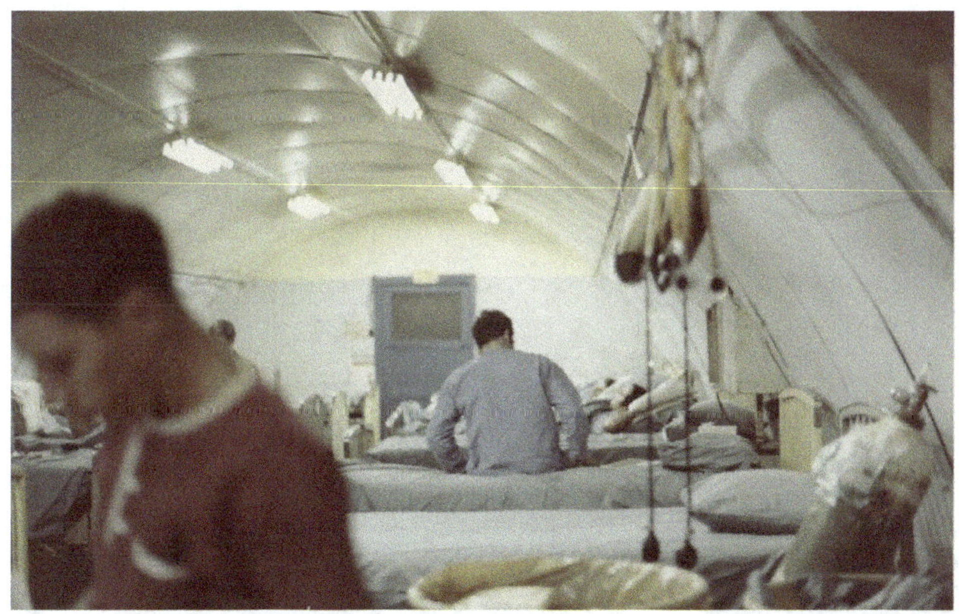

Patient Ward.

Chapel at the 85th Evacuation Hospital.

Repair of quarters after a hurricane.

Photographs

Contributed by John Martin Streeby

In the ER at the 85th.

Choppers!

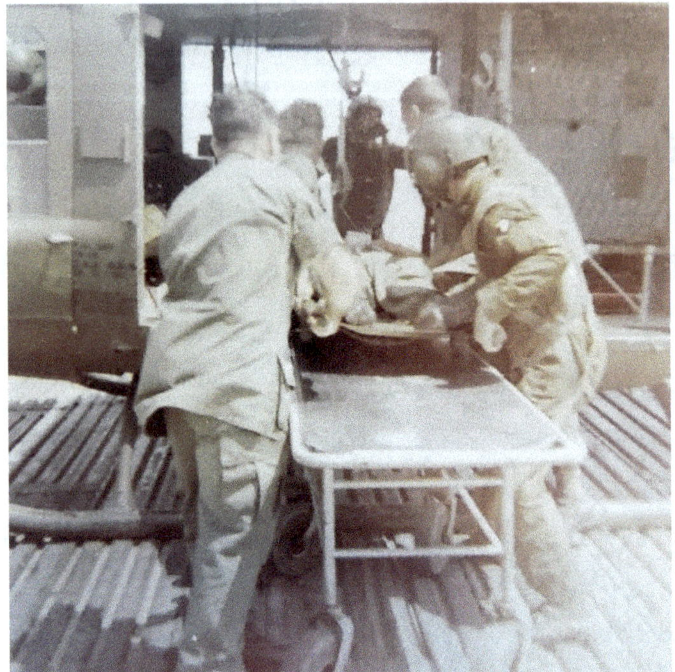

Bringing a patient in from the helipad.

The Dead Shed.

Peace!

Photographs

Contributed by Michael Tucker

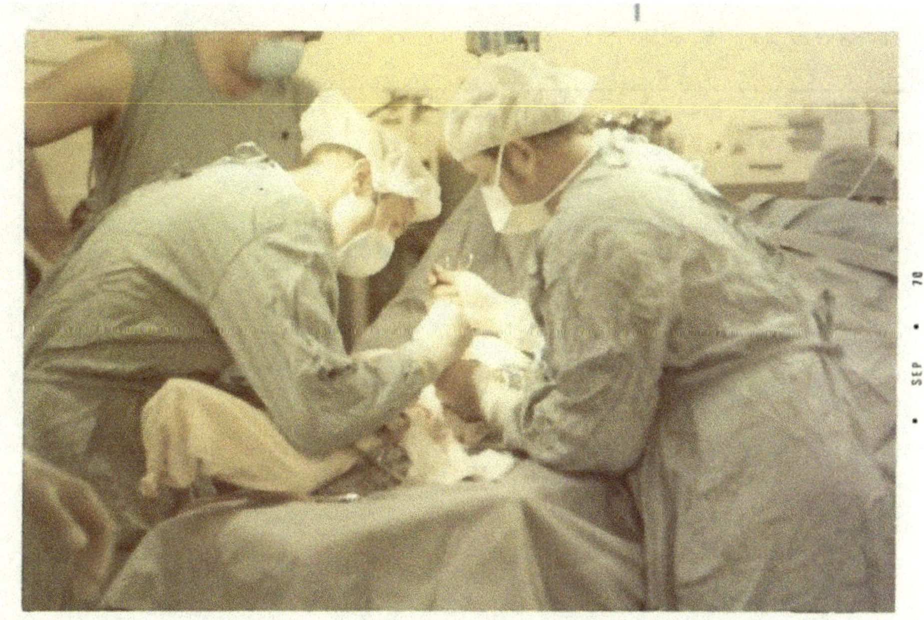
• SEP • 70

Photographs
Maps

101st Airborne Division Area

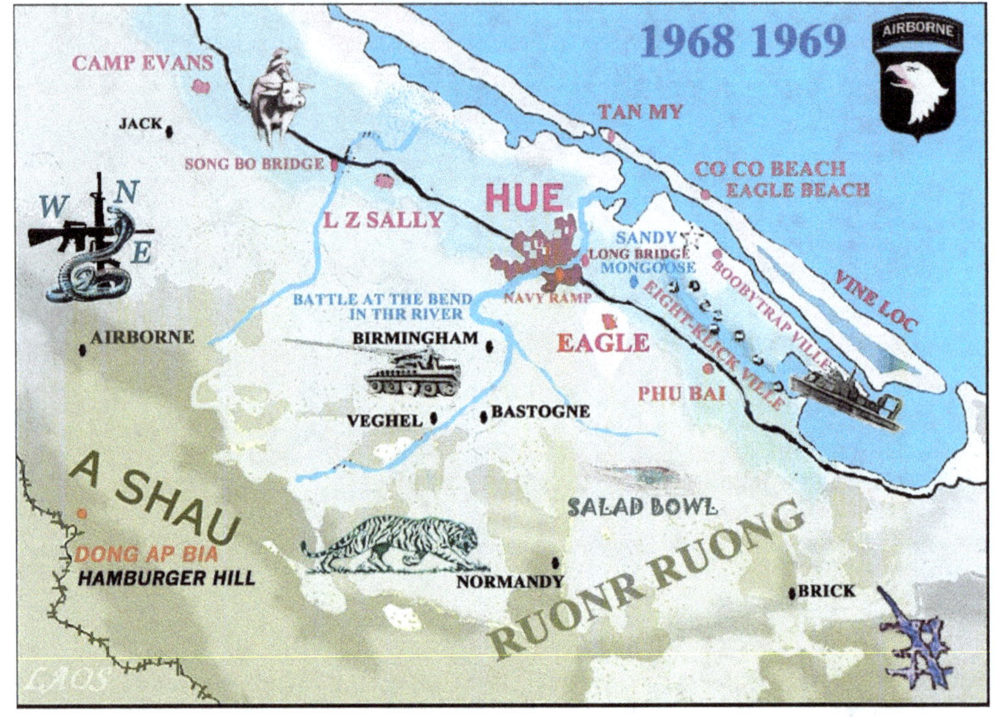

The Face of Vietnam Map

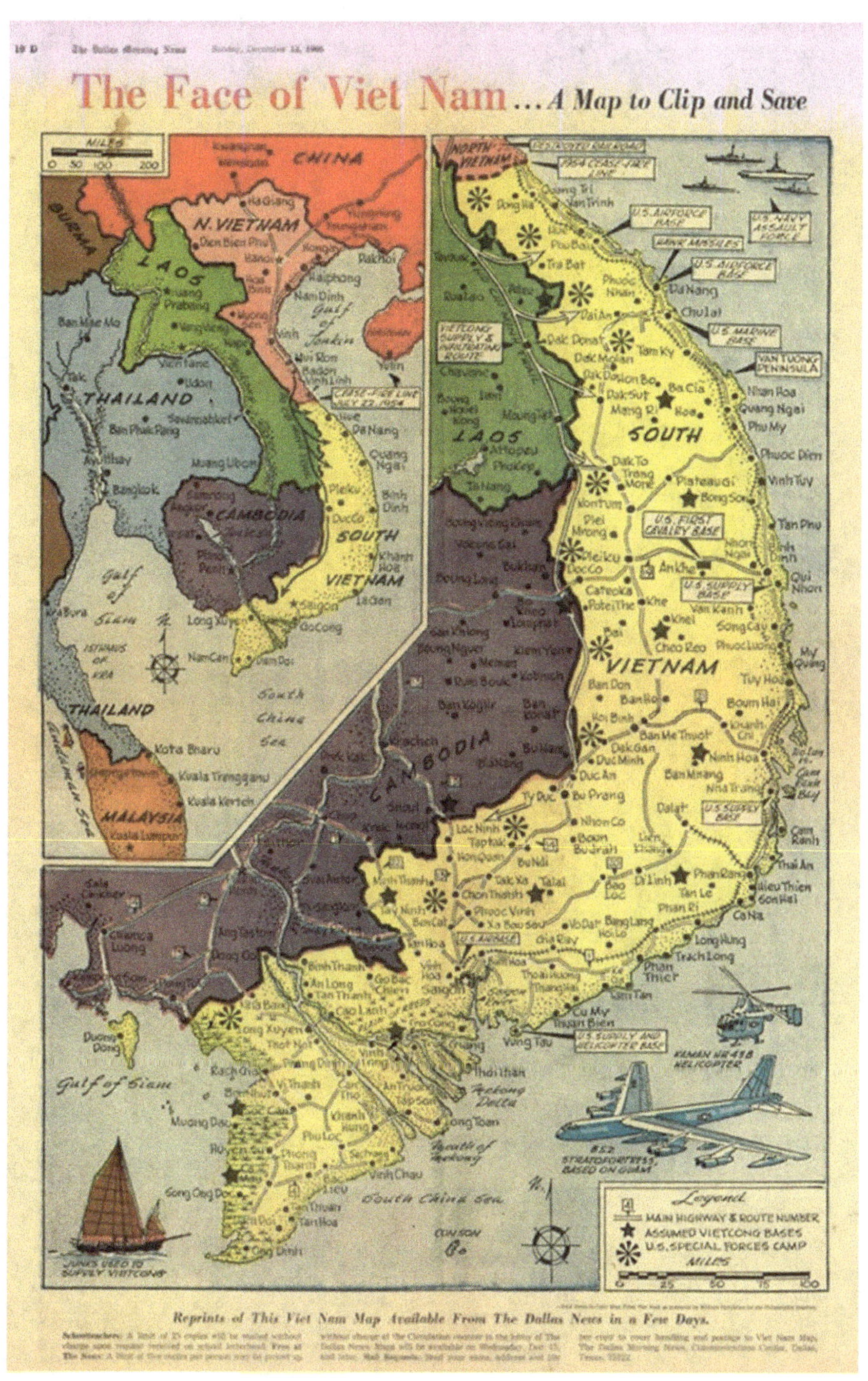

U.S. Army Commands of the Vietnam War

www.ingramcontent.com/pod-product-compliance
Lightning Source LLC
LaVergne TN
LVHW050517100826
845148LV00002B/363

* 9 7 9 8 9 8 7 4 7 4 4 3 3 *